AF876840

Clinical Sociology: Research and Practice

Series Editor

Jan Marie Fritz, University of Cincinnati, Cincinnati, OH, USA

The series explores key research and practice in this rapidly expanding field. Topics include ethical and legal aspects; the nature of client relationships; methods of intervention and evaluation; and the role of clinical sociology in specific settings. This open-ended series appeals to students and teachers in sociology, social work, community psychology, public health, health education, and counseling.

More information about this series at http://www.springer.com/series/5805

Puspa Melati Wan • Abdul Halim Wan

Clinical Sociology

Moving from Theory to Practice

Springer

Puspa Melati Wan
Taman Tun Dr Ismail
Kuala Lumpur, Malaysia

Abdul Halim Wan
Taman Tun Dr Ismail
Kuala Lumpur, Malaysia

ISSN 1566-7847
Clinical Sociology: Research and Practice
ISBN 978-3-030-49082-9 ISBN 978-3-030-49083-6 (eBook)
https://doi.org/10.1007/978-3-030-49083-6

© Springer Nature Switzerland AG 2020
This work is subject to copyright. All rights are reserved by the Publisher, whether the whole or part of the material is concerned, specifically the rights of translation, reprinting, reuse of illustrations, recitation, broadcasting, reproduction on microfilms or in any other physical way, and transmission or information storage and retrieval, electronic adaptation, computer software, or by similar or dissimilar methodology now known or hereafter developed.
The use of general descriptive names, registered names, trademarks, service marks, etc. in this publication does not imply, even in the absence of a specific statement, that such names are exempt from the relevant protective laws and regulations and therefore free for general use.
The publisher, the authors, and the editors are safe to assume that the advice and information in this book are believed to be true and accurate at the date of publication. Neither the publisher nor the authors or the editors give a warranty, expressed or implied, with respect to the material contained herein or for any errors or omissions that may have been made. The publisher remains neutral with regard to jurisdictional claims in published maps and institutional affiliations.

This Springer imprint is published by the registered company Springer Nature Switzerland AG.
The registered company address is: Gewerbestrasse 11, 6330 Cham, Switzerland

Contents

About the Authors

Abdul Halim Wan is one of the pioneers and a champion of Clinical Sociology in Malaysia. Academically, he was trained at Monash University, Australia for his bachelor's degree and at the University of Bristol, England for his MSc and PhD in Sociology. He has developed various community-based and empowerment programs at institutional, state, and national levels such as Social Problem Management System (PINTAS), national family development program: a Social Relations Management System (SRMS), women service center and single mother support group, peer-based rehabilitation program for drug addicts and hospice program for individuals with AIDS, to name a few. Wan Halim is also known for his contribution toward community mediation in Malaysia through his training of community leaders using sociological lens and tools to manage communal conflict. His email address is wanhalim@gmail.com

Puspa Melati Wan is a senior lecturer at Taylor's University, Malaysia. She holds a PhD in Sociology and Anthropology from International Islamic University Malaysia (IIUM). She completed her MSc in Sociology from the University of Oxford, UK (Oxford) and her BA in Sociology and Psychology from the University of San Francisco, US (USF). Identifies herself as a Clinical Sociologist and passionate about the community, Wan Puspa Melati has worked with both local and international NGOs as well as managed grassroots empowerment programs for various target groups such as single mothers, children of low-income households, abused women and children, juvenile delinquents, transgendered individuals, senior citizens as well as deaf community. Her email address is wanpuspamelati@gmail.com

Part I
Introduction to Clinical Sociology

Chapter 1
Introduction: Setting the Stage for Clinical Sociology

Sociologists all over the world had worked diligently throughout the twentieth century to establish their discipline as a reputable social science within the academic world. In order to achieve this, mainstream sociologists have modeled their discipline as an empirical and academic social science, based on common "scientific" methodologies as defined and developed by other social scientists as well. The sociologists see themselves as scientists who maintain intellectual objectivity and detachment when examining and explaining the nature of social phenomena. Sociology is, after all, a logo, a Greek term meaning "a field of study", in this case, a study of society. It is generally held that sociology should be dedicated to the task of researching social life as a means of gaining a better and more accurate understanding of society.

Without doubt, the main objective of any field of study is to enlighten society through accumulation of knowledge, on the assumption that knowledge in itself is a valuable commodity upon which the advancement of the human race rests. How this knowledge is actually utilized and made "useful" and "usable" to improve the human condition is something that is not of primary concern to most sociologists. It is often argued that the onus is on the society, the social scientists, to put this knowledge and understanding to good use. Social scientists, it is often argued, should avoid becoming directly involved in the application of academic knowledge to specific social situations deemed "problematic" by society. Such an involvement may not only inadvertently divert the utilization of scarce resources from the main focus, that is, on knowledge generation and transmission. It would also interfere with the pursuit of strict scientific rationality and intellectual objectivity.

Upon achieving the status as a legitimate social science within the academic world, sociology continues to develop within the confines of academia. Sociologists continue to do what they do best for more than a century, which was primarily to continue teaching sociology, supervising students, and conducting social research. After a century of successfully developing and fine-tuning sociological theories and perspectives, and the accumulation of considerable research data on practically all

© Springer Nature Switzerland AG 2020

P. M. Wan, A. H. Wan, *Clinical Sociology*, Clinical Sociology: Research and Practice, https://doi.org/10.1007/978-3-030-49083-6_1

aspects of the human society throughout the world, an obvious question naturally arises: What is next for sociology?

For some sociologists the answer to the question seems equally obvious. What does one do after having accumulated so much sociological materials, data, and analyses? Sociological theories, perspectives, abstract concepts, and academic discourse need to be put to the final test that is to apply them to real-life social situations. The desire to apply sociological knowledge to improve social situations is not something new to sociology. The early founders of sociology had always believed that the acquired sociological knowledge should be utilized for this ultimate purpose. Not only the move to apply sociology is considered long overdue by its proponents, it is also deemed essential for its future survival as an academic discipline. These concerned sociologists have always been perturbed by the realization that sociology has been shackled by imaginary limitations imposed by the sociologists themselves. An obvious direction for change should be toward making sociology ***directly*** relevant and applicable to resolve social issues and challenges of the day. In other words, sociology should be both a field of academic study as well as a field of social action. The development of specific skills and tools to perform this important task has been ignored or overlooked by mainstream sociology.

Fortunately, there have always been individuals and groups of sociologists who were unwavering in their quest for applied sociology. They had never deviated from their life mission that is to see the sociologist's role going beyond that of merely generating insights into aspects of the human society to that of the sociologist actively involved in social activism and intervention, which the needs arise. They want sociologists to venture beyond merely toying with their "sociological imagination" through their lectures, writings, and public discourses (i.e. Joseph, 2011; Nack, 2011; Schuyler, 2011; Wittner, 2011). For sociologists in developing countries or in countries faced with unrelenting social issues and crisis, the feeling of impotence was particularly unbearable as they observe social chaos and human suffering occurring all around them and yet as sociologists they are only supposed to carry out research and merely talk about their findings. Should they decide to be involved in some form of social activism, they are at a lost as to what exactly should sociologists do to improve the troubling social situation since they were not exposed to social activism and intervention strategies in their training as sociologists. And yet they see other professionals, such as psychologists, social workers, counsellors, medical personnel religious leaders, and the like ever-ready to get involved and play their respective roles without much hesitation. It dawn upon them that in order for sociologists to become a useful and responsible citizens, they need to be trained on how to directly apply sociological skills and tools for resolving social issues and challenges.

Groups of sociologists in many countries have, over many decades, been developing their own approaches, by a "trial-and-error" method, in performing a variety of social intervention activities. They are also continually being vocal in advocating for the urgent need for sociology training to incorporate applied skills and approaches that can be utilized by their graduates. To date, their passionate appeals have largely fallen on deaf ears of mainstream sociology. By the 1980s two sociologists, Swan

(1980) and Rossi (1980) simultaneously announced in their separate articles that the time was ripe for sociologists to "come out of the closet" to apply their knowledge and the courage to face and deal with the real issues facing the society within which they lived.

Practitioners of practical or interventional sociology, although small in numbers, have continued to practice their craft patiently in the backwaters of sociology for all those decades. They may seem to have failed to attract the attention of their peers although from time to time some occasional half-hearted references are made by the latter concerning the need to make sociology more relevant and practical in order to attract more potential students to enter the field of sociology. The practical sociologists quietly continue their practice in the field of social intervention and social problem-solving, learning, and fine-tuning their methodologies as they go along. The demand for, and the marketability of, sociological activism within the private and public sectors of most societies have always existed, enabling those with this inclination to pursue it as their life-long careers.

Their fellow sociologists appear to be oblivious to this fact as they occasionally lament what they see as a stagnant or even a decline in the ability of sociology to attract public interest as reflected in the number of students enrolling as sociology majors or the numbers of job advertisements seeking graduates in sociology. The various forms of sociological practice all over the world have remained largely undetected and undocumented although there is some indication of a growing wider interest and curiosity among sociologists. This is reflected by the emergence of several associations representing this movement alongside the appearance of several books and journals dealing with the applied and clinical aspects of sociological work. Groups of sociologists, principally those in North America, and to some extent in Europe, have continued to keep alive interests in practical sociology as a legitimate and distinct niche and career option that sociologists can opt for.

Without waiting for mainstream sociology to respond to their pleas, some sociologists have tentatively ventured ahead to develop and apply their own approaches toward social intervention based on what they understood as the basic sociological principles, theories, and perspectives. The main crux of this book illustrates the pervasiveness of this quest for applied sociology, with a special emphasis on clinical sociology. The book uncovers the deep schism within sociology between those who plead for a radical re-evaluation of the role of sociology in society and those who sees sociology in its traditional mold as an academic pursuit. It exposes the undying and inextinguishable passion, predominantly in English language sources, by exponents of applied sociology to ensure that their specialty is accepted as a legitimate component of "sociology proper." The book presents the salient arguments and counter-arguments of a continuing verbal "civil war" within sociology that remains unabated and one that will determine the future direction of the discipline.

This book clearly advocates for the general inclusion and adoption of applied approaches and the special position that clinical sociology can contribute to the realm of sociology. A "clinical" addendum to the existing sociology curriculum will complement other approaches that sociologists have often reiterated, from time to time, under the rubric of "applied" sociology. There are sociologists, including the writers, who, for reasons to be explained later in the book, choose to label themselves as "clinical sociologists," practicing a specialty that complements that of the 'clinical psychologists' and yet is distinctly built upon sociological principles and approaches of social intervention.

This book begins with a brief review of the genesis of the various applied approaches within sociology and subsequently explains the emergence of "clinical sociology" as one particularly promising applied specialty. This book highlights the efforts and contributions of many committed sociologists who have, throughout the last millennium, steadfastly held to the unshakable belief that sociology without practice would be an ineffective and incomplete field of intellectual pursuit. This book discusses in a general manner the ideas and practices, as well as the dreams and the hopes, of the ardent exponents of this "clinical" specialty. Some of the sociologists referred to briefly in this book are relatively unknown and may well be regarded as being "marginal," existing on the fringe of mainstream sociology, whose names and works are seldom mentioned in common sociology discourse. What is particularly striking is the realization that, as one re-reads the early writings of the pioneers of sociology, was how passionate were their pleas for some form of interventional or clinical specialty within sociology. They were dedicated to the idea that sociology needed to, and was capable of, integrating some form of practice as a legitimate and essential component of the discipline.

The motivation for writing this book springs from the authors' own personal and professional experiences of working as practicing clinical sociologists in Malaysia. The authors began using the label when working on intervention teams alongside clinical psychologists as well as the participation of other professionals. Since we were often working within clinical settings or dealing with issues generally identified as "clinical," such as with drug addicts, people with HIV or children with physical and mental handicaps, the usual question that was asked by members of the public was "Are you a clinical psychologist?" When the response given was "No, a sociologist," this was often followed by the comment "I see, a clinical sociologist!" After some time the public often refers to the authors as "clinical sociologists." This usage became acceptable to the public because every time the views of a clinical psychologist were solicited, the audience wanted to hear from the "clinical sociologist" on the matter. When sociologists intervenes in what the public regard as clinical issues, they automatically regard the sociologist as "clinical sociologist." Consequently, the label was adopted by the authors even before discovering the existence of other sociologists in other parts of the world who were similarly using the label "clinical sociologists." Since the idea of a clinical specialty within the field of sociology had not been widely propagated or formalized throughout the last century, it was left very much to the ingenuity and innovativeness of individual sociologists to do so. The need for such innovation, especially dawned on those who were employed in nonacademic positions where there were occasional demands from their employers to perform and apply sociological ideas and tools to socially define "problematic" social situations.

This book is purposefully rhetoric, at times personal and not excessively academic, in its approach. It is a merely starting point to generate interests and polemics, where general ideas concerning clinical sociology are discussed without going into too much details of the specific mechanics of clinical practice as envisaged by the authors. It is hoped that this book will serve as a new addition to other earlier attempts propagating this specialty among sociologists. It is aimed at arousing the latent interests of sociologists and students who, consciously or otherwise, are inclined toward, or are already facing real-life challenges, which their previous training did not prepare them for. As sociologists experiment with different approaches in their diverse social settings, the field of clinical sociology will be further enriched and elaborated. Some degree of verification and standardization of approaches, processes, and procedures; the development of specific skills, tools, and protocols; the drawing up of ethical, legal, and professional guidelines, become feasible through an accumulation of recorded real cases and experiences. This is, after all, the way all clinical professions had developed in the past, including the medical profession, which went through decades of trail-and-error resulting in both success and failures. A clinical field undoubtedly undergoes a continuous process of growth through accumulated insights gained through supervised experimentation, action research, and professional peer-evaluation. Intangible as well as tangible rewards will undoubtedly await those who wish to venture as pioneers into this demanding and yet exciting new specialty within sociology.

Basic–Applied Continuum

Sociologists have been continuously deliberating as to whether they should or should not "apply" what they have learned and taught to their students. The primary dichotomy between **basic** versus **applied** sociology has always been a popular way of categorizing the two wings of the discipline. Sztompka (1979) pointed out that sociological research had 4 functions to fulfil. The **descriptive** function used research results to answer the **'what's'** of social phenomena and social processes. The **explanatory** function provided answers to the more complex question of **why** particular social phenomena or processes occurred. The **predictive** function provided answers to the question of what the **trend** in the future would be. Finally, the **practical** function answered the question of what could be done to induce a **change** in a particular social situation.

The first three functions, Sztompka (1979) suggested, could be placed under the ambit of basic or academic sociology, while the fourth belonged to the domain of the applied. Sztompka (1979) and many other sociologists generally agreed that sociology had generally fared well with the first function—the **descriptive** function, while the other three functions were less adequately attempted. Zetterberg (1962) was similarly of the opinion that while the three last functions were relatively neglected, the last, the **practical** function, was the most neglected of all due to the obvious failure of sociology to produce the **know-how** for social intervention. He pointed out that of the hundreds of sociological research papers published in the professional journals, the majority invariably concluded by calling for further research to be conducted, while only a handful of them suggested the need for more practical action.

By dichotomizing sociology into the two camps or wings, the different assumptions and objectives between the two can be more easily contrasted. The so-called **basic** arm or wing of sociology is also described as "pure," "scientific," "cognitivistic," "academic," or "empirical" sociology by different writers. The other arm, the **applied** wing is often referred to as "activistic," "practical," "engineering," "action," "practice," "professional," and "clinical" aspects of sociology. The former category refers to the sociological work that aims at providing a better understanding of the nature of society and human social behavior (Berelson, 1966). Basic sociologists are said to choose to study what is considered as "problematic" to sociology and sociologists, rather than studying what the general society considers as problematic.

The sociologist's choice of the appropriate sociological problems to study is generally based on their personal interests in the subject. Little regard was given to the question of whether these problems were of immediate relevance or of high priority for those outside the academic circle. Jones (1971) made this similar observation when he stated in his writing that basic or academic researchers strived for information and knowledge alone without going beyond this to consider how the findings could contribute to the solution of specific problems. Another writer, De Bie (1970) similarly defined basic research as the search for knowledge for its own sake without responding to "stimulants other than the research itself" (p. 584). He further described basic research as an activity that was independent and autonomous in nature usually originating from "mere curiosity or even a flight of fancy" (p. 585) on the part of the researcher.

The applied wing, in contrast, focuses on the notion that sociology serves as an instrument for directly dealing with resolving social problems. Berelson (1966) saw **action** sociologists as those who focused on problems that had important social consequences and which ordinary citizens were concerned with. Their first allegiance was toward making decisions concerning intervention even if they might not initially have an exact notion or a complete plan for action beforehand. The basic difference between the two groups, he summarized, rested in the emphasis given by the former on the need to understand the ***why*** of a social phenomenon, while the latter focused on the ***how*** of it. According to another sociologist, Perlstadt (1998), sociological **practice** helped to transform knowledge into a form that could be used as a tool for solving concrete social problems, the act of applying knowledge to social situations in order to diagnose, advise, counsel, intervene, and/or treat.

Several writers had pointed out to a certain ambiguity between what could be defined as applied and non-applied sociological **research**. Jones (1971) believed that, in practice, the boundary between the two was nebulous, and that the distinctions might have existed "more in the eye of the beholder" (p. 50) than in reality. Rossi (1980) similarly concluded that the line between basic and applied research was "a fuzzy one" (p. 893) since a particular research work could be recategorized with the passage of time. He pointed out that what might be initially considered as a **basic** research might well later qualify to be relabeled as an **applied** research. For example, academicians may initially conduct their research in order to satisfy their own academic curiosity without any intention of it being utilized for any particular problem-solving purpose. However, it may later be found to be relevant as input into a particular problem-solving situation, thus qualifying it as an **applied** research. Conversely, particular research reports, after having been utilized for some problem-solving efforts, might end up as an article or book that attracted interests from the academic community. Due to this possible transformation, Braude (1974) argued that no research could be considered as being truly **pure** since all sociological research involved some "reference to particular human concerns" (p.74), with the inherent potential of being either directly or indirectly relevant for bringing about social change.

The alleged difference between the two genres of research perhaps does not seem to lie so much in the nature of the research work **per se,** but rather more in the external social circumstances within which the research is conducted. In the so-called **applied** cases, there are usually interested parties that engage sociologists to undertake specific research projects, usually by providing financial sponsorship. In **academic** research projects, the motive for conducting them appears to come from the personal interests of the researchers themselves. The basic sociologist defines the problem which he or she is personally concerned with, while the applied sociologist works on a problem that is perceived as such by another party.

It is possible than when two social scientists embark on exactly the same research topic, the findings from the work of one researcher are expected by its sponsor to be utilized for some problem-solving purpose, while the findings of the other researcher is purely for the purpose of enlightening the curiosity of the researcher. The former can easily be categorized as **applied** research while the latter is described as **basic** research. This clearly demonstrates that the initial difference does not seem to lie primarily in the nature of the work as such, but rather in the circumstances and the intention behind the execution of the research. The secondary differentiation of the so-called applied from the basic research appears to be based on certain assumptions of what is expected to happen after the research has been completed and its findings published. Realistically, there is no guarantee that a particular research finding initially intended for problem-solving will eventually be applied, nor is it predictable that one which is done out of academic interest is not being considered by some interested parties as relevant for some form of application.

Mayo and France (1980) offered to overcome the ambiguity associated with the term **applied** by suggesting that perhaps it should be labeled as **applicable** research instead. They thought the latter term could better capture and evoke an image of sociology as a "pliable" discipline that was flexible and responsive. They felt that the past tense in the adjective "applied" was inappropriate since it was not possible to consider something as "applied" before even deciding on the exact nature of the research and what it is expected to uncover. However, their suggestion may not diminish the ambiguity. The question still remains: how is one to know whether the outcome of a research effort *will* be applicable since it involves predicting the future? Even if a research outcome is initially expected to be applied, there is no guarantee that it will be. Consultancy research reports often end up on the shelves and in the archives without ever being used for any useful problem-solving efforts, despite the initial stated intention.

Perhaps the nature of all sociological *research* work, however, one may wish to label it, remains basically similar, regardless of the larger context within which they are conducted. Research have to conform to the principles and procedures of scientific objectivity as defined by certain agreed standards. A scientific research process typically begins with the selection of a problem considered worthy of study. This is followed by a review of the pertinent theories and already existing data. Then comes the formulation of hypotheses; the formulation of a research design; the actual collection and analysis of data; and finally the report writing. Other factors, such as the choice of the topic and the motivation behind the research; the availability of funds; the disciplinary and ideological leanings of the members of the research team; as well as the political and moral framework are, or should be, **exogenous** to the research process itself. This reality makes some writers feel that it is futile to try to label research as being either pure or applied. They suggest instead that the focus should be on examining the actual utilization of sociological knowledge without being too concerned with the reasons and the conditions, which set the research into motion (Scott & Shore, 1979).

Olsen (1981) stressed the need to avoid what he saw as the role segregation between pure and applied sociologists. Instead, he wanted to see efforts to promote role integration within an integrated sociology by "merging the scientist and the practitioner roles into one" (p. 565). The somewhat vague separation of **knowledge** from **practice** that has raised concern among many present-day social scientists had equally bothered the sociologists of the past. Swan (1984), for example, quoted a renowned Chinese philosopher in the distant past, Wang-Yang-Ming (1447–1579), who saw this very dichotomy as a social disease. He wrote: "Knowledge is the beginning of practice; doing is the completion of knowing." He disagreed with the notion that knowledge had to reach a certain advanced stage before one could go about applying and utilizing it. "Those who to the very end of life fail to practice," he wrote "also fail to understand." The "remedy for the disease" would then be the ability to see knowledge and practice as inseparable components of a single entity.

Sociological work that involves some degree of application can generally subsumed under the general category of **applied sociology** or that of **sociological practice**. Of the two terms, the use of the former has had a wider usage among sociologists, going back to the early writings of Ward in 1906. The term **sociological practice,** however, has also been used by some as analogous or synonymous to **applied sociology** and has gained some currency recently. Clark (1990) defined **sociological practice** as the inclusive umbrella term covering all forms of nonbasic sociology. She wrote: "Both applied sociologists and clinical sociologists are sociological practitioners. Practice is the broad, umbrella category, and clinical and applied sociology are approaches to practice" (p. 107). This definition sees applied sociology as being subsumed under the rubric of sociological practice, a categorization that remains salient among sociologists in the United States to date. Another term that is less commonly used is **engaged public sociology** that refers to either or both applied and/or clinical sociology.

As an alternative to seeing basic and applied sociology in terms of a distinct black-and-white dichotomy is to employ the notion of a basic–applied **continuum** instead. Payne and Cross (1993) agree that instead of seeing the existence of a "firm divide" (p. 7), one can identify a wide range of sociological work that exhibits different degrees of applied-ness. Along with the basic–applied continuum of sociological activities is several types of roles that sociologists choose as their preference. Sociologists have generally been relatively vague in describing the various applied approaches and models they espoused. They seldom explain their preferred approaches in great detail and with sufficient illustrations. One has to resort to making assumptions and presumptions as to what they actually mean by the labels they choose. It is possible that the use of the different terms by different sociologists does not necessarily reflect distinctly different approaches or models. Nevertheless, one can still attempt to locate the various approaches along a hypothetical **basic–applied continuum** in order to make some sense of them.

At one end of the continuum are to be found the basic approaches in sociological work while at the opposite end are located the applied ones. At the basic end are located the first three roles, the **theoretical** sociologist, the **basic researcher**, and the **social critic** who are seen to focus on the task of helping the public to understand better, analytically and critically, social contexts. At the applied end are located the next five, the **social analyst,** the **policy** sociologist, the social **engineer,** the **clinical** sociologist, and the **social therapist**. These categories house those who participate directly in the field of practice performing social intervention in different forms and with different degrees of involvement. As in other continuums, considerable overlapping and blurring of boundaries can be expected between the linear points along the continuum.

The continuum with its varied and balanced repertoire of roles is largely an idealized imaginary dream that has not yet been realized in its ideal form. Sadly, in real life when one envisages sociology one can only see with clarity one end of the continuum, the **basic** end. The other end, the **applied**, is hidden somewhere in the clouds of obscurity in the faint distance. When one conceives of sociology one invariably finds oneself seated at the basic end of the continuum. At this end is found the **first** and most dominant role that sociologists had chosen for themselves for over a century. This is where the sociologists assume the role of theoreticians or **theoretical sociologists**. Some critics may derogatorily refer to them as **armchair** sociologists. They usually develop their ideas based on some research that others had performed together with other secondary resources and personal reflections based on years of academic work and experience. They focus on what they see as **sociological** problems, problems that are considered as the gaps in sociological knowledge or the controversies needing clarifications through stimulating polemics within the discipline. Their role is to disseminate concepts and ideas with the objective of explaining the dynamics of the social phenomena to students. They make attempts to synthesize sociological research findings and draw general theoretical implications from them, identifying **universalities** of human social existence. They may choose to take different ideological stands and espousing different schools of thought, or they may opt for an **eclectic** stand, as they try to make sense of the particularities and dynamics of the social phenomenon.

The **second** role along the continuum is that of the **basic researcher**. When we see sociologists as researchers who are referring to research to produce primary data. Although sociologists do assemble and examine secondary data, it does not require a sociologist to perform this task. Everybody involved in planning an action program needs to familiarize themselves with the existing or published secondary data. If the data need to be reprocessed or reformulated, it usually involves computer scientists, statisticians or mathematicians who are more qualified than the ordinary sociologists to carry out this task. In this role, sociologists do not merely rely on other sociologists' research findings. They prefer to perform original research either motivated by personal curiosities as a researcher or they may be commissioned or sponsored to conduct research by an interested party. A basic researcher's main concern is to demonstrate scientific and academic excellence through his or her impressive and faultless research abilities and acumen. To question of what the research will produce and whether and how the research findings will be utilized is not a primary concern for a researcher. They are concerned with the research **process** itself being impeccable and unblemished rather than with the **outcome** of research, which is beyond their control and of little academic interest. Basic researchers believe that their findings are valuable in themselves, capable of elucidating the true nature of some aspects of the particular phenomenon under study. Students' research projects and theses are usually in the form of basic research and they are rarely linked to a specific or particular problem-solving objective. For some research projects the sponsors may specifically state that they **do not** want the sociologist to go beyond providing basic data and analyses for reasons of guarding confidentiality, anonymity, or avoiding political sensitivities.

The basic researcher usually does not go beyond present their findings to offer social and policy criticisms as this would tarnish their reputation as social scientific researchers *par excellence*. This task is usually left to those in the **third** role on the sociology continuum, the **social critic**. Sociologists included in this latter category are those who offer public commentaries on what they perceive as social issues or problems needing to be remedied. Their objective is usually to create a critical awareness among the public on particular issues which hopefully will serve as a stimulus for social change. Their audience is the general public rather than a particular interested party or client. In order to gain credibility for their critique they usually present relevant research data to support their views but unlike the basic researcher, they discuss the merits and weaknesses of the existing implementation and problem-solving strategies of which they are free to criticize because they are not directly involved in them. Their critiques typically go beyond a mere presentation of research findings. They blend and combine facts and findings with their own personal and professional views, often colored by their own ideological and theoretical perspectives.

Unlike academic sociologists, their channel for presenting their critiques is usually through the public mass media and the Internet, requiring them to use clear non-sociological jargon that appeals to the general public. This role is intended to stimulate critical thinking among the general public who tends to take social reality for granted or as something that is incapable of change. Social critics, however, generally may not go into the practical details of how to change a particular situation although some may suggest some general practical course of action to take toward achieving the desired change. Although critics are supposed to point out both positive and negative aspects of a particular situation or issue, the common practice is to point out the weaknesses and deficits, leading some of them to be labeled as social agitators or agent provocateurs.

To avoid being labeled as mere critics, sociologists need to go beyond acting as critics, demystifiers, reporters, and clarifiers to be more as **constructive critics**. This brings us to the **fourth** role, a role that brings sociologists closer to the practice of social intervention without actually being directly involved in it. It is that of the **policy-relevant researcher**. This role is so dominant in applied research that when one looks under the topic of "applied sociology" in a dictionary of sociology (Marshalls, 1994), one is directed to see "policy research." According to Scott and Shore (1979) applied sociology is not only narrowly linked to research activity but often used as synonymous with an even narrower field of policy research. The policy-relevant researcher usually goes beyond merely pointing out what is wrong with the present situation, as do social critics, to suggest some concrete ideas toward improving it. The policy-relevant sociologists generally try to limit themselves only to matters relating to public policies and agencies (Scott & Shore, 1979). They are likely to hold the view that sociologists should not merely criticize what they see as "the incompetence, ineptitude, middle-class values" or freely issue sharp critiques of how other people "make a mess of things," since such this can be counter-productive as it will only succeed in generating resentment on the part of those who are criticized (Pahl, 1977).

Sociologists are reminded that they should be able to offer viable and practical future solutions and alternatives every time they point out to other people's past and present inadequacies. In order to preserve their reputation as objective academicians policy-relevant sociologists are not as free as their social critics' siblings to assign blame without carefully contemplating and offering constructive alternatives. Similarly, Szymanski (1971) felt that the sociologist must be seen to be not merely "constant social critic" (p. 105) but rather as intellectuals who were capable of developing strategies for bringing about social change. The **policy-relevant researcher** undertakes research with some ideas on how the findings are meant to be utilized, realizing that an ability to help correct or improve a situation will clearly demonstrate one's true credibility as a professional in the eyes of the society, not that of mere fault finding. In addition, the researcher may be required by their client's terms of reference to offer or submit some concrete policy or action recommendations. However, at this point in the basic–applied research continuum the sociologists are not required to go as far as being directly involved in the actual implementation process of the recommendations they offer.

The roles that we have discussed thus far, including that of the policy researcher, show the sociologist's involvement being rather limited to providing a better understanding of a particular situation besides offering some recommendations for action together with their findings. There is potentially a serious flaw when sociologists, who are basically merely academicians performing research, dabble in policy issues. The reality of policy implementation is usually too complex for sociologists to contemplate without corresponding inputs from economists, political scientists, psychologists, physical planners, stakeholders, and sometimes even social historians. There is the danger that their recommendations may appear to be too simplistic and unpractical capable of potentially harming their reputation. This danger can be less considerable for sociologists who had experiences that go beyond teaching and researching. With considerable practical experience of working alongside other professionals in the applied field, these sociologists may be able to better perform the task. Otherwise, their knowledge of the realities of social action is very much limited, as their critics put it, to their armchairs.

The expertise of the policy-relevant researcher unfortunately is still very limited to the traditional role of **enlightening** clients. To **enlighten**, according to a dictionary, is "to give the light of fact and knowledge to; reveal truths to; free from ignorance, prejudice, or superstition" (Neufeldt & Guralnik, 1991). The above definition appears to describe a person trying to promote an ideal world based on "truths" and "knowledge," a kind of an intellectual dreamer, rather than someone dealing the ignorance, prejudice, or superstition' that abound in the real, real world, a world full of warts and all. Janowitz (1972) pointed out that sociologists in policy-relevant research were guided by this enlightenment model with the focus on the provision of knowledge and understanding of the social context within which a problem existed, emphasizing on the rational, cognitive, and intellectual basis for problem-solving. Scott and Shore (1979) agreed the view that the role of policy-relevant sociologists was basically that of the **enlightener.** Scott and Shore noted that the "enlightener" was expected to contribute, among many tasks, ideas that were relevant for policy deliberation; clarifying and critically examining the assumptions upon which policy decisions were based; evaluating the performance of existing programs, and promoting a better understanding of the decision-making processes. The real world of policy implementation is far more complex than that and yet Hewitt (1991), after them, implored sociologists to continue with this enlightening model. He believed, rather optimistically, that it could create an impact on "the way people see themselves and their society." How can sociologists help people "see themselves and their society" better by merely giving knowledge, facts, and appealing to their noble selves? (p. 105).

As any experienced social practitioner will agree that trying to enlighten people, using common examples often requiring social intervention such as when dealing with individuals bent on committing suicide or homicide, or with a group contemplating social revenge, is unlikely to work. The enlightenment model, after all, is very rudimentary one. It is attractive to the sociologists because it is a **safe** model, not because it is necessarily the best model to emulate. It brings them closer to real societal issues without the need to soil their hands in the actual act of problem-solving, while offering recommendation from afar. Still, Street and Weistein (1981) concurred with the enlightenment model because they believed it provided a **middle-of-the-road** approach. It was, they attested, neither siding too closely with the interests of the clients nor did it create the impression of totally ignoring the client's concerns. This is an excellent example of playing it safe. Certainly there are times when applied sociologists, such as when performing the role of a social mediator, may need to adopt a "middle-of-the road" stance. It is, however, doubtful if middle-of-the-rood strategy always works when deciding on a serious policy change. Besides, being in the middle-of-the-road, if you can forgive the pun, is not always the safest place to be!

The role of the enlightener, however important, remains an *indirect* contribution toward problem-solving. Scott and Shore (1979), in fact, agreed that policy researchers often failed to indicate a deep understanding of the actual influence of policy implementation on a particular situation. They tended to ignore the historical, political and social contexts, and intricacies within which policies were made and implemented, making many policy research appeared to be conceived **in vacuo**. They further pointed out that the policy researcher tended to neglect the crucial problem of what exactly people were supposed to do once they had become enlightened (Scott & Shore, 1979). After analyzing sociological literature on the subject they came to the conclusion that few studies produced policy recommendations of any kind, and where recommendations were advanced, they were often rejected by policy-makers as "politically unrealistic, administratively unworkable, or simply impractical" (p. 12).

Sociological researchers cannot possibly be expected to truly understand the actual requirements of policy-makers and the dilemmas that are faced, should their conceptualization of research projects are based on limited disciplinary perspectives and concerns, as opposed to interdisciplinary ones. Should they become too focused on the need to address and impress their professional colleagues as their main audience, the salient policy aspects of their research tend to be relegated to the status of "merely residual variables" (Scott & Shore, 1979, p. 204). Supporting this criticism of the policy researchers Klien (1982) pointed out that sociologists who were involved in policy research remained marginal to the policy process because of their fondness for time-consuming elaborate research and analysis, considered a luxury by many policy implementers. The latter considered simple and fast basic data gathering exercise sufficient for their needs. They were particularly unimpressed if, after an elaborate analysis, the researcher only managed to advance conclusions that appeared to them impractical or simply naïve.

The **fifth** role along the sociology continuum is that of the **social engineer**, together with the less controversial group that utilize the designation of the **social analyst**. The social engineer and the social analyst may at times perform the role as policy-oriented sociologists but they are often expected to go beyond the basic role of suggesting action alternatives to participate to some degree in the actual implementation process. By going beyond the role of a **policy-relevant** sociologist, the social engineer or the social analyst is required to work more closely with their clients to provide some form of social and management support. Due to the more intimate and continuous nature of their involvement with their clients, the two sociological approaches require practitioners to build and gain the trust of their clients and continuously maintain adequate rapport within the framework of esprit-de-corps or team spirit.

As an attempt to augment the limited traditional roles as theoreticians, researchers, and critics, some adventurous sociologists have chosen more active, direct, and sometimes controversial approaches as **social engineering** and **social analysis**. The idea that the society can be shaped or engineered through the utilization of scientific knowledge and social technology has its appeal. Potentially, social engineers can apply sociology to deal with the issues and problems faced by industry, government, churches, and civic organizations (Lee, 1954). Social engineers, according to Marshall (1990) were **institutional plumbers**, those who were called in to fix social situations, which failed to function properly. This was achieved by tracking down the source of the problem through the performance of research and analysis and by offering suggestions on the appropriate actions needed to "repair" it. As Bryant (1991) put it, these sociologists helped to engineer the situation by utilizing their expertise in research designs and techniques in order "to obtain relevant information and by drawing upon the stock of sociological knowledge" (p. 177). Bulmer (1990) described the social engineering model as a **linear** problem-solving process. It began with the sociologist being approached by a client who perceived a situation as problematic. The sociologist, if he or she concurred with the existence of the problem, collected the relevant information, data, and analysis through appropriate research. This was followed by recommendations as to the appropriate solutions and actions for the client to implement (Bulmer, 1990). Bryant (1995) described the social engineering process in a similarly **linear** fashion, involving the following steps: the definition of a social problem; the identification of the missing knowledge; the acquisition of social research data and relationships; the interpretation of problem solution; and finally the implementation of policy change.

The social engineering model came under severe criticisms in the 1960s with the accusation that its practitioners, in the words of Lee (1954), were sometimes committing "intellectual misadventures" (p. 61) due to their tendency to serve the personal interests of their clients, with little or no regard for the broader social interests. Gouldner and Miller (1965) and, two decades later, Olsen and Micklin (1981), echoed the same critiques of the social engineer adding that they had very little influence over the "kinds of data he will analyze, the questions he will ask of the information that is available, or the uses to which his analysis will be put" (p. xx). The critics felt that this flaw seriously limited the validity and effectiveness of the sociologist's input. Allen (1975), in the following decade, continued to bombard the social engineers with more criticisms, accusing them of working "with an abandon which befitted adolescence rather than scientific maturity" (p. 78). He also repeated the earlier criticisms made by others concerning the alleged tendency to accept blindly the terms set by their clients, adding to the criticism that the social engineers failed to critically evaluate the relevance and the usefulness of their efforts, and the impact they have on the long-term reputation of their profession as sociologists.

As social engineering came under fire from its critics, often without much concrete justification, Popper (1966) came to the rescue by offering to differentiate between two models of that approach. He differentiates between what he termed as **piecemeal** social engineering and that of the **utopian** model. According to him, the former was a more positive form because it had a more limited and realistic focus on particular situations that needed to be changed based on the best knowledge and skills available. The **utopian** social engineering model, on the other hand, was a more negative one because it could be used as an instrument employed by the State to remodel the overall society. With the help rendered by the social engineer, the particular blueprint for the future drawn by the State was in fact a form of social manipulation that was deemed to fail. The social **analysis** model, on the other hand, was developed by sociologists who were interested in introducing some semblance of clinical practice into sociology. In a lecture in Sept 1933, Mannheim introduced the idea of **socio-analysis** which he considered as a complement to **psychoanalysis**. While psychoanalysis involved the study of the micro-processes and components of the human personality, social analysis chose to see the human phenomenon as a totality. It was to be based on the sociological perspective that linked persons to their wider context, the social structure of the situation (Kettler et al. 1984). For example Bockstaele, Bockstaele, Malbos, Godard-Plasman and Bockstaele-Theilhaber (2008) developed technical instruments that provide the possibility of "intervening and interpreting, and, for the requested, of carrying out... an analysis of the entity and the action" by socioanalysts (pp. 170–171).

For those who wanted to disassociate themselves from the rather poor reputation that social engineering had gained, social analysis appeared to offer a somewhat less controversial alternative. However, the basic similarity between the two approaches remained salient. Etzioni (1965) considered **social analysis** as a systematic exploration of societal issues based on a "desire to help" rather than merely based on a "desire to know." However, he advised social analysts to stick to the task of exploring the nature of problems without venturing beyond this to become directly involved in trying to solve them. He also limited his concept of social analysis to macro-level social problems, where the client was society itself, rather than the specific micro- and meso-level social situations where the client was usually an individual, a group or an organization. This advice was unheeded by Rowbottom (1977) who, some years later, saw social analysis as something sociologists should freely venture into. He saw it as being very similar to **social engineering**, perhaps the form which Popper (1966) labeled as **piecemeal social engineering**. Quite similar to the social engineering model, he envisaged social analysis as an approach that would help researchers move away from the traditional quantitative research toward one that was capable of producing knowledge that could be immediately "usable" (Rowbottom, 1977, p. vii). He expanded the application of social analysis to a wider and more inclusive framework to include meso-level problems, mainly at the level of **organizations**. At this level the social analyst could play the role of a consultant-cum-researcher helping to analyze organizational problems with the idea of change in mind.

Social analysis was seen as a means of helping people to understand better the social reality of the specific social institutions they were in, at the same time as attempting to "modify and improve them in a controlled way" (Rowbottom, 1977,

p. 3). Despite the enthusiasm exhibited by social analysts in the idea of changing situations and solving problems there remained some apprehension as to how involved sociologists should be in such interventional activities. Rowbottom (1977) himself, for example, despite his support for social analysis, advised the practitioners to restrict themselves to their **elucidatory** role rather than venturing into a **prescriptive** one. The role of the analyst, according to him, was to encourage the client to explore possibilities and even to offer some alternative course of action without resorting to prescribing what course of action clients should take.

Despite the call for a more social involved sociology, those who were inclined toward the idea of an **applied sociology** in the past continued to focus on basic research as its core activity. Whether they chose to perform social engineering, social analysis, or policy research, they were still basically tied to this main role as a researcher. It is true that, occasionally and cautiously, they might venture beyond this to offer some recommendations for their clients to consider. With a few exceptions, this is where they typically stop. Being research-bound, they usually did not go all the way to help in the implementation process because they often lacked the skills and experience necessary for it. And yet, the tendency to equate **applied sociology** with **applied research** was so prevalent that sociologists who performed the latter consider themselves, and were considered by others, as **applied sociologists**.

One basic question that was seldom posed was were primary data acquired through research before the implementation of action a necessary perquisite for practice? For researchers the answer to this question is a yes. They had the tendency to assume sociologists should always begin by undertaking systematic statistical research of some sort. In fact they were warned not to attempt to do anything before they have acquired new research findings to base their ideas on (Schuman, 1975). What was seldom recognized was that it was not *always* an essential prerequisite in all or even in most situations. Social action often only required secondary research data. If additional data is required, these can be obtained through action research where information and statistics were generated during the process of implementation of intervention, or as a product of the intervention itself (i.e., Flores-González & Rodríguez-Muiz, 2011). Fernandez (1975) noted that although statistical methods did often have an important role to play in sociology, it was not necessarily a primary one. Trying to use statistics to describe social reality, to him, was like trying to "squeeze a round peg into a square hole" (p. 19) since human behavior simply refused "to submit to straitjackets" (p. 20) in the form of statistical analyses. According to him, the increased incursion of mathematical and statistical models in sociology was merely a way of convincing its critics that sociology was unquestionably and truly a scientific enterprise. The implication out of this was that research and action needed to go hand in hand, often with action being the precedent, and only rarely every action needs an initial primary research. This does not stop sociologists from insisting on carrying out primary research before action states. It is almost a standing house joke among members of a multidisciplinary intervention team that sociologists will invariably ask to perform primary research and then more research to elucidate further the findings of the first research.

If the intention of sociologists was to impress others with their statistical abilities, Braude (1974) contended that this was not always working. To him not many non-sociologists, including clients, were easily impressed with elaborate statistical procedures, questionnaires, and interview procedures of the applied sociologist. In fact, he claimed that these people were often bemused at the way sociologists became so obsessed with their abstruse terminologies, tools and techniques which were alien to the "honest-to-goodness interacting people" (Braude, 1974, p. 136). The overwhelming interests are shown toward data and statistical techniques often made the applied sociologist appeared to be seemingly uninterested in people and individuals as such. It was ironic, Braude (1974) wrote, that the more sociologists studied society, the farther they seemed to remove themselves from the subject of their studies, "incapacitating them from seeing the true nature of the people behind the punches in the IBM cards (p. 139). Braude (1974) reminded sociologists that "statistical reality" with its "sterile, even lifeless, quality about them" (p. 140) was not equivalent to the reality as experienced by their subjects. Horowitz (1968) almost mirrored the same view when he said that in the social sciences the sociologist who was charged with the study of society was probably "further removed from the sources and object of his study" (p. 207) than any comparable group of scholars. The simplistic and naïve idea of social reality as something that is reducible to mere statistics to him was untenable. Try to imagine what a 2.45 person household, a typical statistic describing an average family size, would look like in real life. It would certainly be laughable to literally visualize an image of 2 members of a household being accompanied by another member with perhaps missing body parts! While this is clearly an absurdity, sociologists presenting statistics to the layperson appears to be presenting an abstract, contrived and imaginary versions of "reality," while the latter operates and struggles on a daily basis at another level of reality. Berelson (1966) felt that statistician sociologists got so carried away with the new "reality" that they had just created that they began to assign and read "significant" meanings even to minute statistical variations. Sociologists are often more concerned with whether the analysis which they extracted from tiny subsamples is **statistically significant** or otherwise, rather than dealing with what an ordinary person would consider as **socially significant**.

Lindesmith (1960) was similarly concerned with what he saw as the **trivialization** of research where sociologists used sophisticated statistical tools to create the impression of having achieved great precision in answering questions which in reality might be neither important nor relevant. He was concerned with the tendency for sociologists to divorce themselves from the everyday realities and problems as they preoccupied themselves with statistical techniques while the actual subject matter, human beings, remained neglected. The sociologist, he contended, projected the image of being a "clever technician, available for hire, flitting from one problem to another as research subsidies become available" (Lindesmith, 1960, p. 272). Etzkowitz and Schaflander (1968) expressed rather succinctly their distaste of the excessive quantification of sociology: "We are nauseous over the continual replication of meaningless, microscopic quantifications of 'what's wrong or right with...

society' from sterile, neutral, non-involved, objective research-sociologists!" (p. 399).

Similarly, Lee (1973) expressed his disapproval with the way sociologists became fixated with "computerization and complex mathematical formulas" (p. 8), while failing to evaluate the actual "accuracy, novelty, scientific significance, and social importance" (p. 9) of the data they considered as important contributions to sociological knowledge. Lee (1973) felt that sociologists should not allow statistical **virtuosity** to become an end in itself, instead quantification should be used merely as a means toward the crucial task of helping people to cope with their problems. Lee (1973) identified two types of sociologists. The first, of which he approved, were the sociologists who wanted to help people to function more "effectively and satisfying" (p. 29) as members of the society. The second type which he derogatively termed the "games-playing" (p. 29) statisticians were those who seemed to learn very little about society and instead were concerned with "how to determine that little bit in a most correct fashion" (p. 29). Schuman (1975), commenting on the research findings of independent studies carried out for the National Advisory Commission on Civil Disorders in the wake of the 1967 urban riots in the United States, came to the conclusion that social research did not seem to produce much in discovering new relationships, beyond merely disconfirming existing ones. This lead him to conclude that sociology was better at "bursting balloons than at launching rockets" (Schuman, 1975, p. 42).

Those who continue to assume that quantitative basic research work represents the core of sociological work, that anything else is secondary or peripheral to this, seem to seriously overlook one crucial fact—that sociology does not have a monopoly on statistical research expertise. Most social scientists, as well as some natural scientists, possess the ability to perform quantitative social research. It can even be argued that many non-sociologists are even more knowledgeable and skillful than many sociologists in applying this ability. The research methods and statistical analysis tools that sociology students learn are the very ones learned by other social science students. It is not unusual to see a sociologist being the principal researcher who eventually writes the final report while those performing the actual data collection and analysis are non-sociologists, such as statisticians or mathematicians. Upon a close examination of the people commissioned to perform any social research projects, at least according to the experiences of the authors, one will find that sociologists are not necessarily considered as the research expert. In fact Bulmer (1993) speculated the reason why the term "applied sociology" was seldom used in British sociology was possibly due to the fact that a great number of social researchers in present-day Britain were not trained as sociologists. It does appear rather precarious for a discipline or profession to continue to claim superiority in a particular field of knowledge or skill that is in fact commonly possessed, or even surpassed, by many others.

The above criticisms of the excessive love affair that sociologists seem to have with statistical methods are not meant to deny its rightful role in sociology. What exasperated the critics was that the obsession with quantitative sociology as an end in itself which effectively excluded sociologists from interacting with the real world of living human beings. Certainly some forms of **quantitative** data gathering activities are often highly relevant to problem-solving situations, but similarly are **qualitative** ones. Whatever methods, knowledge or skills being employed, whether they are quantitative or qualitative in nature, that can be proven to be effective and efficient in improving social conditions, **should be given equal recognition.** Schein (2001) wanted sociologists to consider all forms of research as legitimate and important in sociology, rather than adopting a rigid and **imperialistic** view that some forms of research are valid while others are not. Midgley (2000) supported the idea of methodological pluralism which asserted that not only the so-called scientific methods were valid for interventional purposes. Equally so were the combined use of many different methods, including "the methods for clarifying values, exploring subjective viewpoints, facilitating participation, visioning possible future scenarios, etc." (p. 6).

Enters Clinical Sociology

We have so far discussed the main roles that sociologists can play in society, beginning at the basic theoretical end of the sociology continuum and moving toward the applied end of it. The first three roles as of **theoretical** sociologist, **basic researcher**, and **social critic** involve the task of enlightening the general public so as to enable them understand better, analytically and critically, the dynamics of human society. The next two roles, that of the **policy** sociologist and the **social engineer** or **social analyst** involve going beyond mere promoting a better understanding of a social phenomenon or situation, to directly address with some degrees of involvement into specific issues. However, as a social engineer or social analyst, one is usually not expected to be responsible for the whole process of problem-solving, a role that tends to be expected of the next and final category of sociologists, the **clinical sociologist**.

Zetterberg (1962) identified 5 elements of social practice that any social science consultants needed to perform. These are the following: conducting **exploratory inquiry** where the consultant explored the details of a problem through informal interviews, observing, and researching; promoting **scholarly understanding** where a client's problem was translated into scientific terms, theoretical problems formulated, and important variables identified; engaging in **scholarly confrontation** where the client was provided a tentative theoretical perspective of the situation and invited to respond and give feedback; helping in the **discovery of solution** that involved the weighting of the alternative solutions; and finally the offering of **scientific advice.** In this final step a theoretical solution is translated into the client's language where "he is told what to do, given the complications and unintended consequences of the solutions proposed" (Zetterberg, 1962, p. 135). Zetterberg (1962) felt that consultants should only go this far, that is, as far as advice giving, a stop-short from entering the truly clinical world of actual implementation and direct intervention in the client's situation.

The idea that advice giving is **safer**, less demanding in nature, and therefore pose a lesser risk to the professional image of the consultant, appears to non-practitioners to be a sensible assumption to make. After all, there is the possibility that the advice given is inappropriate and the efforts to implement may fail. If the consultant is not directly involved in the implementation, it would be easy to blame the failure on the implementers. Why should sociologists give **advice** in the first place? **Advice** encompasses many nonobjective elements and as such there is no such thing as **a scientific advice**. The term "advice" is rather unfortunate since it means making a specific recommendation as to what concrete action the "advisee" needs to take. This role is fraught with inherent dangers as well as other potential ethical, moral, and legal improprieties.

As consultants, alternative courses of action can be presented to the client who alone is qualified to choose what appropriate action to take. In other words the decision maker should be the client, the not consultant. Stopping at the point of advice giving and not going beyond it, as suggested by Zetterberg, does not necessarily absolve one totally from blame should the advice given turn out to be inappropriate or ineffective. In reality, consultants may still be blamed for giving a specific "bad advice." They stand a better chance of defending themselves should the clients themselves are allowed to choose their own course of action selected from the several alternatives offered by the consultants. They also stand a better chance of salvaging their professional reputation should they choose to guide and work alongside their clients throughout the implementation process. Advice giving is often a little more than conjuring a simplistic end-result **vision** as a destination to be achieved while the implementation process is a **mission** that involves a complex interaction of actors and interrelated factors, foreseeable and unforeseeable ones. It requires implementers to be able to continuously navigate, negotiate, redirect, and reformulate, modifying not only the planned mission but perhaps even part of the original vision. The implementation journeys provide valuable learning experiences with which textbooks and armchair theorizing cannot possibly compete.

Where is the applied end of the continuum where the sociologist truly "applies" rather than contemplate and advise others on **what** and **how** to apply? The applied end of the continuum should be extended further to include what we suggest in this book as a **clinical** specialty. At this extended point of the applied continuum sociologists can play the role as direct applicators of knowledge and skills through direct intervention with the objective of achieving some specific form of the desired change. This will be the role of the **clinical sociologist,** the main focus of this book. This additional role of the clinical sociologist helps to complete the spectrum of role positions along the sociology continuum. In this clinical role sociologists are committed to working in tandem with their clients throughout the whole process of problem-solving. This involvement may be in response to an invitation by clients or interest groups, but no invitation is needed to intervene in situations involving critical public interests and concerns. It may involve the drawing up of formal contracts or alternatively not involving any contractual agreement of any kind. Clinical sociologists and their clients go through a systematic process of problem-solving while at the same time gradually empowering the latter to be able to function optimally and effectively after the involvement of the sociologist officially ends.

A typical sociologist may choose to combine several of the roles along the continuum, performing them in succession or concurrently depending on the sociologist's professional assessment of their appropriateness to the specific task at hand. For example, basic sociologists may decide to play the role of a **social critic** offering public commentaries on particular social issues, They may choose to conduct **basic research** projects, partly as a part of their academic responsibility while at the same time elucidating the general public with their research findings on topics of public interest. These first two roles may be fused together since the academic world often requires one to perform both roles simultaneously. More adventurous sociologists may add policy-relevant research as an additional role. They may perform commissioned research projects that require them to address specific problems that need solutions and recommendations. However, should they find this role as too superficial and wish to become more involved in the problem-solving process they may add the role as **social engineers** or as **social analysts** to their repertoire. Over time, they will accumulate considerable experience in providing them with valuable insights regarding the complexities and dynamics of an implementation process. Some sociologists may want to go beyond this self-imposed limitation that sociologists have placed upon themselves to embark upon even more direct role of social intervention.

As the social engineering model faced mounting criticisms, Gouldner and Miller (1965) took the opportunity to promote **clinical sociology** as a new and viable alternative. A clinical sociology model, they assured, would be able to avoid the major pitfalls of the social engineering approach, reputed as allowing clients too much leeway in determining how intervention was to be performed. They saw a clinical approach as a more holistic approach that treated a client's definition of a situation as constituting "part of the problem" (p. 13) to be resolved while incorporating other "definitions" of the situation, including that of the sociologist. According to them, clinical sociologists considered their clients' complaints and self-formulations as only one among a number of inputs, not as the main input, for diagnosing the clients' problem. What they probably meant was that clinical sociologists would consult with all the parties affected, or potentially to be impacted, by their intervention strategies. This is to ensure a more systemic sociological perspective is maintained, rather than being unduly influenced by only the clients' limited perspective. While heaping praise on clinical sociology as a viable alternative, Gouldner and Miller (1965) did not disapprove of the social engineering model in its entirety. On the contrary Gouldner and Miller (1965) did not see the clinical and engineering as total opposites. They recognized that both models had their own strengths and weaknesses.

In order to strike a harmonious coexistence between the two models of applied sociology, Rossi and Whyte (1983) suggested that both approaches should continue to complement each other. The social engineer, they suggested, could focus on "institutional arrangements and design" while the clinician could concentrate on the "specific problems of concrete social entities." They provided some specific examples to help illustrate the difference between the two models. In one example, they suggested that the social engineer could work with clients for the purpose of drawing up a marriage contract, while the clinical sociologist could advise the married couple on how to work out a division of labor between the couple during the marriage period. In another example, a social engineer might propose a new form of work group in an assembly plant while the clinical sociologist might work on how to improve worker morale in the workplace. They, however, did realize that it was often difficult to distinguish clearly between the two approaches. The authors of this book agree that it may be difficult in actual practice to do so, and even more importantly, it is not necessary to impose such an arbitrary distinction between the two.

Using the example given above, it will indeed be difficult to ask a social engineer only to work with a prospective married couple on a marriage contract and to suggest that the issues that may arise *after* the marriage should be handled by someone else by a clinical sociologist. It will be more realistic to allow *both* approaches to be equally applicable to any of the situations depending on the interests and inclinations of both the practitioner and the client. Despite the popular criticism of the social engineering model as being too submissive toward the demands of the clients, it is not clear whether this is merely a criticism of the performance of some particular social engineers, or whether there is a genuine inherent defect in the social engineering approach itself. It is difficult even to ascertain whether there is such a thing as a definitive approach in social engineering since efforts ascribed under this rubric were relatively experimental or pioneering in nature with no clearly established protocols, standards or *modus operandi* to guide the work of its practitioners.

Although the idea of a clinical specialty within sociology had always attracted some sociologists who had from time to time toyed and experimented with it, it failed to attract the serious attention and substantial support from mainstream sociology beyond some occasional academic polemics on the subject. The authors of this book feel very much as **closet sociologists**, cautiously practicing and promoting clinical sociology without being able to make open public declarations about it. There is not much vocal opposition or outright rejection to the idea of clinical sociology, but rather indifference to it. The majority of sociologists either do not see the need for it, unsure as to what it is all about and yet not wanting its probe further what exactly clinical sociologists do. This general demonstration of disinterest and apathy within the sociology fraternity is reflected in the conspicuous absence of course offerings related to clinical sociology theory and practice in almost all sociology curriculum worldwide. Due to a real and pressing need for clinical sociology, the lack of support and recognition received from the larger sociology community does not in any way diminish the commitment of its practitioners. Its exponents tirelessly continue to develop the field to the point where it had achieved some form of official recognition.

What are the roots of clinical sociology? Fritz (1985) traced the historical development of clinical sociology with considerable detail in her two main works, in her book ***The Clinical Sociology Handbook*** and in her article "The Emergence of American Clinical Sociology." Fritz (1985) considered an Arab statesperson, Ibn Khaldun (1332–1406), as one of the forerunners of this specialty for what she saw as his clinical observations of the social conditions and problems of his contemporary society. Ibn Khaldun (1377), centuries before Comte (1798–1857) propagated the idea of having a rational and analytical approach toward understanding society, expressed his misgivings toward the traditional historical approach toward understanding society. Although Ibn Khaldun's writings, and some of Comte's (1798–1857) ideas, can be considered as somewhat naïve by today's standards, he presented some thoughts on such issues as man's relation with the physical world; presenting an analysis of primitive social organization; discussing the nature of leadership; exploring the relationship among different societies; and theorizing the evolution of early human society into "higher, urban form of society."

The ideas of this early Arab scholar could have subsequently influenced those of the French sociologist, Comte (1798–1857), the inventor of the term "sociology." Comte, Martineau, and Harrison (1896) visualized sociology as capable of helping to prepare the society of his time for the new Industrial Age. He was convinced that by studying and identifying the laws of social phenomena one could foresee and modify them to one's advantage. This was reflected in his famous dictum "Savoir pour prevoir; prevoir pour prevenir," which approximately meant the **acquisition** of sociological knowledge was for the sake of **prediction** which in turn enabled sociologists to undertake the appropriate action for **prevention,** or according to Berger and Berger (1972) as meaning "to know in order to predict in order to control" (p. 33).

Not much later, Karl Marx (1818–1893) introduced the concept of **praxis**, which could be defined as purposive social action capable of bringing about radical social change in society, made him equally eligible for being considered as one of the forerunners of clinical sociology. In approximately the same period, in the United States, Small (1895) strongly subscribed to the view that the raison d'etre of sociology was that of using sociological knowledge for the purpose of transforming society (Fritz, 1985). In another source Small (1896) eloquently advocated the need to ensure that the idea of sociology as a science went hand in hand with the idea of sociology as a practice, where "the wisdom which comes from knowing" was to be combined with "the larger wisdom which comes from doing" (p. 564). He expressed his disapproval for the "do-nothing traditions," declaring that it was time to "repeal the law of custom which bars marriage of thought with action" (p. 564). At the turn of the twentieth century, in his book on general sociology, Small (1905) expressed his confidence that sociology was capable of bringing about practical changes in society, and that sociologists had to have a vision of what the future society should be.

At about the same time, another American sociologist, Ward published two books. The first was entitled ***Pure Sociology*** and published in 1903, followed by a book entitled ***Applied Sociology*** in 1906. The appearance of the two publications was highly significant since they signaled the emergence of two distinct wings within sociology. He conceptualized **applied** sociology as the systematic study of social forces with the objective of bringing about social synergy that would eventually benefit society, based on the belief that man was capable of **intelligent foresight**. Ward (1906) did not want sociologists to be fooled by the notion that social structures they saw around them were stable and unchanging, as were emphasized by "pure" sociologists. He was of the view that only a few of the social structures, if *any*, were incapable of modification. He believed that even if some aspects of the social structures could not be changed by the use of direct methods they could still be gradually transformed by the use of appropriate indirect methods.

While "pure" sociology considered the development of society as a spontaneous process, he wanted applied sociologists to develop the "artificial means of accelerating the spontaneous processes of nature," which would produce social improvement and the achievement of social ideals. He placed an emphasis on the idea that social structure was modifiable and he was optimistic that humans possess the capacity for planned social change. This notion of dynamic and ever-changing social structures tended to be lost to later sociologists of the structural–functionalist persuasion who tended to favor the idea of social structures as permanent features that were beyond the capability of the individual or small human groups to change. The eventual emergence of a distinctly applied, practical and clinically oriented sociology on American soil was hardly surprising since, as pointed out by Berger and Berger (1972), sociology in America grew as a response to a different social milieu when compared to that of the Old World Europe. According to them the experiences and challenges faced by the American nation as a relatively new immigrant society, undergoing a rapid rate of industrialization and urbanization, forced its native-born sociology to offer societal analysis and an understanding of the practical needs for social reform and social work.

Looking for the origins of the term "clinical sociology," Fritz (1985, 1991) identified Winternitz, a pathologist, as the first person to link together the words **clinical** and **sociology** in print in 1930. Winternitz proposed the offering of a course to be named **clinical sociology** and he even suggested the setting-up of a whole department of clinical sociology within his medical school. This was to enable medical students to have the chance to discuss medical cases using clinical sociology lens. This dream, however, turned out to be somewhat premature for his time. Following this the first known university course offered under the name of **clinical sociology** was one that was taught by Burgess in the University of Chicago (1928–1933), followed by a clinical sociology course offered at the Tulane University in Louisiana in 1929 (Fritz, 1991).

The first most significant effort to explain the idea of clinical sociology was found in an article contributed by Wirth (1897–1952) in an academic journal published in 1931. In this article Wirth (1931) announced the genesis of a new division of sociology which he suggested should most appropriately be called **clinical sociology**. Wirth (1931) was himself a practitioner unlike many others before and after him who merely expounded the theoretical potentials of clinical sociology. Wirth (1931) personally entered the world of practice in order to obtain a more intimate understanding of how a sociologist could contribute to the clinical field alongside other practitioners. The next outstanding exponent of clinical sociology after Wirth (1931) was probably Gouldner (1956) who pointed out the potentials of clinical sociology as an alternative to the controversial and much maligned social engineering approach as mentioned earlier. He himself offered an undergraduate course in clinical sociology at Antioch College, Ohio (1953–1954) wherein its course description he described clinical sociology as "a sociological counterpart to clinical psychology" (Fritz, 1991, p. 21). After Wirth's (1931) article, Gouldner's (1956) exposition of clinical sociology in 1956 helped to keep the idea of clinical sociology alive among its supporters as well as attracting the attention of those who were still unfamiliar with the nature of this specialty.

Throughout the 1960s and 1970s an occasional individual and small groups of sociologists, who were convinced of the potentials of clinical sociology, began to quietly introduce it as part of their university course offerings. Each one of them had the liberty and flexibility of experimenting with their own approaches in what was a relatively a virgin territory within sociology. This low-profile and incremental propagation of the specialty culminated finally with the establishment of the **Clinical Sociology Association** in 1978 in the United States. This event brought together the clinical sociologists, who had hitherto been performing individually and whose existence had not obtained the recognition it deserved, to pool their ideas and resources on a scale not witnessed before. The establishment of the Association encouraged an unprecedented flurry of books, journals, and articles on clinical sociology. Among the books written on the topic of clinical sociology included ***Clinical Sociology*** by Glassner and Freedman (1979); ***The Practice of Clinical Sociology and Sociotherapy*** by Swan (1984); ***Using Sociology: An Introduction from a Clinical Perspective*** by Straus (Ed.) (1985); ***Sociology for Whom*** (1978) and ***Sociology for People*** (1988) by Lee; and ***Handbook of Clinical Sociology*** by Rebach and Bruhn (Eds.) (1991). The main journals for the Clinical Sociology Association were the ***Clinical Sociology Review*** that began publication 1982 as well as ***Sociological Practice*** through which new articles and reprinting of previous articles on the subject were annually published. These two journals were later replaced by ***Sociological Practice: A Journal of Clinical and Applied Sociology***, which publishes quarterly.

In 1986, all sociological practitioners, regardless of whether they consider themselves as clinical sociologists, social analysts, social engineers, or simply applied sociologists, were brought together and the previously **Clinical Sociology Association** (CSA) was renamed the **Sociological Practice Association** (SPA). The change in the name from that of **clinical** to that of **practice** could be seen as a step backward for clinical sociologists who had been dreaming of an organization that could organize and promote their distinct specialty from other applied approaches. This change, however, was justified on the grounds that it was a good strategy to bring together **all** sociological practitioners at a time when the number of clinical sociologists was still relatively small. Clark (1990) the fourth president of the CSA explained the change as partly due to the need to broaden the membership base of the Association as well as the fact that, historically speaking, "practical sociology" (p. 107) which began in 1900, could be considered as the precursor of both applied and clinical sociologies. The attractiveness of bringing all sociology practitioners together under an umbrella was plausible since they were all concerned with a similar objective: to achieve a resolution of problems with a therapeutic objective in mind. However, for those who saw clinical sociology as a distinct approach and who dreamt of developing it as a distinct training program and profession, the change left it once again without a clear sense of identity and direction. However, a new momentum to push clinical sociology to the front had been unleashed and interests in it among sociologists had been galvanized.

Although a temporary setback had occurred in the United States, important events in the development of clinical sociology occurred in other parts of the world. At the international level, the International Sociological Association (ISA) set up a separate Working Group on Clinical sociology (R46) was initiated in 1982, in the ISA World Congress held in Mexico City signaling at last, the legitimate importance of this specialty on the international scene. Papers on the subjects were regularly presented during the Association's World Congresses, organized every 4 years and the International forum, every 2 years following the Congress attracting the curiosity and attention of sociologists with clinical interests all over the world. At about the same time, back in the United States, the name of "clinical sociology" was about to make a comeback. A renewed recognition of clinical sociology as a specialty was seen in the setting-up of a Commission on Applied and Clinical Sociology (CACS) in 1995 by the combined efforts of the Sociological Practice Association and the Society for Applied Sociology.

The coming together of the two associations to drop the term **practice** and to replace it with the term **clinical** instead certainly placated those who were adamant that the clinical specialty should not drown in the sea of practical sociology. This Commission was given the task of giving accreditation for clinical and applied sociological practice programs in universities throughout the United States. It involved registering graduates who had successfully completed the accredited programs in clinical and applied sociology. It also advocated for sociology in the areas of occupational licensing and certification and finally disseminating program models and resources to sociology departments interested in developing applied and clinical programs. The commission was later renamed as The Commission on the Accreditation of Programs in Applied and Clinical Sociology (CAPACS) in 2010 to better represent both applied and clinical wings of the profession.

Another positive step forward toward re-establishing the coexistence between the two was when the Sociological Practice Association and the Society for Applied Sociology were eventually merged into a single **Association for Applied and Clinical Sociology (AACS).** It was created as a platform that brought the applied, clinical, and engaged sociologists together aimed at promoting "integrative approaches and systems perspectives for analyzing complex problems and developing creative, practical solutions" (**Association for Applied and Clinical Sociology**, 2019). The newly established AACS was arguably a major milestone for the advancement of clinical sociology. A certification of recognition was issued to clinical sociologists and other practitioners who were able to demonstrate an adequate level of field experience and expertise as well as a high level of commitment and involvement in social services They also have to pass an evaluation of their work by a certified professional in the field. Consequently, they would then be awarded the title of Certified Clinical Sociologists (CCS) or Certified Sociological Practitioners (CSP). Mentorship for young scholars was also another important development toward quenching the thirst of clinically inclined students. However, the emphasis on research which was still prevalent in the association's code of practice which tended to distract sociologists from moving beyond research to do work that qualifies as **real** clinical work.

The above brief discussion on the development of clinical sociology has concentrated almost solely on its development in the United States, a bias which hopefully will be redressed when more information concerning the actual practice of clinical sociologists in every corner of the world are documented. Other than the United States, there were other parallel strands of interest and development in this specialty, such as among French and Francophone sociologists as well as by their counterparts in Italy. They all played an important part in making clinical sociology as an emergent specialty on the international scene, no longer limiting the interests in it to the American scene.

It is evident that considerable efforts have been made recently to establish organizations, publications, and committees particularly in both with the Anglophone and with the francophone academic circles to promote the idea and advancement of clinical sociology (ISA-RC46, 2014). In 1988, a workshop within the Internationale des sociologues de langue française that discusses clinical sociology was spearheaded by Sevigny, Houle, Enriquez, and Gaulejac in Geneva. This was followed by the first clinical sociology conference in France (1992) at Universite Paris Diderot and subsequently the setting-up of the foundation of the Institut International de Sociologie Clinique in 1999, Paris as well as Clinical sociology committee in Internationale des sociologues de langue française and l'Association française de sociologie in 2004 (Gaulejac, 2008). Numerous articles are written by those who choose to consider themselves as clinical sociology practitioners within wide range of subfields and settings dealing with such issues and projects such as in health education, rehabilitation, and prevention (Cote, Renaud, Rhéaume, & Zanchetta, 2010; Rhéaume, 2009; Sévigny, Sheying, & Chen, 2010).

Some work as case workers assessing the effectiveness as well as providing direct social services to numerous target groups. Some work as counsellors and even as psychiatric social workers dealing with target groups such as troubled youths, homeless adults, and people with disabilities. Some of them work as marriage and family therapists. Many of them see the conducting of innovative research and the program evaluation of existing practices as their introduction into the world of clinical sociology. Some others choose to deal with organization development and change efforts as well as other organizational issues with the belief that a sociological perspective can help to improve the effectiveness of organizations (Enriquez, 1992). Recently a clinical sociology dictionary in French that was contributed by sociologists across the globe and compiled by Vandevelde-Rougale and Fugier (2019) is another development that signals the acceptance and growth of clinical sociology.

This deluge of material subsumed under the rubric of clinical sociology, however, is deceptive because most of them qualify as a preparation for the eventual entry into the world of social intervention, an early exploratory phase which hopefully will lead to the full future potential of clinical sociology. A great number of work, mainly in both the Anglophone and the francophone traditions, is still very theoretical and research in nature. Even those who are directly involved in direct intervention seem to fail to develop and fully explain the so-claimed uniqueness of their clinical sociology approaches in comparison with the existing approaches adopted by the other professions. Until and unless the additional benefits of new and innovative clinical sociology approaches can be demonstrated as beneficial and effective in the actual performances and the actual outcomes of social intervention, clinical sociology will continue to remain an immense potential for the future. Most clinical sociologists need to accept the reality that they are only preparing themselves for clinical practice, not actually performing it. The sad reality is that no amount of preparation will equip them, psychologically and experientially, to enter the field of actual interventional practice other than entering the field of practice at the shallow end before becoming adequately confident and equipped with the necessary skills and tools to survive and thrive at the deeper end of the social whirlpool.

There are also some literature written on clinical sociology in non-English languages, particularly those written by Francophone, Italian, and sociologists of other nationalities, most of which have not been translated and made available to Anglophone sociologists. There are some materials available on what are referred to as **clinical sociology** written by Francophone sociologists available in several French-speaking countries, principally of France, Belgium, and Quebec, Canada. Gurdin (1986), for example, provided some overview of how the term **clinical sociology** was used in conjunction with other ideas and approaches in applied sociology, namely that of **socio-analysis**, **psycho-sociology, psychiatric sociology**, **social psychiatry, ethno-psychiatry**, etc. There was no clear-cut differentiation in how the various terms were used although Gurdin (1986), did summarize the several differences found between the clinical sociology in the French-speaking countries and that of the American approach. He noted that the former tended to have a more psychoanalytical bias. At the same time they tended to address macro political processes where the sociologists were employed as governmental policy analysts, commentators, and civil servants. The American approach, he observed, especially the one acknowledged by the members of the American Clinical Sociological Association (CSA), tended to focus more on small-scale micro-level intervention in localized settings. He predicted that the differences would diminish as clinical sociologists became more connected with one another as **global villagers**.

Though the trend now is changing, according to Herreros (2002) Francophone sociologists generally shied away from using the term **clinical sociology**. Touraine (1984), an exponent of sociological intervention or social action, did not use the term **clinical** to describe it. According to Herreros (2002) even the psycho-sociologists, the psychiatric sociologists, and the social psychiatrists who were familiar with the psychological and psychoanalytical approaches did not want to take the **risk** by applying the word **clinical** to sociological practice. Bourdieu (1997), a renowned French sociologist, however, was among those who were supportive of the idea of clinical sociology. However, in his **Les usages sociaux de la science: Pour une sociologie clinique du champ scientifique,** he did not elaborate on what exactly clinical sociology meant to him. This is true for most sociologists who seldom go beyond offering definitions and brief explanations without elaborating on exactly how clinical sociology is to be put into practice. The place of clinical sociology in the grand scheme of things will not be understood unless and until it can be shown to contrast and differ, complement and supplement, the roles of its close cousins—**clinical psychology** and **clinical social work**. Future historians of clinical sociology hopefully will reveal with greater detail the important role played by non-Americans in promoting the field of clinical sociology although early efforts have already been done by Fritz and a few others, beyond research work.

References

Allen, V. L. (1975). *Social analysis: A Marxist critique and alternative*. London: Longman.

Association for Applied and Clinical Sociology. (2019). Retrieved from https://www.aacsnet.net/

Berelson, B. (1966). Sociology in action: In population and in general. In A. B. Shostak (Ed.), *Sociology in action: Case studies in social problems and directed social change* (pp. 15–21). Illinois: The Dorsey Press.

Berger, P. L., & Berger, B. (1972). *Sociology: A biographical approach*. Harmondsworth: Basic Books.

Bockstaele, J. V., Bockstaele, M. V., Malbos, J., Godard-Plasman, M., & Bockstaele-Theilhaber, N. V. (2008). Socioanalysis and clinical intervention. In J. M. Fritz (Ed.), *International clinical sociology* (pp. 170–187). New York: Springer.

Bourdieu, P. (1997). *Les usage sociaux de la science. Pour une sociologie clinique du champ scientifique*. Paris: Institut Nasional De La Recherche Agronomique.

Braude, L. (1974). *A sense of sociology*. New York: Praeger Publishers.

Bryant, C. G. A. (1991). The dialogical model of applied sociology. In C. G. A. Bryant & D. Jary (Eds.), *Giddens' theory of structuration: A critical appreciation* (pp. 176–200). London: Routledge.

Bryant, C. G. A. (1995). *Practical sociology: Post-empiricism and the reconstruction of theory and application*. Cambridge: Polity Press.

Bulmer, M. (1990). Successful applications of sociology. In C. G. A. Bryant & H. A. Becker (Eds.), *What has sociology achieved?* (pp. 117–142). London: The Macmillan Press.

Bulmer, M. (1993). The apotheosis of liberalism? An American dilemma after fifty years in the context of the lives of Gunnar and Alva Myrdal. *Ethnic and Racial Studies, 16*(2), 345–357.

Clark, E. J. (1990). The development of contemporary clinical sociology. *Clinical Sociological Review, 8*, 100–115.

Comte, A., Martineau, H., & Harrison, F. (1896). *The positive philosophy of Auguste Comte*. London: G. Bell & Sons.

Cote, R., Renaud, L., Rheaume, J., & Zanchetta, M. (2010). Retour de mission: visite au brésil pour disséminer de l'information sur les determinants sociaux de la santé et les vulnérabilitiés sociales. *Cahiers METISS, 5*(1), 47–60.

De Bie, P. (1970). *Problem-focused research. In main trends in the social and human sciences* (pp. 578–644). Paris: Mouton UNESCO.

Enriquez, E. (1992). Remarques terminales vers Une sociologie clinique d'inspiration psychanalytique [final remarks toward a clinical sociology with psychoanalytic inspiration]. In *L'organisation en analyse*. Paris: Fevrier.

Etzioni, A. (1965). Social analysis as a sociological vocation. *The American Journal of Sociology, 70*, 317–323.

Etzkowitz, H., & Schaflander, G. M. (1968). A manifesto for sociologists: Institution formation – A new sociology. *Social Problems, 15*(4), 399–408.

Fernandez, R. (1975). *The promise of sociology*. New York: Praeger Publishers.

Flores-González, N., & Rodríguez-Muiz, M. (2011). Youth culture, identity, and resistance: Participatory action research in a Puerto Rican Barrio. In K. O. Korgen, J. M. White, & S. K. White (Eds.), *Sociologists in action: Sociology, social change and social justice*. Thousand Oaks, CA: Pine Forge Press.

Fritz, J. M. (1985). *The clinical sociology handbook*. New York: Garland Publishing.

Fritz, J. M. (1991). Emergence of American clinical sociology. In H. M. Rebach & J. G. Bruhn (Eds.), *Handbook of clinical sociology* (pp. 17–27). New York: Plenum Press.

Gaulejac, V. (2008). On the origins of clinical sociology in France: Some milestones. In J. M. Fritz (Ed.), *International clinical sociology* (pp. 54–71). New York: Springer.

Glassner, B., & Freedman, J. A. (1979). *Clinical sociology*. New York: Longman.

Gouldner, A. W. (1956). Explorations in applied social science. *Social Problems, 3*, 169–181.

Gouldner, A., & Miller, S. M. (Eds.). (1965). *Applied sociology: Opportunities and problems*. New York: Free Press.

Gurdin, B. J. (1986). Clinical sociology in France and Quebec: A primer and commentar. *Clinical Sociology Review, 4*, 46–56.

Herreros, G. (2002). Pour une sociologie d'intervention. *Sociologie du travail, 46*(3), 407–408.

Hewitt, J. P. (1991). *Self and society: A symbolic interactionist social psychology*. Boston, MA: Allyn and Bacon.

Horowitz, I. L. (1968). *Professing sociology: Studies in the life cycle of social science*. Chicago: Aldine Publishing Company.

International Sociological Association – RC46. (2014). *Links*. Retrieved from https://clinical-sociology.org/

Janowitz, M. (1972). *Sociological models and social policy*. Morristown, NJ: The General Learning Press.

Jones, G. (1971). *The role of science and technology in developing countries*. London: Oxford University Press.

Joseph, C. (2011). Sociology: Promise and potential through praxis. In K. O. Korgen, J. M. White, & S. K. White (Eds.), *Sociologists in action: Sociology, social change and social justice*. Thousand Oaks, CA: Pine Forge Press.

Kettler, D., Meja, V., & Stehr, N. (1984). *Karl Mannheim: Key sociologists*. Milton Keynes: The Open University.

Ibn Khaldun. (1377). *The muqaddimah: An introduction to history*. Translated from Arabic by F. Rosenthal, abridged and edited by N. J. Dawood (1967). Princeton, NJ: Princeton University Press.

Klien, G. C., Dentler, R. A., Hunter, R. M., Catton, W. E., Jr., & Dynes, R. R. (1982). Let's not be lecturing on navigation while the ship is going down: On the creation of public interest sociology. *The American Sociologist, 17*(3), 120–136.

Lee, A. M. (1954). Sociologists in an integrating society: Significance and satisfaction in sociological work. *Social Problems, 2*(1), 57–66.

Lee, A. M. (1973). *Toward humanist sociology*. New Jersey: Prentice-Hall.

Lee, A. M. (1978). *Sociology for whom?* New York: Oxford University Press.

Lindesmith, A. R. (1960). *Social problems and sociological theory*. Reproduced in A. B. Shostak (Ed.) (1966), *Sociology in action: Case studies in social problems and directed social change* (pp. 270–275). Illinois: The Dorsey Press.

Marshall, G. (1990). *In praise of sociology*. London: Unwin Hyman.

Marshall, G. (1994). *Oxford concise dictionary of sociology*. Oxford: Oxford University Press.

Mayo, C., & La France, M. (1980). Toward an applicable social psychology. In R. F. Kidd & M. J. Saks (Eds.), *Advances in applied social psychology* (Vol. 1, pp. 81–96). Hillsdale, NJ: Erlbaum.

Midgley, G. (2000). *Systemic intervention: Philosophy, methodology, and practice*. New York: Kluwer Academic Plenum Publishers.

Nack, A. (2011). From *damaged goods* to empowered patients. In K. O. Korgen, J. M. White, & S. K. White (Eds.), *Sociologists in action: Sociology, social change and social justice*. Thousand Oaks, CA: Pine Forge Press.

Neufeldt, V., & Guralnik, D. B. (1991). *Webster's new world dictionary*. New York: Prentice-Hall.

Olsen, M. E. (1981). Epilogue: The future of applied sociology. In M. E. Olsen & M. Micklin (Eds.), *Handbook of applied sociology* (pp. 561–581). New York: Praeger Publishers.

Olsen, M. E., & Micklin, M. (1981). *Handbook of applied sociology*. New York: Praeger Publishers.

Pahl, R. E. (1977). Playing the rationality game: The sociologist as a hired expert. In C. Bell & H. Newby (Eds.), *Doing sociological research* (pp. 130–148). New York: The Free Press.

Payne, G., & Cross, M. C. (Eds.). (1993). *Sociology in action: Applications and opportunities for the 1990s*. London: The Macmillan Press.

Perlstadt, H. (1998). Bringing sociological theory and practice together: A pragmatic solution. *Sociological Perspectives, 41*(2), 268–271.

Popper, K. R. (1966). *The open society and its enemies* (5th ed.). London: Routledge.

Rhéaume, J. (2009). La sociologie clinique comme pratique de recherché en institution. Le cas d'un Centre de sante et services sociaux. *Sociologie & sociétés, 41*(1), 195–215.

Rossi, P. H. (1980). The presidential address: The challenge and opportunities of applied social research. *American Sociological Review, 45*, 889–904.

Rossi, P. H., & Whyte, W. F. (1983). The applied side of sociology. In H. E. Freeman, R. D. Russell, P. H. Rossi, & W. F. Whyte (Eds.), *Applied sociology* (pp. 5–31). San Francisco: Jossey-Bass Publishers.

Rowbottom, R. (1977). *Social analysis: A collaborative method of gaining usable scientific knowledge of social institutions*. London: Heinemann.

Schein, E. H. (2001). Clinical inquiry/research. In P. Reason & H. Bradbury (Eds.), *Handbook of action research: Participative inquiry and practice* (pp. 228–237). London: Sage.

Schuman, H. (1975). Race relations: Some policy implications, proximate and remote, of a negative finding. In N. J. Demerath, O. Larsen, & K. F. Schuessler (Eds.), *Social policy and sociology* (pp. 37–44). New York: Academic Press.

Schuyler, K. G. (2011). Organizational consulting: A passion for meaningful sociological work. In K. O. Korgen, J. M. White, & S. K. White (Eds.), *Sociologists in action: Sociology, social change and social justice*. Thousand Oaks, CA: Pine Forge Press.

Scott, R. A., & Shore, A. R. (1979). *Why sociology does not apply*. New York: Elsevier North Holland.

Sévigny, R., Sheying, C., & Chen, E. Y. (2010). Explanatory models of illness and psychiatric rehabilitation: A clinical sociology approach. *Qualitative Sociology Review, 6*(3), 63–80.

Small, A. (1895). The era of sociology. *American Journal of Sociology, 1*, 1–15.

Small, A. W. (1896). Scholarship and social agitation. *American Journal of Sociology, 5*, 564–582.

Small, A. (1905). *General sociology*. Chicago: University of Chicago.

Straus, R. A. (Ed.). (1985). *Using sociology: An introduction from the clinical perspective*. New York: General Hall.

Street, D. P., & Weistein, E. A. (1981). Prologue: Problems and prospects of applied sociology. In M. E. Olsen & M. Micklin (Eds.), *Handbook of applied sociology* (pp. xiii–xxiv). New York: Praeger.

Swan, L. A. (1980). Clinical sociologists: Coming out of the closet. *Mid-Atlantic Review of Sociology, 5*(1), 87–98.

Swan, L. A. (1984). *The practice of clinical sociology and sociotherapy*. Cambridge, Mass: Schenkman Publishing Company.

Sztompka, P. (1979). *Sociological dilemmas*. New York: Academic Press.

Szymanski, A. (1971). Toward a radical sociology. In J. D. Colfax & J. L. Roach (Eds.), *Radical sociology* (pp. 93–107). New York: Basic Books.

Touraine, A. (1984). *Le retour de l'acteur: Essai de sociologie*. Paris: librairie artheme fayard. Translated in English by M. Godzich (1988). Return of the actor. Minneapolis: University of Minnesota.

Vandevelde-Rougale, A., & Fugier, P. (Eds.). (2019). *Dictionnaire de sociologie Clinique*. Toulouse: ERES.

Ward, L. F. (1906). *Applied sociology: A treatise on the conscious improvement of society by society*. Boston: Ginn and Company.
Wirth, L. (1931). Sociology and clinical procedure. *American Journal of Sociology, 37*, 49–66.
Wittner, J. (2011). Stand up and speak out. In K. O. Korgen, J. M. White, & S. K. White (Eds.), *Sociologists in action: Sociology, social change and social justice*. Thousand Oaks, CA: Pine Forge Press.
Zetterberg, F. (1962). *Social theory and social practice*. New York: Bedminster Press.

Part II
The Fundamentals of Clinical Sociology

Chapter 2
Defining "Clinical Sociology"

For some unclear reasons, many sociologists appeared to be uncomfortable with the term **clinical** to refer to sociological practice. The typical reaction encountered by the authors would be "why **clinical**" to which the authors would retort "why **not** clinical?" Many have generally not been at ease with the term because of the belief simply that it essentially belonged to other disciplines, principally to medicine and psychology. Michel Foucault (1963), a non-sociologist who had somehow earned respect for his sociological observations, in his book's entitled ***Naissance de la clinique*** examined how the concept of **la clinique** developed within the medical profession. He did not elaborate on the need for a broader scope of application to nonmedical situations.

Even in dictionaries of sociological terms the appropriateness of applying the term **clinical** to sociology (Jary & Jary, 1999) is questioned. The dictionaries generally associate the term **clinic** with the medical profession, not acknowledging the fact that the word had long entered everyday language used to refer to nonmedical activities as well, as examples, to refer to "car-care clinics" and "legal advisory clinics." Politicians in Britain perform weekly or monthly "clinics" when they conduct face-to-face encounters with their constituents to resolve local issues and demands. Similarly, the derivative word **clinical** is used in everyday expressions with nonmedical connotations, in such expressions as "clinical detachment" which means "being coldly objective." The term is used in the dictionaries to refer to an activity that is based on actual observation that is strictly objective and realistic; "dispassionately analytic"; "unemotionally critical"; and "purely scientific" in nature. In summary, a sociologist can be considered to be a clinical worker when he or she approaches a social phenomenon in a scientific, objective, realistic, and analytic manner to bring about changes that can be clinically evaluated and assessed. In other words, for an activity to be clinical it needs to be linked to the idea of "improving" a particular social situation. In the case of the medical and psychology professions, it is for the purpose of "treatment" or "cure." Clearly, an adversity to the use of the term **clinical** is clearly emotional and habitual rather than rational in nature.

© Springer Nature Switzerland AG 2020

P. M. Wan, A. H. Wan, *Clinical Sociology*, Clinical Sociology: Research and Practice, https://doi.org/10.1007/978-3-030-49083-6_2

The earliest definition of **clinical sociology** offered by Wirth (1931), a sociologist, as "the insights, methods of approach, and techniques which the science of sociology can contribute to the understanding and treatment of persons facing some forms of problems." According to Wirth (1931), the clinical sociologist uses a **cultural** approach that involved taking into consideration the wider social context in which the person exists and functions, rather than merely focusing on the individual in isolation. According to this sociological perspective, a person is perceived and diagnosed as being part of "a constellation of a number of roles." Each role in turn needs to be understood with reference to a specific social group or social system within which it exists. Wirth (1931) gave the assurance that the focus on the **social** did not degrade the importance of the physical and psychological characteristics of a person, which obviously needed to be given equal consideration. However these considerations were to be interpreted in terms of their social significance, rather than as being significant in themselves. Wirth (1931) also asserted that the term **clinical** did not necessarily refer to social pathology where behaviors and situations are labeled as abnormal or diseased requiring **treatment** or **rehabilitation** the way other clinical professions defined the term. Instead of using the pathological or abnormality perspective, which Wirth (1931) saw as belonging to "the older conception of medicine," clinical sociologists offered a perspective that interpreted problematic human behaviors as normal responses to the social context (pp. 7–15).

Gouldner (1956) described a clinical approach as one where professionals or specialists apply their knowledge to the diagnosis of a problem after assessing all relevant factors, including the clients' definition of the situation. Swan (1984) considered a sociologist as being clinical in approach when he or she was involved in "direct observation, assessment and measurement" (p.51) of a particular social situation or phenomenon, perceived by the sociologist's **professional eye** or **insight**. Most importantly, what differentiated the clinician from the basic sociologist, according to Swan (1984), was that the former performed all these functions with the purpose of diagnosis and treatment of a particular situation, while the latter did not. Similarly, Schein (2001) saw the role of the clinician as one who went beyond data manipulation and diagnosis to combine clinical approaches and participant–observer ethnographic models. Intervention and diagnosis become inseparable as two sides of the same coin with the clinician performing research for the purpose of making diagnoses, which then led to intervention.

The first dictionary definition of "clinical sociology" was provided by Alfred McClung Lee (Fairchild, 1944) who described it as a division of practical or applied sociology which stressed the development of "effective manipulative and therapeutic techniques and of accurate functional information concerning society and social relationships" (p. 303). Lee considered a clinical sociologist as someone who synthesized the experiences of two categories of practitioners. The first was what he termed as the **social psychiatrists** including the social workers, personnel managers, psychiatrists, career guidance experts, who focused on individuals who were facing functional and adaptation problems. The second was the **societal technicians** including the public relations counselors, professional politicians, sentiment and opinion analysts, propagandists, advertisers, etc., who dealt with institutional problems and adjustment (Fairchild, 1944). In other words, clinical sociology was seen as a practical-oriented approach through the performance of professional intervention in social life.

Glassner and Freedman (1979) defined the field of clinical sociology as involving "the application of a variety of critically applied practices which attempt sociological diagnosis and treatment of groups and group members in communities" (p. 5). Freedman (1982) gave a list of what he saw as the basic characteristics of clinical sociology, including being practice-oriented; case-focused; involving the individuals, groups, organization, and community levels; diagnostic; change-oriented; humanistic; behavior change, and growth as objectives. Dunham (1982) offered his conception of clinical sociology as dealing with "the problem personality" and on how social structure, historical events, interpersonal relations, and cultural patterns affected the development of the personality. According to him, the clinical sociologist's central concern was to explore the influence of those variables on a person's self-image, role style, behavior pattern, and psychic orientation as being part of a larger social system.

Swan (1984) defined clinical sociology as a specialty in sociology that applied sociological knowledge, principles, and analysis at the group, community, organization, and individual levels, with the objective of "reducing distress, managing conflicts and assisting in achieving meaningful and effective functioning" (p. 34). Swan (1984) considered sociologists as being clinical practitioners or **socio-therapists** when they interpreted and manipulated sociological information for the purpose of promoting optimal activity, growth, and development at all levels of social reality. He perceived clinical sociology as capable of **liberating** what he saw as the **oppressive** and narrow approaches to such practices as marital and family therapy offered by the traditional psychiatrists, psychologists, and psychotherapists. The latter group of practitioners, Swan (1984) felt, did not have "the disciplinary base and content-focus to diagnose social situations, social interactions, and interpersonal relationships" (p. 28). Marshall (1994) offered a short description of **clinical sociology** in his dictionary, describing it as the application of sociological knowledge to aid diagnosis, treatment, teaching, and research. Fritz (1991) defined this specialty as "the creation of new systems as well as the intervention in existing systems for purposes of assessment and/or change" (p. 18). Clinical sociologists were seen as **humanistic** scientists whose approach was multidisciplinary, engaging in planned social change at any system level while utilizing a sociological frame of reference.

Many sociologists are familiar with the use of the term **clinical** but in a slightly different context. The term "clinical" has been used to refer to a genre of social research categorized as **clinical research**. Sociologists sometimes refer to some forms of research as **clinical inquiry**, **clinical research**, or **clinical study**. Lee (1955) defined a clinical study of society as one that employed "first-hand experience with group responses to therapeutic efforts." Lee (1955) described a clinical study as one that was diagnostic in approach and which involved "informed and critical judgment, driving curiosity, and integrity" as crucial elements in the development of reliable knowledge concerning society. He saw **clinical** students of society as being involved in studying society, focusing on social aggregates rather than solely on the individual.

Clinical studies utilize observations, techniques, and insights that have points of similarity with the clinical practice as performed by psychiatrists and clinical psychologists. A **clinical** study of society deals with social aggregates in its natural setting, existing in time and place, and having unique historical and functional facets which need to be diagnosed. It can also have a therapeutic impact that requires the scientist to be particularly sensitive and analytical in the way she or he approaches the study. Jayaratne and Levy (1979) pointed out that the idea of a research–practice dichotomy is **unnecessary** since they were convinced that clinical research can and should be made directly relevant to clinical practice. They described the **clinician-researcher** as one who, among other characteristics, had a clear apprehension of the **treatment methods** being employed; a detailed knowledge of the client system and its environment; an empirical and objective orientation toward the process of intervention; as well as the ability to incorporate empirical feedback and the research findings of others into the intervention process.

Ramondt (1994) described a **clinical-oriented research** as a particular approach where the clinical researcher approached a particular situation with an open mind rather than allowing the thinking process to be circumscribed by a particular theoretical perspective or ideology. To him clinical researchers studied reality by observing the processes involved with analytical precision and intensity. They needed to establish a close collaborative working relationship with their clients without abandoning an "objective academic attachment" (p. 93). He saw clinical researchers as playing two different roles simultaneously: the role as **ethnographers** who allocated priority to the discovery of academic knowledge as the object of the research effort, and as **experts** who gave due consideration to the client as the problem owner.

Schein (2001) considered clinical research as an act of data-gathering in settings that were "created by people seeking help" (p. 228). The researcher in these settings was engaged because he or she was considered as having the necessary helping skills to deal with the subject matter presented to them by their client. If **clinical research** or **clinical study** is already being performed by sociologists, why is clinical sociology still needed? Although both former terms utilize the word **clinical** they are basically research approaches and are not used to refer to clinical practice as such. The role of a practitioner is distinctly different from that of a researcher. While the latter is involved in generating data and analysis for the purpose of obtaining a better understanding of a situation, a clinical practitioner is involved in the implementation of strategies and efforts to achieve concrete and specific solutions. In clinical practice, research is merely one of the many supportive tools which may, or may not, be relevant for resolving problems.

Sieving through the various definitions and descriptions of clinical sociology offered by its practitioners mainly within the English language literature, there appears to be a general agreement that the practice involves five basic components or desired characteristics. **Firstly**, clinical sociology synthesizes the distinct sociological **perspectives**, **concepts**, **theories**, and **tools** to be applied to a situation that is perceived as existing within a wider social framework. **Secondly**, clinical sociology is seen as part of a wider **interdisciplinary** effort where it is able to complement the contributions of other existing clinical professionals, reflecting real-life situations that exist in its totality, integrating all facets of social existence. **Thirdly**, clinical sociology involves a systematic effort at finding an optimal solution to a specific problem or **case**. **Fourthly**, clinical sociology involves the management of **clients** and **client systems**. **Lastly**, clinical practice should be capable of providing some theoretical inputs and insights into the development of the sociology discipline over time. Instead of merely moving from case to case without synthesizing their methods and harvesting their experiences, the practitioners help to contribute to a continuous process of upgrading the methodologies and the skills required for other clinical sociologists and for the general students of sociology to emulate. The following five chapters will examine each of the aspects of clinical sociology mentioned above in greater detail.

Open Comprehensive Systemic Perspective

The main justification for developing clinical practice within sociology is the conviction that the discipline has something unique to contribute while other professionals are deemed to be less equipped to do it with equal degree of effectiveness. The clinical approaches of the physician, the psychiatrist, the psychologist, and the social worker are seen as different approaches from that of a clinical sociologist. The uniqueness of the sociological approach has always been its insistence that social issues and problems are seen within a holistic framework of an overall social structure. This holistic approach is clearly reflected in the contents of basic sociology textbooks which typically touch on all the major social institutions and social processes as these books introduce a sociological overview of society to students. They offer an overarching view of the whole social landscape with such topics as culture, personality, social stratification, ethnicity, family, religion, laws, politics, economics, education, group, organizations, community, society, population, human ecology, collective behavior, social change, theories, research methods, and many others. In contrast to this holistic perspective, other social sciences tend to focus on particular niches or sectors of the society. The basic psychology textbooks, for example, generally focus on the internal aspects and components of the human personality; basic economics focuses on how resources are optimized, distributed, and consumed; social geography studies the human population and its relationship with its physical environment; and social history traces the stages and phases of past events to ascertain their influence on the present situation needed resolution.

First-year sociology students are typically taken on a magic carpet ride for a comprehensive tour of the whole society. The introduction to the discipline in this comprehensive manner provides sociology students with what management **gurus** call a **helicopter's view** of a phenomenon. It is only later that the students are allowed to focus on more specific aspects of society but by then the basic backdrop of the holistic perspective would have been well-established in the psyche of a conscientious sociology student. McGregor (1961) used the analogy of the sociologists as adventurers or explorers who decided to explore their chosen territory by using **aerial photography** should they wish to acquire a panoramic picture of the social terrain. However, they can also decide to "stay on the ground and to cut their way through small thickets" (p. 33) should they need a more detailed narrative of the situation. It is this ability to focus on a particular social phenomenon, while at the same time being able to take into account the large social context that constitutes the unique contribution of sociology to social problem-solving.

This **comprehensive** perspective that only sociology offers its students has both potential strengths as well as weaknesses. Its main strength lies in its ability to demonstrate the complex interplay of all facets of society. At the same time it clearly underscores the crucial fact that sociology cannot ignore the fundamental need to establish linkages and interfaces with ALL other disciplines that study human existence. Other disciplines may choose to ignore or minimize the social context when performing intervention, such as a medical doctor only deal mainly with an obese patient while ignoring the **enablers**, or a psychologist dealing directly with a suicidal client with minimal attention given to the **significant others**. When dealing with such cases the sociologist will take into consideration the medical and psychological aspects without brushing aside the client's social context. This is a necessity, not an option. Who else is in the position to do it if not the sociologist, or its close biological sibling, the social anthropologist? For the above reason, according to the authors' personal experiences, sociologists will need to deal with so many aspects of a social situation that usually they are the last to leave the scene. The sociologist needs to focus while at the same time able not to be too focused on what is at hand. Using the analogy of a bird flying high in the sky, a sociologist can be seen to land occasionally on the solid ground briefly to obtain nourishment, in the case of the sociologist for the purpose of data and narrative-gathering, before taking off again to hunt for **preys** in the wide stratosphere of sociological generalities.

Mainstream sociologists are often accused, and not totally without justification, of being more comfortable with the bird-eye view of the world, extracting generalizations, and abstractions, while the specifics and the concretes on the ground are treated as insignificant and trivial. Clinical sociology attempts to correct this lop-sidedness by requiring sociologists to leave their helicopters and their aerial cameras, to **walk the walk** of their clients, entering and experiencing the latter's world long enough to affect real changes. Occasionally they can zoom out to the bird-eye view in order to gain a broader perspective of the overall phenomenon. The bird and the helicopter analogies are useful since clinical practice needs to adopt a flexibility of approaches requiring the practitioner to rapidly change one's altitudes and latitudes to alternatively **zoom in** and **zoom out** one's focus, as the situation demands it.

This sociological perspective may be labeled as an **open comprehensive systemic approach**. What is meant by a **comprehensive** approach is that any social phenomenon which a sociologist focuses on needs to be conceived of as being dynamic, multifactor, and multi-level. Mills (1959) referred to this ability to perceive the comprehensiveness of social reality through the use of one's **sociological imagination**. He expounded that the possession of this ability was precisely what differentiates a social scientist, who possessed "a playfulness of mind" (p. 211) in making sense of the world, from that of a "mere technician" (p. 211) who typically lacked this ability. Mills (1959) believed that the use of a sociological imagination enabled sociologists to shift their foci with ease. The examples he gave included the ability to shift from the political to the psychological; from the examination of a single individual or family to comparative studies at the societal level; from studying a theology school to studying a large military establishment; or from studying the sociology of the oil industry to a study of contemporary poetry.

According to Chodak (1973) a comprehensive theory of society was indispensable to any efforts to promote a better understanding of the intricacies and interdependencies between man and social structures. It provided a more complete view of the social phenomena than when viewed from the single vantage of an individual or a group. This means that while a general sociological training provided the general perspective, the action or **clinical** component provided the specifics. To reiterate the point made earlier, the combination of the two within the specialty of clinical sociology enabled the practitioner to see the whole while at the same time being able to focus on the specifics. It is a combination that was often lacking among many other clinical practitioners who do not wish to venture beyond their comfort zones provided by their professional training. While the idea of **comprehensiveness** requires the practitioner to include as many components, factors, or processes as possible, the use of the concept **systemic** emphasizes on the linkages and relationships that exist between these elements. The term **systemic** can be defined as a way of perceiving, recognizing, or conceiving something as forming a coherent whole. By putting together the components of a social system, like putting together the pieces of a jigsaw puzzle, practitioners are able to gain a clearer picture of the overall situation even if the pieces do not fit perfectly, before they may even attempt at intervention. Charon (1992) used this jigsaw puzzle analogy to describe the sociological search for knowledge where events that superficially and initially appeared to be separate and unconnected, when seen together actually presents a more complete, often a different, and more complete understanding of a social phenomenon.

The basis of a systemic approach rests upon a fundamental concept in sociology that of the **social system**. A **system** is referred to the arrangement of things that forms a unity or organic whole. If summarized from several dictionaries, the concept of **system** can be seen as referring to some form of interrelationship, combination, network, or cooperation between several objects, individuals, or ideas. These elements are complementary and supplementary to one another, functioning as an integral part of a bigger entity. Although originally the concept of **system** was used by natural scientists to refer to the biological and mechanical phenomena, when applied to human society it refers to groups of people who exhibit "a relatively persistent, patterning of social relations" (Neufeldt & Guralnik, 1991). All aspects of individual and group human behavior are seen as mutually interacting and responding to one another. It does not mean that there is necessarily some rational and logical basis for these relationships although the sociologist can try to understand the patterns and factors which affect the individuals or groups involved. According to Compton and Galaway (1984), the interrelationships among the components create a whole that is greater than the sum of its parts. Due to the wholeness of the system a change in any part of the system is capable of eventually affecting and changing the system as a whole and all of its parts.

The concept of social systems, although generally accepted as a basic sociological framework among many prominent sociologists (Talcott Parsons comes automatically to mind) others were more critical toward its usage. The exponents of the idea of **social systems** initially had the tendency to import and apply the characteristics of a natural organism or mechanistic entity, such as the concepts of **feedback**, **entropy**, and **homeostasis**, to social systems. Sociologists and social anthropologists of the functionalist or structural–functionalist persuasion were therefore accused of overemphasizing the image of social phenomena as well-structured and well-integrated social systems in which every component of the system performs specific functions and that they are indispensable to its overall functioning.

The idea of human social life exhibiting systems and subsystems, directly compares society to the mechanical human-made machines, which are believed to be so intricately linked and balanced that a slight change in one will produce change in others in predictable ways, capable of threatening the machines functioning. When this organicist model is applied to human society, every component of the society is perceived as harmoniously coexisting in a highly integrated and optimally functioning social order. To anyone living in any society at any time in human history, it is apparently clear that this utopian dream is far from reality. Consequently, this **organicist or mechanical** perspective of society is accused by its critics of being unrealistic, of gross underemphasizing the importance of the social realities of conflict, social change, and cultural lags. The human society somehow does not, and need not, exhibit the characteristics of an integrated and internally harmonious organism in order for it to survive or thrive. While the idea of a stable and integrated social system may be attractive to idealists, it becomes an obvious bone of contention among sociologists who questioned the assumption that in order to continue existing a system must be a smooth functioning and integrated entity. The organic analogy of social systems is accused of having a built-in conservative bias toward the need for social order while ignoring the realities of social conflict and social change. **The very imperfection of the social system is exactly the reason why sociologists need to intervene!**

Practitioners in social intervention are aware of coexistence of apparently opposing aspects of integration and conflict in social life. The fact that integration and conflict do coexist, sometimes rather harmoniously and with little enduring negative outcomes, is the reason why external social intervention is deemed necessary to resolve the sources of social tension. Social conflicts are usually capable of resolving by themselves through existing internally inbuilt conflict-resolution mechanisms. Only when that fails that the need for new mechanisms, such as the need for external intervention, may be necessary. While working with spouses, family, community, or organizational members, practitioners will have to identify *both* aspects of integration and conflict simultaneously. For example, it would be unproductive to assume that openly conflictive couples are no longer willing or are incapable of resolving their differences without external help. Similarly, an apparently harmonious spousal or family system is equally likely to be experiencing some covert sources of conflict which may need to be addressed with the help of an external intervenor.

The criticisms against the **organicist** or **mechanical** model of social system may make some sociologists decide to avoid using the concept altogether. Others, including many practitioners, may consider the concept to be too useful and to be totally discarded. One way of salvaging the concept is to offer alternative explanations to it. One of these was the **ecology** model. Auerswald (1968) advanced his alternative which he named the **ecological phenomenology** model. This model offered a less rigid concept of social systems as consisting of components that did not need to be in a continuous synchronized interaction with one another. Instead social systems are envisaged as a loosely structured social context within which people or problems can coexist.

Straus (1987) agreed that an ecology model was a viable alternative since it provided a more holistic and total picture of the social phenomenon under observation. According to them, social systems could only be understood and analyzed in terms of the total pattern of interrelationships as human groups interact "with their social and material environments in pursuit of optimal survival in a world of limited resources" (Straus, 1987, p. 68). After considering the various models of a social system in sociology, Turner (1991) concluded that the human ecology model was the most viable perspective since it did not construct "majestic and cumbersome conceptual edifices" (p. 151) and that its prepositions were more testable than other alternatives. Flexible notions of social systems were easier for practitioners to work with rather the highly dogmatic and prescriptive conceptions of **either** integrative **or** conflictive perspectives.

Are Social Systems Real?

Are social systems an objective reality? Is it something that exists **out there** that can be observed, measured, and touched or is it merely a useful abstract mental construct? The question of whether the sociologist is dealing with an **objective** social reality or whether it is just a **subjective** analytical construct in the mind of the sociologist may influence the approach one takes as one tries to intervene in the social system. The idea that systems were real, according to Flood (2001) was borrowed from the natural sciences which assumed that all phenomena were real systems. The implication of this idea was that people, with the help of the change agent could and needed to bring about real changes in their social environments. Such changes include initiating a change in the interactional and behavioral patterns between individuals, groups, and institutions. Or it could bring about changes in particular aspects of the physical–technical environment such as changes in specific legislations and administrative procedures. Some writers refer to the **objective** or

hard social system as a product of what they label as **systems (not systemic) thinking.**

An alternative to the idea of social systems as **real** societal mechanisms, is the view that it is an **analytical construct**, a subjective mental or conceptual construction of the world, not as something that actually exists **out there**. Flood (2001) viewed a social system as a product of **systemic thinking,** in contrast to the earlier mentioned **systems thinking**. The **systemic** or **soft systems** thinking saw the assumed interrelatedness within the social phenomena as a mere interpretation and product of the way the human mind organizes and makes sense of the world. The most important implication of this **systemic** thinking is that the social intervention performed by clinical sociologists is for the purpose of changing people's worldviews rather than changing the social situations or environment they are in. Supporting the systemic form of thinking, Midgley (2000) asserted that whatever the social scientist thinks about reality was in fact merely a **knowledge** of it—not reality itself.

Upon closer examination, it is clear that both the **systems** and the **systemic** views can be seen as coexisting realities rather than as incompatible alternatives. The clinical sociologist needs to work with both ideas—the idea of social system as a social reality as well as an analytical construct. Both realities can contribute to the process of resolving a problematic situation. Changing an objective reality involves changing the parts of the social, economic, legal, and political structures that are attributed as **causes** responsible for the perpetuation of an undesirable social condition. Flood (2001) felt that this change could be done preceding, as well as concurrent with, the efforts at changing the way people subjectively perceive and evaluate their world. People's worldviews can be changed by increasing their understanding of the dynamics of the social systems and structures within which they exist through such efforts as the enhancement of their cognitive capabilities; a reevaluation of their value systems which in turn influences their objectives and priorities; as well as helping them to make critical and radical paradigm shifts relevant to the problem at hand.

At the level of concrete reality, the clinical sociologist is involved in observing and inducing changes in the patterns of social relationships at the level of concrete behaviors. The practitioner needs to translate the somewhat abstract notion of **system** into a more concrete form of reality. At the level of a **theoretical construct** clinical sociologists can choose to focus on the abstract manifestations of a social system. These include such components as beliefs, sentiments, goals, norms, status-role, rank, power, sanction, facility, communication, boundary maintenance, systemic linkage, institutionalization, socialization, social control, social change, territoriality, time, and size, as listed by Loomis (1960), with an additional component of "action" appended this list by Ritzer (1981).

According to the systemic perspective, any intervention at any point in the system, whether directly or indirectly, changing any or a combination of several of its elements, is capable of bringing about systemic change. This perspective requires the sociologist to assemble all possible relevant factors and components which make up the social context or human ecology of the situation requiring intervention. A change in one element or one relationship within a system, effectively executed, is capable of causing a ripple effect of changing other elements and relationships. Its impact is not in a simple and totally predictable manner since the factors and dynamism of a particularly unique situation tend to produce different possible outcomes. In any social system, the relationship between the individuals within it forms the **socius**, which locates a person at an intersection of "an indefinite number of circles representing social groups, having as many arcs passing through him as there are groups" (Wiese, 1932, p. 23). The **socius** represents a person's social world, "a condensation or nexus of countless processes of sociation" (Wiese, 1932, p. 84). The results of an accumulation of human activities from the past up to the present.

Going Beyond Dichotomous Thinking

By assuming that social systems are both real as well as analytical, the clinical sociologist stays faithful to the idea of the comprehensiveness of the social phenomenon. By maintaining an open and critical mind, a practitioner can avoid becoming entangled in nonproductive academic polemics based on narrow dichotomous thinking. When clinical sociologists talk about the social reality they are aware of the fact that social scientists are always dealing with only **partial reality**, never with **total reality**. This is because reality is too complex to be captured in its entirety. Yet, the idea of problem-solving involves efforts in trying to simplify the complex, clarifying the ambiguous as well as measuring the unquantifiable wherever possible. A social science model is a deliberate effort at simplification and approximation of the real thing for the purpose of making it easier for the human mind to visualize and conceptualize.

The clinical sociologist needs to deal with many apparent basic contradictions found within the social sciences. One of them, as pointed out by Easton (1972) was the contradiction that while all social sciences use analysis as its basic tool, all understanding of social phenomena requires synthesis as its basic tool for seeing them in their totality. This means that as social scientists focus on identifying and describing as accurately and as minutely as possible single elements or variables, the total understanding of the social reality remains elusive and unattainable. And yet, no social intervention can be truly effective if a particular social situation is not comprehended within a framework that is as holistic and systemic as is possible. Bruyn (1966) expressed his concern with the excessive preoccupation shown by social scientists, including sociologists, with **analysis** while **synthesis** was often neglected. Social scientists love to dissect and examine parts of their social data separately and critically, imputing artificial statistical relationships between variables misleading the audience as if they are real relationships existing between real **things**. According to him sociologists tended to model their discipline along the lines of the natural sciences with the latter's **atomistic** tendencies, isolating distinct variables, and studying them separately in the greatest possible detail. No amount of sophisticated statistical multivariate analysis can reflect the actual nebulous nature of social reality.

For this reason, Auerswald (1968) implored social science clinicians to avoid treating social reality in the same manner physical scientists regard their domain. For the latter, specific atoms, DNA, viruses, and the like are laboriously separated and dissected for the purpose of studying them at the minutest molecular level. Successful physical scientists may earn their Nobel prizes, financial gains, and professional recognition but in order to apply their newly acquired knowledge to good use, others, the applied scientists, or clinicians need to conduct human clinical trials on real-life subjects—highly complex human bodies existing within complex social contexts. A medical practitioner, for example, will need to not only analyze a specific physical dysfunction with a great degree of accuracy but also needs to see how intervention with this dysfunction will affect the overall organism and its post-intervention functioning.

Gillin noted in 1954 that it was ironical that while scientific knowledge had increased our knowledge of nature and its processes, our understanding of man in society had made little progress due to the tendency to divide knowledge into separate and often rival disciplines which consequently produced a "obfuscation of thought and theory that passeth all understanding" (Gillin, 1954a, b, p. 5). This trend, according to him, had serious consequences because it failed those who expected "science and humanistic studies to provide some guidance toward the fuller realization of human potentialities" (Gillin, 1954a, b, p. 5).

It is this concern for the need to understand better the total man, as opposed to examining separately components of the Man (and then forgetting to assemble them back together again) that inspired some sociologists to develop what they termed as **humanistic sociology**. It appears somewhat paradoxical that a humanist sociology needs to be created in order to allay this concern. How is it possible that sociology, the study of human society, should ever adopt anything but a humanistic perspective where members of a society are treated as indivisible human beings whose lives are intricately interwoven with the life of others? The emphasis given in the past on abstract concepts, social categories, and statistical generalizations tended to make human beings as mere statistical things to be studied from afar in an emotionally detached manner. Very little of humanity is revealed in most sociological work although there are exceptions where sociologists adopt the social anthropological method of "living with the natives" while conducting participation–observation research. The negative consequences of fragmenting research subjects are probably not as objectionable in the work of the physical scientists, such as those who are striving to discover the minute and detailed sequence in a DNA chain or to isolate an elusive virus. After all, the physical scientists are not required, generally speaking, to relate their findings and the analyses of the parts to the analysis of the whole.

Briefly, in order to achieve a comprehensive understanding of a social phenomenon clinical sociologists need to avoid the tendency to regard ideas, theories, and perspectives as dichotomous and mutually exclusive in nature. As practitioners they need to be able to strike a healthy and realistic balance between the ability to analyze ideas and the ability to synthesize them. In other words, they need to be able to achieve an integration between **synthetic** and **analytic** modes of thinking. Through the **analysis** of certain aspects of reality practitioners and their clients are able to see and identify specific aspects of human existence in greater detail, while through the process of **synthesis** they can understand how parts of the social systems work in synchronization or in conflict within a wider perspective. By going beyond analysis to synthesize clinical sociologists can avoid or minimize what is labeled as **reductionism**. Flood (2001) described reductionism as the generation of knowledge and understanding of social phenomena "by breaking them down to constituent parts and studying these simple elements in terms of cause and effect" (p. 133). He contrasted this with systems thinking which viewed the social phenomenon as an interrelated whole that could not be fully comprehended only in terms of the properties of its constituent parts.

Sociologists fear that reductionist tendency would make social scientists know "more and more about less and less" (Manis, 1976, p. 26) instead of trying to "put it all together' to present the bigger picture" (Manis, 1976, p. 27). While sociologists often criticize psychologists for their reductionist explanation of social behavior at the level of the individual personality, it can also be counter-argued that many sociologists are equally guilty of being **reductionists**. This occurs when sociologists consider social structure as the only main cause of all social behavior, which is clearly a form of reductionist thinking. Sociologists who are obsessed with measuring and transforming social facts and findings into statistics can also be seen as exhibiting **reductionist** tendencies.

While reductionist thinking may help in the analytical process by enabling practitioners to generate greater details of a particular aspect of interest, systemic thinking should provide the default larger holistic perspective that is in-built in a sociologist's psyche. According to Bruyn (1966) in clinical sociological work, the practitioner went beyond the analytic toward the synthetic process of discovering patterns of uniformity and linkages existing between "disparate elements of data that relates them into a coherent whole" (p. 35). The systemic view helps the sociologist to assemble or synthesize all possible relevant factors that make up the social context or ecology of a particular phenomenon before attempts are made to intervene in it. Clinical sociologists may choose to begin with a **synthesis** of the wider social context before doing some **analysis** of specific problematic parts of the system. Alternatively, they may choose to perform an **analysis** before synthesizing it. More likely they will need to continuously alternate between analysis and synthesis in order to maintain a proper perspective of the problem. Marshall (1963) asserted that the need for sociologists to synthesize their ideas and findings by no means implies that analysis is unnecessary or outmoded. He believed that a science that did not itself engage in analysis "would lack discipline and assurance in handling its materials" (Marshall, 1963, p. 6). For that reason, it is important to ensure that synthesis should occur at both levels, the concrete interpersonal and inter-group levels, as well as at the abstract level of the overall components and processes of a system as listed out by Loomis (1960).

Working with Open Systems

The use of the terms **comprehensive** and **systemic** naturally implies the idea of an all-inclusive perspective. Why then do sociologists find it necessary to include the term **open** in the expression **open** comprehensive systemic approach? The answer is that it is often necessary to emphasize the openness of social systems since some practitioners who claim to adopt a systemic approach are in fact using a rather limited version of system approach that lacks comprehensiveness. They tend to adopt a **closed system** approach that focuses on what happens **within** a specific social system while ignoring or minimizing the relevance of the other adjacent, sub- and supra-level systems. For example, practitioners claiming to adopt a systemic approach in dealing with, let's say, a juvenile delinquent's misconduct, may adopt a family work approach where only members of the delinquent's immediate family are considered as relevant to the case. By doing so they focus on the internal dynamics of the immediate family system, identifying its members and examine the relationships and interactions among them.

The potential roles played by other adjacent and adjunct systems, such as the school system, the peer group system, or the community system, are largely ignored. Other practitioners in a similar situation may choose another social system as their main focus. If they conceptualize the etiology of the problem as being due to poor academic performance, they may choose to work with the school system instead of dealing with the family system. Their **closed system** perspective leads them to consider the family system as of secondary importance and is therefore not given the same amount of attention. This limited approach can be termed as a **simple closed systemic approach** that conceptualizes a particular problem within a particular social system as if the social system of choice is relatively closed to external influences. An **open comprehensive systemic approach**, on the other hand, considers all the influence of all systems on the problem as possible solutions and as possible points of intervention. It also considers the *relationships* between all systems as potentially of even greater significance and importance than the dynamics within one particular closed system.

According to the **open** perspective, each social system is never totally closed or insulated for a long period from its immediate environment. When applied to the case of the child mentioned above, it is possible that the practitioner will have to help their clients to be able to deal with the school system, the peer system, the workplace, the political system, etc. If the main clients are the parents, the clinical sociologist will need to go beyond focusing on the client's immediate family system. Similarly if the clients are teachers or school administrators, they will need to look at the child's interactions beyond the school and family environments to include other influencing systems. Loomis (1960) had pointed out to the crucial role of the **systemic linkage** component of a social system, which allowed one or more elements of at least two social systems to be linked in such a manner that the two systems might be viewed at a higher level as forming a single unit. An example of this is when a member of a family attends school, participates in a community activity, or being newly employed in an organization, effectively establishing a link between several systems.

All social systems are basically open in nature with the **systemic linkage** component keeping all the systems linked to one another to form larger and more complex social systems. The term **supra-system** is used to refer to a larger and more inclusive system, larger in terms of the number of members and the degree of complexity involved. In a **supra-system**, several smaller and more exclusive **subsystems** can be identified based on certain criteria. According to Loomis (1960), the practitioner who is using an open systems approach will be able to move from a given subsystem to a larger system and back again—alternating between macro-level social realities and micro-level ones. When the concept of **systemic linkage** is ignored, every component of a system will appear to be in itself a closed independent system. The linking of the various levels, subsystems, and supra-systems and their interfaces is the basic contribution that clinical sociology can make to professional practice. It is a perspective that counteracts the tendency toward simplistic reductionism, fragmentation, and isolation of persons and situations from their social context.

An open systemic perspective requires the clinical sociologist to deal with both **first-** and **second-order** changes. Seidman (1983) had pointed out that a **first-order** change involved the act of inducing change by manipulating particular components **within** a particular system, while the supra-system was left untouched. A **second-order** change, on the other hand, involved a change in the premises, rules, or assumptions governing the relationships of a subsystem with other systems because the latter were seen as influencing the way the former functioned. The second-order change was less concerned with what went on inside a system than within the larger framework of external relationships. It required practitioners to shift their foci from one level of the social system to the next. As change agents, clinical sociologists needed to work with both the first- and the second-order change instead of merely focusing on the former and ignoring the latter.

Practitioners who focus only on **first-order** changes are working with a closed social system perspective. They may view the idea of an open social system as being too cumbersome and ambitious to handle or simply too bewildering and perplexing for humans to comprehend and manage. They may be concerned that adopting an open comprehensive system approach will unnecessarily dissipate their limited resources and capabilities. For the inexperienced practitioners an all-compassing framework may appear to be confusing to both the practitioner and the client. The practitioner may experience what is referred to as "interventionist despair" or what has been described by others as "paralysis by analysis." This malaise strikes when one becomes overwhelmed by the complexity of a problem to the point of de-motivating one from continuing to deal with it. The critics of open systems may, therefore, conclude that practitioners should only deal with "small bites" of manageable reality. This is a bit like the proverbial search for a lost key under a streetlight even though one knows that it was lost in the adjacent dark area simply because it is much easier to search in a flood-lit area!

Midgley (2000) gave the skeptics assurance that systems thinking needed not necessarily be perplexing. He argued that it was capable of enabling practitioners to consider as much relevant information, helping to paint a rich and complex picture of a particular situation, without necessarily **paralyzing** the practitioner. The authors do agree that this reservation is somewhat overdramatized. After all, seeing a problem within its comprehensive context does not mean that the whole of the social context needs to be changed concurrently or even sequentially. In fact, a systemic approach implies that an intervention at only one or a few highly strategic points is capable of producing an optimal impact on the rest of the system, sufficient to bring about important systemic changes. As an analogy, a physician applies his or her systemic knowledge of the human body in deciding on the best single point to begin intervention.

The decision may be to introduce some medication at particular chosen points of the patient's body, rather than to intervene in every or simply any part of the body. The idea of a system is that there is a flow of energy and information between its parts which keeps the system alive and functioning. Although the nonorganic nature of a social system makes it less possible to predict with a high level of accuracy the exact impact of an intervention it is nevertheless valid to expect an overall systemic impact of an appropriate intervention at an appropriate point of a system. Of course appropriate intervention at the client's personal level is likely to bring about some, but not necessarily sufficient, changes at the family, career, and community life levels. If intervention is performed on several points or at several levels of the system hierarchy, instead of only at one point or level, the impact of the intervention may be considerably enhanced. By now, it is obvious to the reader that the clinical sociology is so simple that anyone with basic sociology can perform. No one says that it will be easy!

Unlike the academic sociologists who are free to offer many hypothetical, ideological, and radical suggestions as solutions to some problems, the practitioner is seldom privileged to such a generous license to act. Practitioners need to be constantly cautious with their recommendations and actions. They, unlike their academic cousins, soon realize that their effectiveness is judged by the concrete results their intervention produces. Lindblom (1959) recommended adopting an **incremental** approach toward comprehending and intervening in a particular social situation. He suggested that one should immerse oneself in the situation at hand before beginning to initiate some form of tentative action. **Incrementalism** is a gradual process of learning from personal experiences, and those of others, both their successes and failures. According to Wan (1988) while short of the ideal, the incremental approach often helped researchers to avoid committing serious and expensive mistakes simply be allowing themselves to tentatively "test the water" (p. 34) as they go along, avoiding the risk of tarnishing their reputation should they rush in to act in some "foolhardy and risky" (p. 34) manner.

The definition of the word **practice** in a dictionary denotes something that is being done "repeatedly in order to learn or become proficient" (Neufeldt & Guralnik, 1991) reflecting the underlying idea of incrementalism. Through incrementalism, intellectual and professional maturity can be enhanced. Etzioni (1965) and Dror

(1964) suggested that applied social scientists should attempt to combine both elements of the rational-comprehensive model with that of **muddling through**, in other words combining both the rational and the extra-rational elements in decision-making. Such a mixture involved the combined use of judgment, creative invention, brainstorming, and other alternatives in addition to scientifically rigorous methods of arriving at decisions and action.

Those who consider themselves as **radical** sociologists contend that their main goal, and perhaps their only reason to be involved in practice, or what they refer to as **praxis**, is to eventually change **the whole system**. Clinicians do have their ideals of achieving a better society but they do not necessarily see total societal change within a short time span, as an achievable objective, not that they would not do it if they could. Even achieving small limited changes is an onerous task for the practitioner. The limited change objective set by the clinical sociologist may indeed appear to be too timid and insignificant to those who believe in radical social revolutions. However, the clinical sociologist is convinced that bringing about some changes, no matter how small it may appear to some, is better than mere theorizing, conducting research, presenting social criticisms, and preaching revolutions. Clinical sociologists are too busy with small challenges at hand to wait and hope for the **oppressed masses** of the world to raise in revolt to change the system with one swift swoop. They will have to content themselves with only fond memories of their radical sociology professors, compulsory radical literature, and heated polemics of their college days. They may still harbor the notion of a silent and a long-drawn-out world revolution but, much to the chagrin of their radical colleagues, they will settle for small incremental not particularly earth-shattering social changes.

Some radical sociologists are disappointed with clinical sociologists who generally do not seem to be committed to the Revolution, making insignificant and inconsequential social changes while working alongside and cooperating with people and institutions they deemed as the status quo symbols of social oppression and exploitation. Performing clinical sociology can appear to them to be a **sell-out** motivated by financial gains and career advancement, nothing short of a betrayal to the ideals of social radicalism of past college days. History and personal experiences teach these sociologists that systemic changes occur over time and generations and that there is no real alternative to gradualism. If I may engage in a little bit of sarcasm, to the radical sociologists we would say, worry not, clinical sociologists will join the bandwagon when the Revolution finally comes!

When one studies social phenomena utilizing a systemic framework, one comes to the realization that practitioners are mere outsiders who, initially at least, are the person least knowledgeable of the social system they are entering. Midgley (2000) saw the need to move away from the traditional view, which considered professionals as **experts** in a situation. The systemic approach requires a radical change in the way practitioners function within the system. They need to remind themselves that most members of the system possess information, skills, and **expertise** which they do not. They do possess some potentially useful skills and expertise and they do have a role to play, but only potentially. This means that the practitioner fulfill **one** function among many within the system and all functions are equally important for the viability of the system. The systemic approach acknowledges and encourages the contribution of all members of the system, including the practitioners as its latest addition. The labeling of professionals as **experts** while the clients are **non-experts** is incompatible with the systemic approach adopted by clinical sociologists. Clients are not mere as targets and beneficiaries of change (Hoffman, 1995). They are the active actors of change, while the practitioners are more of a **primus inter pares** (first among equals).

With the use of an open comprehensive systemic approach clinical sociology can help to promote a **non-pathological** view of human problems, avoiding the tendency often seen among other practitioners—the psychologists and the physicians in particular—to be influenced heavily by the pathological and therapeutic models which see human problems as pathological. The latter tend to view them as therapists who performed **treatments** and **therapies**. However, some psychologists and social workers openly disapprove of the **medicalization** of their professions and prefer a more systemic approach. Goldenberg (1973) expressed the view that clinical psychology could not become a truly autonomous discipline until it disassociated itself from the medical model. Jackson (1969), a psychiatrist, appreciated the need for psychiatry to incorporate wider perspectives of looking at human problems rather than the usual narrow focus given by clinicians to their clients as being relatively isolated and autonomous entities. He wrote of the need to move "from individual assessment to analysis of the contexts, or more precisely, the **system** from which individual conduct is inseparable" (Jackson, 1969, p. 387).

Another psychiatrist, Kolb (1977) recognized the important role that sociologists could play in changing the personality system through what he termed as **sociotherapy**. He could see the enormous potential the sociological approach would bring to his profession, providing a comprehensive approach when dealing with personality issues, an alternative to traditional psychotherapy. By utilizing a social system approach situations labeled as problematic can be seen as natural or understandable consequences of the normal dynamics within social systems. Of course, many sociologists themselves in the past are also guilty of expounding a pathological perspective of social problems. This perspective has, in fact, been espoused by many sociologists who see human problems as **pathology**, of seeing individuals and social systems as **disorganized**, **entropic**, and **dysfunctional**, implying that they are **abnormal** based on some criteria of social normalcy. As an alternative, a non-pathological approach allows practitioners to see situations that may be defined as **problematic** by certain people, rather than as situations involving **problematic people**. This implies that what is seen as problematic to one party may be quite contrary to others.

If clients are not seen as being in a **pathological** state of being, then the role of a clinical sociologist cannot strictly be that of a **therapist**. A systemic perspective sees clients in their **total** social milieu as capable of producing some forms of **therapeutic effect** by themselves rather than relying on so-called experts who somehow have a monopoly over therapeutic know-how. Certainly, the presence of the so-called experts, can trigger a therapeutic effect but it is not appropriate or misleading for anyone to claim to "performing therapy" or of "curing" clients. The failure of therapy as a treatment in many cases, even when performed by so-called experts, clearly indicates that practitioners only play a role in the process of therapy, not the main or the most important one. Of course, a therapeutic outcome is nevertheless important for clinical sociologists. No practitioner can ignore the need to contribute in some way toward some form of therapeutic effect on their clients. It is just that therapy is an **outcome**, not an **effort**. It is the ultimate result achieved, not what one does or hopes to achieve. Clinical sociologists see the therapeutic effect as the outcome of the total systemic effect of the social context within which clients have successfully created with the help of outside help. Therapy should not be the main goal for clinical sociologists, the way other practitioners claim it as their main objective.

References

Auerswald, E. H. (1968). Interdisciplinary versus ecological approach. *Family Process, 7*(2), 202–215.

Bruyn, S. T. (1966). *The human perspective in sociology*. New Jersey: Prentice-Hall.

Charon, J. M. (1992). *Ten questions: A sociological perspective*. Belmont, CA: Wadsworth.

Chodak, S. (1973). *Societal development*. New York: Oxford University Press.

Compton, B. R., & Galaway, B. (1984). *Social work processes*. Chicago, IL: Dorsey Press.

Dror, Y. (1964). Muddling through – science or inertia? *Public Administration Review, 24*, 79–88.

Dunham, H. W. (1982). Clinical sociology: Its nature and function. *Clinical Sociology Review, 1*, 23–33.

Easton, D. (1972). Comment on Robert Lane's political science and policy analysis. In J. C. Charlesworth (Ed.), *Integration of the social sciences through policy analysis.*. AAPSS monograph 14. Philadelphia, PA: AAPSS.

Etzioni, A. (1965). Social analysis as a sociological vocation. *The American Journal of Sociology, 70*, 317–323.

Fairchild, H. P. (Ed.). (1944). *Dictionary of sociology*. New York: Philosophical Library.

Flood, R. L. (2001). The relationship of 'systems thinking' to action research. In P. Reason & H. Bradbury (Eds.), *Handbook of action research: Participative inquiry and practice* (pp. 133–144). London: Sage.

Foucault, M. (1963). *Naissance de la Clinique*. Paris: Presses Universitaires de France.

Freedman, J. A. (1982). Clinical sociology: What is it and what it isn't – A perspective. *Clinical Sociology Review, 1*, 34–49.

Fritz, J. M. (1991). Emergence of American clinical sociology. In H. M. Rebach & J. G. Bruhn (Eds.), *Handbook of clinical sociology* (pp. 17–27). New York: Plenum Press.

Gillin, J. (1954a). Grounds for a science of social man. In J. Gillin (Ed.), *For a science of social man* (pp. 3–13). New York: Macmillan.

Gillin, J. (1954b). The forward view. In J. Gillin (Ed.), *For a science of social man* (pp. 257–276). New York: Macmillan.

Glassner, B., & Freedman, J. A. (1979). *Clinical sociology*. New York: Longman.

Goldenberg, H. (1973). *Contemporary clinical psychology*. Monterey, CA: Brooks/Cole Publishing Company.

Gouldner, A. W. (1956). Explorations in applied social science. *Social Problems, 3*, 169–181.

Hoffman, L. (1995). *Exchanging voices: A collaborative approach to family therapy*. London: Karnac.

Jackson, D. D. (1969). The individual and the larger contexts. In W. Gray, F. J. Duhl, & N. D. Rizzo (Eds.), *General systems theory and psychiatry* (pp. 387–408). Boston, MA: Little, Brown And Company.

Jary, D., & Jary, J. (1999). *Dictionary of sociology*. Glasgow: Harper Collins.

Jayaratne, S., & Levy, R. L. (1979). *Empirical clinical practice*. New York: Columbia University Press.

Kolb, L. (1977). Personality assets and social rehabilitation: Overlooked aspects of personality functioning. Paper prepared for statewide rehabilitation conference, 11 May 1977. New York: Albany.

Lee, A. M. (1955). The clinical study of society. *American Sociological Review, 20*(6), 648–653.

Lindblom, C. E. (1959). The science of muddling through. *Public Administration Review, 19*, 79–88.

Loomis, C. P. (1960). *Social systems: Essays on their persistence and change*. Princeton, NJ: D. Van Nostrand Company.

Manis, J. G. (1976). *Analyzing social problems*. New York: Praeger.

Marshall, T. H. (1963). *Sociology at the crossroads: And other essays*. London: Heinemann.

Marshall, G. (1994). *Oxford concise dictionary of sociology*. Oxford: Oxford University Press.

McGregor, O. (1961). Sociology and welfare. In P. Halmos (Ed.), *Sociological Review Monograph No. 4*. Keele: Keele University Press.

Midgley, G. (2000). *Systemic intervention: Philosophy, methodology, and practice*. New York: Kluwer Academic Plenum.

Mills, C. W. (1959). *The sociological imagination*. Oxford: Oxford University Press.

Neufeldt, V., & Guralnik, D. B. (1991). *Webster's new world dictionary*. New York: Prentice-Hall.

Ramondt, J. J. (1994). Methodological observations on clinical organization research. *Clinical Sociology Review, 12*, 83–101.

Ritzer, G. (1981). *Toward an integrated sociological paradigm*. Boston, MA: Allyn and Bacon.

Schein, E. H. (2001). Clinical inquiry/research. In P. Reason & H. Bradbury (Eds.), *Handbook of action research: Participative inquiry and practice* (pp. 228–237). London: Sage.

Seidman, E. (1983). Unexamined premises of social problem solving. In E. Seidman (Ed.), *Handbook of social intervention* (pp. 48–67). Beverly Hills, CA: Sage.

Straus, R. A. (1987). The theoretical base of clinical sociology: Root metaphors and key principles. *Clinical Sociology Review, 5*, 65–82.

Swan, L. A. (1984). *The practice of clinical sociology and sociotherapy*. Cambridge, MA: Schenkman.

Turner, J. H. (1991). *The structure of sociological theory*. Belmont, CA: Wadsworth.

Wan, A. H. (1988). The role of basic and applied research in developing countries. In Proceedings of the research utilization seminar, Institute for Development Studies (Sabah) and the Konrad Adeneur Foundation (Germany).

Wirth, L. (1931). Sociology and clinical procedure. *American Journal of Sociology, 37*, 49–66.

Chapter 3
Interdisciplinary Collaboration

As long as sociologists perform solely within their ivory tower, focusing only on teaching, researching, and administration activities, there is little need or opportunity to work in interdisciplinary teams. Academic departments are often required to compete rather than cooperate with one another. They are more likely to highlight and exaggerate their unique identities and their relative importance. They need to stake their claims to a specific piece of the academic territory since this will help them to survive the competition for limited resources available within their institution as well as for resources from outside. For practitioners out in the nonacademic world, the reality is somewhat different. Clinical sociologists, for example, do not have much choice but to function beyond the limits of their disciplinary specialization and organizational concerns. As practitioners, clinical sociologists are required to deal with a whole range of issues rather than with only one particular situation typically involving a **social** aspect. Traditionally, sociologists lay claim to the **social** niche as their rightful property and that sociologists are the most competent persons to deal with it. By the same token psychologists and economists stake their claims, respectively, in the psychological and economic niches.

Upon graduation, should social scientists choose to walk the nonacademic path, they soon realize that the narrow disciplinary specializations which they were conditioned to accept tended to unnecessarily restrict their understanding of a particular social situation (Lynd, 1939). Phillips (1973) lamented that when academic social scientists claimed that a particular problem was under the jurisdiction of their discipline they began to be less able and willing "to let the problem guide" their focus and efforts. Instead, he noticed, it was the discipline that tended to guide the problem rather than the other way round. Practitioners who do not avoid this pitfall are likely to face dire consequences since their disciplinary blinders will hinder their ability to look at a situation in its entirety.

Imagine a practitioner who tells his client not to talk about the latter's financial problems or about cancer the latter is currently suffering from just because sociologists believed that they should not encroach onto the territory of other professionals. Certainly sociologists may not be able to offer sound financial and medical

© Springer Nature Switzerland AG 2020

P. M. Wan, A. H. Wan, *Clinical Sociology*, Clinical Sociology: Research and Practice, https://doi.org/10.1007/978-3-030-49083-6_3

advice, but as practitioners they will have to take these aspects into consideration as an integral part of the intervention plan. Practicing clinical sociologists do not have much choice but to transcend their own imaginary boundary of **exclusive sociology** to work in tandem with other disciplines and professions. The reality is such that real-life problems involve diverse and overlapping dimensions including those of politics, economics, history, race, class, gender, sexuality, and many others, where "personal troubles and public issues become entangled in a social labyrinth" (Wardell & Zajicek, 1995, p. 312).

By the same token, clinical sociologists cannot stake a claim and label a problem as a **sociological** one and then to declare it as out-of-bounds to other social scientists. Other practitioners have a right to intervene in a situation, especially if sociologists themselves do not do so, or should sociologists themselves fail to intervene effectively. Clinical sociologists working on a team soon realize that they face the same issue as other scientists, although they may approach it from different angles of vision due to their distinct academic training. Swan (1984) reminded social scientists that they belonged to a single science that had the overall behavior of mankind as its common subject matter. For this reason, any one discipline would always be inadequate in its attempts should it ignored the contributions of other disciplines. The Frankfurt Institute for Social Research (1956) made this point rather succinctly:

> There exists no more a pure sociology than a pure history, psychology, or economics: even that substrate of psychology, the individual, is a mere abstraction when removed from his societal conditions. The scientific division of labor cannot be ignored if intellectual chaos is not to arise; however, it is certain that its division into disciplines cannot be equated with the structure of the thing in itself. That all the disciplines which concern themselves with man are linked and forced to refer to each other need hardly be stressed specifically, now that the concept of totality has come to be a cliché. (p. 11)

More recently, Rossi and Whyte (1983) echoed the same sentiment when they advised sociologists to stop harboring a biased attitude toward other disciplines since that would only be "dysfunctional" (p. 18) to themselves. Instead they had to learn to communicate with specialists from the other disciplines, in the process of learning about the special knowledge and skills possessed by these other disciplines. Swan (1984) agreed that the knowledge and skills developed by the social sciences, in general, had the potential of being used by what he categorized as all **social clinicians**. One way of working closely with those from other disciplines is through **multidisciplinary** research projects where specialists from two or more disciplines are jointly involved in one particular research activity. The involvement of researchers from various disciplines doing their own work separately qualifies it as a multidisciplinary research activity as long there are some efforts to bring together the results and recommendations. However, the outcome of such efforts still belies a **silo** mode of thinking, disciplinary trenches are half-buried but remain salient.

A more integrated alternative to a multidisciplinary approach is that of an **interdisciplinary** collaboration effort. This approach requires the formation of a team of specialists whose members are required to consolidate their efforts right from the beginning up to the end where a combined product or service is eventually produced. In an interdisciplinary team, researchers may borrow each other's tools and techniques, importing or exporting concepts, methods, and approaches across disciplinary boundaries. The team members are required to brainstorm ideas and to agree on their findings and recommendations (Wan, 1988). Interdisciplinary activities, according to Smelser (2000) may lead to the creation of a new subfield out of several disciplines as well as the synthesizing of theories and the development of metatheories, the purpose of which is to obtain a more comprehensive understanding of a particular empirical or theoretical problem.

Some sociologists may want to go even further on this point. They may feel that even the interdisciplinary approach is not integrative enough because the disciplinary boundaries remain apparent and often impenetrable. According to Auerswald (1968) in the interdisciplinary approach there was still the tendency for each contributor to view a problem from the vantage point of their own disciplines. Although each member of a team tried to expand the boundaries of their discipline to include the theories and concepts from other disciplines, they tended to be highly selective, choosing ideas that were nonthreatening to their disciplinary assumptions and worldviews. They tended to avoid those that directly challenge their discipline's assumptions and narrow theories and perspectives. In order to overcome this weakness Auerswald (1968) suggested an **ecological phenomenology** model, which had been mentioned earlier in this book, which does not need interfacing between the conceptual frameworks of different disciplines. Clinical sociologists may want to try out the ecological approach at some stage of their collaborative efforts with other specialists. At particular stages of the intervention process they may revert back to the more traditional interdisciplinary or even the multidisciplinary mode of cooperation.

The Societal "Cake"

The need for collaboration between the social science disciplines requires a clear notion of how the various aspects of the social phenomenon are perceived and conceptualized. Social scientists try to visualize the total social phenomenon by using concrete analogies, such as the analogy of human society as a **cake** that can be apportioned as slices to be distributed among the various disciplines. For example, a political scientist may lay claim to the **power** slice; the psychologist inherits the **psyche** slice; the economist is allocated the **resources** slice; the anthropologist settles for the **cultural** slice while the sociologist end up with the **social** slice. This sectoral division-of-labor helps the above claimants to accentuate the separateness of their respective disciplines while collectively they realize that they make up a whole societal **cake**.

The **economic**, **political**, and **psyche** components appear to have established themselves in distinct and uncontestable niches: the first deals with society's materialistic and human resources; the second with power allocation system; and the third with personality dynamics, respectively. The **social** or **cultural** components however are less easily distinguished since they overlap considerably with the first three societal sectors. This is clearly reflected in the existence of such specializations within sociology as that of **political sociology**, **social psychology**, **economic sociology**, **medical sociology**, **social anthropology**, and many others. Carr (1948) felt that the way the cake was distributed did not benefit sociology since after other disciplines had laid claim to their portions "there is very little that is left behind for the sociologist" (p. 2).

The identification of the various aspects of social life in the form of vertically sliced sectors, although is commonly accepted in society, does not seem to clearly explain sociology's niche. An alternative analogy of society would be one that visualizes it being sliced horizontally—society as a multilayered or multi-strata cake. According to this horizontal strata model of society, sociologists may choose to deal with any of the layers of the societal cake. A social scientist may choose to deal with the **individual** stratum while others may choose the **family, group**, **community**, **organization, societal,** or **global** strata as their main focus. The one focusing on, for example, the **individual** layer of the cake will deal with combined politico–economic–psychological dimensions of the individual. Some writers suggest that sociologists should concentrate only on the **group** stratum, studying the composition, forms, structure, functions, and changes of human groups as such Carr (1948) leaving the other layers to other disciplines to deal with. However, based on a social system approach, there is no reason why sociologists should limit themselves only to the **group** level. The **group** is intricately linked to other subsystems, such as the individuals, and supra-systems, such as the community and society. It is quite easy to conclude that no matter how one looks at society, sociologists clearly cannot avoid from having to share the same piece of the cake with other disciplines.

Whether the cake is sliced as vertical portions or as horizontal layers or strata it still involves the sharing of the **cake**. While using the cake analogy lends to visual and conceptual clarity, in actual practice clinical sociologists using a systemic approach invariably find themselves **trespassing** on the territories claimed by other disciplines. Another alternative way of visualizing society is to see it as a series of overlapping concentric circles with nebulous borders, each circle is **owned** by a discipline with areas of overlapping interests. It may better reflect social reality when compared to the cake analogy since the latter seems to suggest a clean-cut partitioning of social reality among disciplines. After all is said and done, an analogy is merely a tool to help us to visualize an abstract idea more succinctly. It is not meant to reflect reality with any degree of accuracy. Clinical practitioners will have to decide on which analogy they personally find helpful in. There is no such thing as right and wrong analogies, only appropriate and less appropriate ones.

Upon the realization that the field of sociology invariably needs to deal with all sectors of society the need for interdisciplinary collaboration is not even a choice to be made. Clinical sociologists must be prepared to function as an active member of an interdisciplinary team instead of isolating themselves from other professions and disciplines. Wirth (1931) had already warned clinical sociologists not to entertain the idea of distancing themselves from, or even less so, of displacing the physician, the psychiatrist, the psychologist, or the social worker. Sociologists should instead concentrate on contributing their insights to other professionals with the objective of influencing the latter's viewpoints and approach in dealing with a particular social phenomenon.

Wirth (1931) realized that one of the most challenging problems in an interdisciplinary team was how to prevent it from becoming a battle-ground between specialists with different training backgrounds. He believed excessive rivalry could be avoided if the members of a team could minimize the usual disciplinary **ritual and dogma** while adopting a more flexible and experimental attitude towards their practice. Wirth (1931) also suggested more humility on the part of the new-kid-on-the-block clinical sociologists so that they could become more acceptable to the other more experienced and established practitioners. They could do this by being more modest in their claims to be able to solve all problems without help from the other disciplines. Although clinical sociology has definitely something unique to contribute, he warned of the dangers of exaggerating this uniqueness to the point of becoming and acting like a **cult member** of the specialty. While sociologists were reminded to be modest when working with other disciplines Berger (1977) warned that they should not let themselves be bullied to the point where other disciplines placed limits on the sociologist by putting up **no trespassing** signs on any social territory that, according to him, was a legitimate **hunting ground** for sociologists.

Interdisciplinary collaboration can bring about a greater sense of mutual respect and exchanges of ideas across disciplinary boundaries. This blurring of boundaries, necessary in the field of practice will not affect the development of the disciplines in the academic world. There will always be a need for compartmentalization of the fields of the various fields of knowledge. The maintenance of disciplinary boundaries helps to make the growth of human knowledge more systematic and manageable. The phenomenal growth of knowledge throughout the twentieth century required man to establish disciplinary boundaries and specialization just in order not to become overwhelmed by it. It is practically impossible, and not even necessary, for social scientists to master *all* the fields of knowledge in order to make interdisciplinary collaboration a success. Gillin (1954b) believed that teamwork, including team research, was a valuable form of **bridge-building** between different disciplines.

Sociologists who were not used to collaborative work were advised to treat others as their equals rather than as their inferiors. Archibald (1976) issued a reminder that although sociologists believe that their own discipline possessed something which others lacked, they should avoid developing what he termed as a **supremacist** attitude—the wish to have one's discipline dominate over other disciplines. Horowitz (1964) used the term **sociological imperialism**—to refer sociologists who did not see a need for the involvement of other social scientists in dealing with social issues. An example of this **imperialistic** attitude, according to him, was when sociologists were only willing to work with other professionals if they are allowed to lead or dominate the team.

The spirit of teamwork should mean that team leadership is shared or rotated in some equalitarian and fair manner, making every member feel that they have a crucial and important part or role to contribute. A true team spirit in interdisciplinary collaboration requires the willingness to offer equal recognition, respect, and responsibilities to all members rather than trying to dominate and dictate the direction of the teamwork. Bringing all parties into direct face-to-face contact and competition may generate a natural sense of defensiveness or that of **besieged mentality** among those who lack a firm sense of self-confidence and professional worthiness. Beginners in this effort often recognize this within themselves or in the responses of their co-practitioners. This negativity is likely to recede as practitioners find themselves focusing on the intricacies of the problem.

Sociology's "Sister" Disciplines

In dealing with complex cases requiring intervention, clinical sociologists invariably find themselves at some point working alongside or collaborating with the various practitioners. These practitioners are from the social sciences, humanities, and the physical sciences, principally the clinical psychologists, social and physical planners, psychiatrists, medical practitioners, educationalists, special education experts, counselors, historians, economists, theologians, geographers, demographers, legal experts, agricultural experts, and so on. However, out of the many disciplines a few have a particularly close association, historically and substantively, with clinical sociology, namely the fields of social anthropology, social work, and psychology. Gillin (1954a) suggested that should the idea of interdisciplinary cooperation involving **all** disciplines appears to be too broad and ambitious, a more limited **modus vivendi** between what he considered as the **core** sciences of human behavior should be given top priority instead, namely between **sociology**, **social anthropology**, and **psychology**.

In the middle of the last century, Gouldner (1956) advised sociologists to learn from the experiences of other clinical disciplines that could be adapted to the specific needs of the clinical sociologists. Rossi and Whyte (1983) advised practicing sociologists not to hesitate from learning what their **sister** social sciences had to offer, especially at the early stage of the development of sociological practice. The existing practitioners, such as the clinical psychologists, counselors, and social workers, had pioneered and documented the relevant interventional skills and had developed training curriculums and programs that ensured their students were adequately equipped with these skills. These were available for the clinical sociologist to adopt, modify, or reject if necessary while they developed new ones that were based on some original sociological theories and perspectives.

Sociology and Social Anthropology

The discipline most akin to sociology is that of **social anthropology**. If the other closely related disciplines can be considered as "sister" disciplines, social anthropology can perhaps be considered as its special "Siamese twin" discipline. This is because the basic perspectives of the two disciplines are almost identical to each other with considerable overlapping of substance and approaches. In the nineteenth century, the fields of sociology and cultural or social anthropology were almost indistinguishable from each other (Gillin, 1954a, 1954b). The most common distinction frequently offered to distinguish the two was that sociology was supposed to focus on the study of complex modern societies while anthropology concentrated on the study of numerically-smaller and technologically-simpler preliterate and nonindustrialized cultures (Jary & Jary, 1999).

By the mid-twentieth century, this distinction began to blur somewhat as social anthropologists included the study of advanced communities as legitimate anthropological concerns. At the same time, some sociologists became increasingly involved in the study of economically undeveloped and developing societies and communities (Mills, 1959). Gillin (1954b), writing in the 1950s, insisted that there was no major difference between the two, and that there were no anthropological or sociological methods as such. The only minor difference that existed, according to him, was merely in the differences of the kinds of data and the techniques used to collect them. Similarly, a decade later, Banton (1964) considered the difference between the two disciplines as having been overstated, asserting that social anthropology had always been interested in studying all types of society, not merely in the study of "pre-literate peoples in out-of-the-way places."

Consequently, generalized statements made to differentiate between the roles of the social anthropologist or ***the*** sociologist were grossly exaggerated. Murdock (1954) similarly noted that only with the passage of time that the academicians of the two disciplines began to drift apart. They began to develop their own separate identities by employing different terminologies and jargons, disguise the underlying commonality between the two disciplines. Sociologists began to develop a fondness for elaborate statistical techniques while the anthropologists focused on ethnographic and participant-observation methods. He agreed with the assertion that anthropology had much to gain should it adopt the research and statistical methodologies developed by sociology but he equally felt that sociology would profit should it revived its interest in the anthropological methods.

Horowitz (1968) too believed that although anthropology was "left behind" (p. 174) in the area of elaborate statistical research methodology (mainly developed by mathematicians and statisticians, not by sociologists) that sociology was fond of using, he admired the anthropological method as "a thing of brilliance and illumination" that sociologists should not overlook. He praised anthropology as a discipline that had faithfully and successfully maintained its focus on peoples and cultures as well as remaining committed to interdisciplinary research. In contrast, he accused sociologists of "mere talk and no action" in these aspects. The observation that the anthropologists were more willing to be involved in interdisciplinary practice in comparison to the sociologist also came from Hyman (1967). He noted that sociologists working in teams in medical settings generally chose not to concern themselves with medical clinical aspects of their work and became less directly involved with patients in a ward, when compared to the psychologists and anthropologists on the team.

According to the personal observations of the authors of this book, graduate students in sociology are not particularly encouraged to adopt anthropological methods in their research apparently the latter are deemed **simplistic** or **unsophisticated.** This reflects the sociologists' disciplinary bias which holds high regard for survey research methods utilizing elaborate statistical techniques as compared to the case study and participant-observation methodologies of the anthropologists. The comparison between the different approaches of the two **twin sister** disciplines is inappropriate for the simple reason that while the anthropological methods may lack quantitative generalizations they surpass in acquiring qualitative details concerning social dynamics. Sociology textbooks do include the use of qualitative methods used by anthropologists as legitimate and equally important sociological methods it is just that they are less frequently utilized.

Clinical sociology has more to gain than to lose by establishing a closer relationship with social anthropology. Anthropologists generally have managed to maintain a close contact and rapport with real **everyday** life of people in different cultural contexts globally, while sociology has the tendency to focus more on the Western society and modern culture. Sociologists have been trying to promote more interests in what anthropologists do through their own **sociology of everyday life** and a microsociology specialty but with limited success. The anthropologist's involvement in detailed ethnography, through the use of the participant-observation method, is a particularly valuable and indispensable asset for sociologists who wish to enter the field of clinical work. It is unfortunate that sociology students are not exposed to basic social anthropology in their undergraduate years, except perhaps where there sociology and anthropology are administered as a single department. This lack of opportunity to be exposed to the dynamics of less complex non-Western societies is lamentable.

An obvious consequence of a lack of exposure to social anthropology is a general lack of appreciation of the potential benefits of the participant-observation approach in the quest for understanding the human condition. This method, much utilized in social anthropology, puts meat on the dry bones of statistical analysis, adding a touch of humanistic realism and a deeper insight into everyday social dynamics. Without this method, sociological findings read like a report written by aliens head counting and categorizing human behavior from afar. Like the aliens, sociologists may not come to truly appreciate the depth and richness of human existence until they leave their space capsules to participate and observe in the midst of humanity around them. An early exposure to the anthropological approach would help to prepare the sociologists as they put on their clinical sociology attire. The participant-observation method combines the two important roles that clinical sociologists cannot afford to avoid, that of a **participant** and an **observer**.

As **participants**, clinicians seek to establish direct and sustained rapport with their clients with whom they need to develop a deep and genuine sense of trust, understanding, and empathy. As an **observer**, they are able to examine the interaction of diverse forces within a particular social situation and how the actors respond to them. Bruyn (1966) made a very important statement when he wrote: "The social scientist cannot understand people scientifically in any adequate sense unless he understands them in particular, and for their own sake" (p. 122). The failure to expose sociology students to social anthropology is particularly regretful especially for those who are working in developing countries. Many sociologists exhibit distinctly Western centric mode of thinking, as reflected in the statements and assumptions they make about human beings and human society, often without them even realizing it. Some modern sociological thoughts have much hidden or inherent Western ethnocentrism due to the predominant influence of the value orientations of modern industrialized societies on sociology in general.

Sociology and Social Work

One of the main justifications given by sociologists for their lack of involvement in social intervention is that sociology has already had a practical specialty in the form of **social work**. Berger (1963) noted that during the early stages of the development of sociology, the need to develop a distinctly applied sociology was not seriously considered due to the belief that social work was the representative or **proxy** of sociology at the practice level. With such a belief it was not surprising that the general public had gained a similar impression. Heraud (1979) noticed that some members of the public tended to see social work as "a kind of applied sociology" (p. 117) and that the sociology discipline was believed to provide the basis for social work practice. Several other writers had described the origins of the social work profession as a sort of offshoot of sociology, or at least in a large part inspired by the latter. According to Dominelli (1997), the fact that the training of early British social workers began within the School of Sociology as early as 1903 was particularly telling. Similarly, in the United States in 1917, Richmond published an influential book entitled ***Social Diagnosis*** in which she defined social work and the social worker's task in mainly sociological terms, emphasizing the importance of social factors in the worker's efforts at understanding social issues and problems.

Throughout the twentieth century, in many universities, sociology graduates who were interested in practical or clinical careers were likely to be advised to register for a postgraduate training in social work. Although social work was seen as having an assumed progeny with sociology, this relationship probably lasted for a very limited time period, if it ever did. This was because even as early as 1931 Wirth (1931) was already critical of the failure of social workers to present a sociological approach in their professional work. Social workers were seen as drifting toward the psychiatric and psychological approaches, emphasizing such factors as biological inheritance, the influence of physical surroundings, and the role of psychological factors to explain the failure of individuals to adjust to and function optimally within their environments. There was the tendency to consider the role of the wider social context, specifically the influence of family dynamics, peer pressure, and occupational stress and community conflicts on social behavior as something of secondary and lesser importance, if at all. Social workers, he lamented, failed to highlight the interplay of personality factors within the larger cultural and interpersonal relationship factors. By the 1960s, the influence of psychology and psychiatry in social work continued to dominate while sociology's contribution diminished considerably. Woodroofe (1962) referred to what he described as a **psychiatric deluge** in social work as new developments emerged within the fields of psychology, psychoanalysis, and psychiatry. Writing in 1968, Leonard commented on what he saw as a **sociological blindness** in social work due to an overemphasis on personality dynamics as the main focus while neglecting the influence of the external social context.

The incorporation of the psychological perspective in social work is understandable due to the obvious fact that psychology, more specifically clinical psychology, provides the essential concepts and tools for measuring and changing behavior, something which sociology does not even try to develop. The social worker is constantly involved in intensive face-to-face interactions with their clients and therefore needs to understand the intrapsychic and the interpersonal dynamics of interpersonal relationships. The social worker can easily apply the psychological and psychiatric inputs directly to their cases. In the meanwhile, macro-sociological offerings appear to be nebulous and academic, without any clear guidelines, which were immediately usable to the social worker. French (1956) provided an example of the difference between how a sociologist and a social worker deal with the task of presenting a lecture to medical students. According to his account, sociologists typically wanted to review the empirical literature on the subject and want to base their lectures on whatever generalizations they managed to abstract from them. Social workers, on the other hand, prefer to give lectures that consisted of detailed descriptions and analyses of individual cases (quoted in Hyman, 1967). Heraud (1970) placed the blame for what he saw as a sad state of affairs on sociologists themselves—for not becoming involved in direct collaboration with practicing social workers. To make it worse, he noted that many sociologists tended to see professional practice as something irrelevant, or as something that distracts attention and resources away from other more "central concerns and essential business of sociology" (Heraud, 1970, p. 277). Consequently most social workers see their relationship with sociology as one between unequals, pointing out to what they saw as the "colonizing aspects of sociology" (Heraud, 1970, p. 277).

Berger (1963), a sociologist, was openly critical of their colleagues who try to **set the agendas** for social workers for the reason that they do not have a sufficiently intimate understanding of the intricacies of practice (Berger, 1963). He wanted sociologists to accept the fact that the so-called role of the sociologist as the social worker's mentor was "misleading" (Berger, 1963, p. 3). This was because of the nature of practice, which was what social work was all about, was very different from merely attempting to understand society, which was what sociologists focused on. He asserted that despite the sociologists' wish to believe that their discipline would be useful to the social worker, there was very little in the efforts of sociologists to provide much that was directly relevant for practice. Heraud (1979) noticed by the late 1970s that both the sociologist and the social worker were becoming inward-looking. Each was focusing on their respective internal interests and concerns, the former remaining distant from **practical concerns** while the latter remained deeply involved in them. As only to be expected, without clinical experiences, sociologists were unable to translate sociological knowledge into action, the crucial task of "making the leap over the gap from knowledge to decision." According to Turner and Turner (1990), the only contribution that sociology could offer the social workers was to provide some general theoretical perspectives, while the main needs of the social workers were supplied by those who were more familiar with psychotherapy or counseling.

Some nonpracticing sociologists remain convinced that their discipline has something tangible to offer to social workers, although it remains unclear what exactly are these resources. Are the sociological theories, concepts, empirical studies, and methods of research in the present form useful offerings to the social worker? Clinical sociologists would probably doubt that. It is unfortunate that not only has sociologists in the past been unable to provide much input to social work practice, but some of them went out of their way to belittle the social work profession. Eversley (1973) noted that sociologists from without and within social work profession had from time to time "mounted swinging critiques" (p. 2) particularly those who pursued a professional status for the profession Sociologists saw this move as unnecessary and damaging. Social workers were naturally puzzled by the sociologists' critiques which they regarded as "patronizing and arrogant" in nature. Most social workers felt that they had no other alternative than to simply ignore the negative comments made by the sociologists (Heraud, 1979).

By now it is quite clear that sociologists need to come to accept one fundamental fact: social work is no longer, or perhaps it never was in the first place, an applied or clinical arm of sociology. For some this inevitable fact is hard to swallow. Some sociologists and even a few social workers find it difficult to accept the idea of the two disciplines becoming uncoupled, developing along separate trajectories. In the mid-1960s, Meyer, Litwak, Thomas, and Vinter (1967) were among those who remained hopeful toward the future relationship between the two, although by then there was not much basis for such optimism. The writers merely expressed wishful thinking when asserted that sociology would remain pertinent for social-work practice and that there were many potential areas of collaboration for the future. Many other writers similarly chose to interpret the drift in the sociology–social work relations as a temporary phenomenon that could eventually be reversed. Lee (1978), for example, referred to the drift as something "invidiously artificial" (p. 76) and as something that was potentially damaging to both disciplines. Heraud (1970) believed that it was **premature** for social work to cut its umbilical cord from sociology (p. 281–282). He insisted that sociology still had an important role to play in educating social workers and helping the latter to **debunk** certain popular views of society (Heraud, 1970, p. 76).

In another book written some years later, Heraud (1979) continued to express his optimism that sociologists could offer help to professional social workers. He tried to patch up the relationship by advising both parties to continue collaborating, to keep the process of "socialization or re-socialization" (Heraud, 1979, p. 193) going which hopefully would facilitate the assimilation of each other's professional values. Similarly, Dominelli (1997), a social worker, tried to save this relationship by suggesting the formulation of a new subfield called **sociological social work**, a specialty that would be based on the sociological perspective, making it different from the **psychological social work**, which appeared then to dominate the practice. The proposed **sociological social work**, she hoped, would ensure that social work could no longer effort to ignore the relevance of the wider social contexts of the society.

It was therefore not too surprising that after decades of drifting apart, by the early 1970s some graduate schools of social work no longer gave much attention to the sociological input in their curriculum (Bates, 1971). According to another source, by the late 1970s the social workers were already well on the way to develop their profession into an autonomous and identifiable profession, instead of remaining as mere "stepchildren of an **omnium-gatherum** college category" of sociology (Lee, 1978, p. 76). Over the decades, slowly but surely the social work profession has developed its own distinct identity and independence. In reality, social workers do not need the help of sociologists any more than sociologists need theirs. Looking through current social work textbooks, sociologists may recognize certain theories, concepts, empirical studies, and methods of research which are perhaps originally developed within sociology, and yet, on referring to the book's index, there is very little reference made to the contribution of sociology.

Some dominant sociological ideas have somehow, through the process of academic **osmosis**, become incorporated as social work ideas. Social workers do their own research and develop their own theories and concepts. If it is any consolation to sociologists, social work has also tried to maintain its distinctness away from psychology. It wants to change its image as a mere applicator of psychological theories, perspectives, and methods, as much as they want to avoid being seen as mere implementers of sociological **praxis** (Lee, 1978). Heraud (1970) noticed the trend whereby social work tried to develop its own social-work theories and methods, eliminating the problems of trying to incorporate borrowed ideas principally from sociology and psychology, thus eliminating the "bewildering variety of frames of reference" (p. 281), which outsiders offered but which did not fit easily into the framework of social work.

Should and could the sociology–social work marriage, if it did ever truly existed and that it was not a forced marriage, be saved? We can see that despite the basic incompatibility between the two disciplines, some sociologists and social workers do, from time to time, work on a common project and remain optimistic about the future of this relationship. Like any divorce, it is always a good omen when ex-spouses keep a good relationship going for the sake of their children, in this case for the sake of the general public who on occasion need them both. Perhaps there is lurking somewhere an underlying fear that without this relationship sociology will end up without a clinical outlet for its theories and findings. If it is the case, there is no need for it.

This is exactly what the whole discussion and main concern of this book are all about. **A clinical outlet in the form of clinical sociology has always existed within sociology**. It is just that this specialty will remain undeveloped as long as sociologists continue to assume that social work is still their clinical proxy. Sociology can celebrate the fact that it always had its own outlet for clinical practice, which is ready to bloom into a fully developed specialty. With the development of clinical sociology, sociology no longer needs a proxy in the clinical arena. The emergence of clinical sociologists on the scene will help to reduce somewhat the credibility gap that exists between sociology and social work. Hopefully, over time, the clinical sociologists while trying to develop and test out their clinical methodologies and tools will find ways of working with social workers as their equals, perhaps engaging social workers in the training programs for clinical sociology. Hopefully, too, that the field of clinical sociology would have been sufficiently developed to make it worthwhile for social workers to invite the former to participate in and contribute to social work training programs. The future requires both disciplines of social work and sociology to continue developing, as separate but equal partners, based on mutual respect rather than where one is considered as a mere appendix or off-shoot of the other. Sociologists and social workers can see the past drift in the relationship as a positive outcome of a healthy future growth process. Just like any good divorce can probably achieve!

Sociology and Psychology

The next obvious discipline that is closely related to sociology is that of psychology. At the risk of oversimplification, the discipline of psychology can be described as dealing the individual **psyche**, referring to the internal dynamics of the human mind and consciousness and how they influence behavior. Sociology, on the other hand, is said to focus on the **socius** which sees the individual as being located in social groupings made up of families, groups, communities, and organizations. According to Lennard and Bernstein (1969), the activities of the psychologists tended to revolve around attempts to change the personal psychological variables, principally the thoughts and behaviors of individuals, rather than changing parts of the wider social systems. They asserted that even when psychologists dealt with groups they were still dealing with the "individuals in the group" rather than "treating groups of individuals" (Lennard & Bernstein, 1969, p. 202). Psychologists of course do not totally ignore the significant role played by the social context in influencing human behavior but they tend to consider it more as a backdrop to the main concern of the discipline.

Moskowitz (2001) too agreed that the popular emphasis given by psychologists to the individual psyche resulted in minimalist regard given to the social, economic, and political factors, which underlie social realities. To illustrate this point she gave the example of a group of juvenile delinquents were being considered as needing psychological treatment by the psychologists although they did not pose any particular social threat. By seeing so-called delinquent behavior as **pathology** the obvious treatment is to deal with their personality deficits. If on the other hand, the so-called problem stemmed from the failures of the local market economy, emphasis should be given to address the issue of youth employment.

Another example provided by Moskowitz (2001) was when psychotherapists examined the psyches of soldiers by tracing their problems to their psychodynamic relationships with their parents while ignoring other environmental factors such as the traumatic impact of the violent context in which the soldiers functioned. While the examples provided may not reflect the weakness of the whole discipline, there is a general agreement that psychology tended to underplay the role of the social context in explaining and treating problematic individuals and groups. Mills (1959) had described psychologists in the late 1950s as promoting what he termed as **psychologism**, a form of **reductionism** which rested upon the idea that, in order to understand social structure, one only needed to study the individual. This, he felt, tantamount to "an explicit metaphysical denial of the reality of social structure" (Mills, 1959, p. 67).

While psychology and psychiatry were seen as focusing too much on the individual and treating the cultural and societal context as a nebulous background concern, Billson (1994) was concerned that the disciplines of sociology and anthropology were equally guilty of downplaying the significant impact of individual differences and intrapsychic processes in their work. According to her, this either-or or dichotomous thinking only obstructed attempts to understand human behavior in its entirety. To be fair to the psychologists, if they are accused of promoting **psychological reductionism** it will be equally appropriate to accuse many sociologists of **sociological reductionism**. This occurs when sociologists reduce all explanations of social behavior to the role of social structure to the point of ignoring the role played by the intrapsychic dynamics of an individual. Sociological reductionism is apparent in the writings of even the great founders of sociology who generally avoided making explicit or direct reference to psychology in their concept of society. Comte, the founder of sociology, appeared to omit totally any direct references to the psychological aspects of human existence in his writings; Spencer seemed to consider individual biology and psychology as being significant only at the earliest stage of social evolution before society became fully developed; and Durkheim and his followers viewed psychological life as entirely a product of society (Znaniecki, 1965).

Some sociologists have openly advocated for closer cooperation between the disciplines of sociology and psychology. Gillin (1954a, 1954b) believed that sociologists did in fact make certain psychological assumptions which, because they were not explicitly examined, tended to be inaccurate. The "sin" that sociologists committed, according to him, was their carelessness in presenting naïve and simplistic psychological assumptions. He felt that it was unforgivable for sociologists to make "psychological error and outright dogmatism" (Gillin, 1954a, p. 232) by minimizing the role that human biology and genetics play in influencing social behavior, or for insisting that human beings were mere passive organisms helplessly placed at the mercy of the society's folkways or culture. Naturally, psychologists considered the psychologizing that sociologists did as "distinctly amateurish and casual," in the same way perhaps sociologists find the **sociologizing** done by psychologists equally naive. It is evident that the sociologist needs to incorporate psychological perspectives as much as they would expect psychologists to incorporate sociological ones. Inkeles (1959) agreed that sociologists could not escape from making certain assumptions, especially implicit ones, concerning the individual psyche. He pointed out that even Durkheim, who was often attributed of being anti-psychology, did in fact make implicit references to personality and psychological variables in his work on suicide.

Unlike the general sociologists, clinical sociologists immediately recognize the need to be familiar with the psychoanalytic concepts and theories. Even if they do not need to use them as tools they cannot ignore the psychological issues involved in the cases they handle. They will invariably experience the intrapersonal psychological dynamics which their relationships with their clients tend to generate. For example, clinical sociologists need to deal with the psychological phenomenon of **transference** and **counter-transference** that are capable of interfering with effective intervention efforts. Experiences shared by Roseneil (2015), a sociology professor who is also a group analyst clearly demonstrated that a combination of psychoanalysis approach with sociology is a "powerful medium for personal change—for encountering the self and others, and for producing better understandings and new ways of being" (p. 63).

Bredemeier and Stephenson (1962) believed that sociologists definitely need to familiarize themselves with such psychological concepts such as the defense mechanisms such as repression, projection, displacement, rationalization, and so on. These mechanisms can help to explain how certain forms of behavior considered by society as **irrational** are not so easily explained by social structure theories alone. Endleman (1981) even suggested the need to develop sub-discipline of **psychoanalytic sociology** for sociologists. He felt that it was important that sociologists recognize and understand the importance of such concepts as defense mechanisms and other unconscious factors in explaining social behavior. He wanted to emphasize the view that one would need to acquire the mastery of both disciplines in order to deal effectively with human behavior.

Similarly, Homans (1987) was convinced that it is not possible to obtain a real and deep understanding of social phenomena without making general propositions about social behavior. He implored sociologists to cease the **intellectual hypocrisy** of keeping psychological explanations "under the table" (Homans, 1987, p. 15) instead of openly acknowledge them. Hunt (1989) agreed that few sociologists were familiar with psychoanalytic thinking, many of whom were only superficially acquainted with the works of Freud and were therefore unaware of the more current developments in the field of psychoanalysis. She believed that the psychoanalytic perspective provided the richness and depth which could enhance the way sociologists conducted their fieldwork research. Fieldwork, she wrote, involved more than just the performance of social roles and cultural symbols. It included a dialogical process, which was "mediated by complex intrapsychic meanings" (Hunt, 1989, p. 81) between the researcher and respondents. Hewitt (1991) identified many other psychological concepts such as that of conformity, person perception, causal attribution, obedience, leadership, and many other topics, as being absolutely indispensable for sociologists. The tendency to mount harsh criticisms of psychology by sociologists was often based on a lack of deep knowledge and understanding of the latest psychological concepts and approaches. This situation can easily be rectified when sociologists begin to collaborate and become more intimately familiar with the field and profession of psychology.

Social Psychology

Prominent sociologists saw enough similarities between them and the psychologists to consider the possibility of a **marriage** that can produce a progeny that inherits both genes. The eminent sociologist Mannheim (1953) believed that since both psychology and sociology dealt with the same material, that of the social and psychic lives of the individual, the differences between the two should not be exaggerated. After all, he argued, even psychologists did take into consideration the role played by the wider social environment, namely the influence of social institutions such as the family, neighborhood and nation, although these aspects might not be pursued in great detail. Similarly, according to him, sociologists did not totally ignore the psychological peculiarities of the individuals as members of social systems. Both were merely adopting different approaches as they followed opposite directions in the chain of causation.

Psychology placed an emphasis on the events which had its source in the individual, while sociology followed up the causal interlinkage in the opposite direction. He noticed how each psychologist appeared to have "a private sociology of his own" and that each sociologist had similarly invented his own "truncated psychology for his private use." Gillin (1954a) agreed that both sociologists and psychologists needed to perform a concerted strategy on their common goal—that of modifying human behavior within its social context. Heraud (1970) agreed with many others mentioned above that it was meaningless to judge the two disciplines in terms of which was superior or more useful since the two dealt with different levels of analysis of the same phenomenon. The sociologist concentrated on the social system level while the psychologist on the personality level.

Finally, a successful attempt to bridge the gap existing between the disciplines of sociology and psychology occurred at the turn of the twentieth century. It was in the form of a new disciplinary specialty named **social psychology**. Coincidently, or perhaps not, in the same year of 1908, both disciplines emerged with their own versions of the new specialty qualifying both disciplines to claim progeny, and perhaps custody, of the new infant sub-discipline. One of the two books was written by a psychologist McDougall (1908) entitled ***Introduction to Social Psychology*** published in London, while the other was written by a sociologist Ross (1908) entitled simply as ***Social Psychology*** published in New York. The emergence of social psychology initially promised to bring the dawn of a new era in sociology–psychology relations. Through this specialty, the sociological and the psychological concepts and perspectives can be interfaced and be made complementary to one another in explaining the social phenomenon.

Instead, it turned out that the two strands that initiated social psychology continued to reflect the separate theoretical, conceptual, and research traditions of their respective parent disciplines, producing what some writers had labeled as two versions of social psychology—a **psychological** social psychology and a **sociological** social psychology. **Psychological social psychology** chooses as its main focus research on basic psychological processes of learning, cognition, or emotion, without denying the important roles that social and cultural forces play in shaping these processes. The individual is considered as the central and main unit of analysis, emphasizing such topics as conformity, interpersonal attraction, the attribution of causality, aggression, altruistic behavior, attitudes, and so on. In contrast, **sociological social psychologist** focuses on the patterns of conduct among larger aggregates of people—groups, communities, social classes, and even whole societies, again without neglecting the processes that operate at the individual level.

Inkeles (1959) noted that the **sociological** social psychologists were not giving sufficient attention to psychological theories, making their studies more, according to him **psychosocial** or **psycho-sociology** rather than **social psychology**. He contended that in order to qualify as social psychology both the psychological make-up of the person as well as the social context and forces which influence the individual's action need to be given equal recognition. Stolte, Fine, and Cook (2001) agreed that sociological social psychology was not fundamentally social psychological, but more of a form of **microsociology**. To appease the situation, Hewitt (1991) appealed to both social psychology camps that despite everything, they shared a common purpose and destiny. They studied the same topics, such as interpersonal attraction, causal attribution, and the relationship between attitudes and behavior, and they both were interested in a broader range of phenomena, including social roles, processes and contexts of socialization, intergroup and collective behavior, deviance and social control, social structure and personality, and public opinion. So like a good marriage counselor he reminded all parties that it was meaningless to dispute which approach was the better one since the disciplines of psychology and sociology "have both common and different goals" (p. 4).

Clearly, the old rivalry between sociologists and psychologists continued to surface from time to time even when the "marriage" was already solemnized and the social psychology offspring was safely delivered. As to be expected in any marriage, one should not hope the arrival of a child to rescue a marriage with preexisting unresolved issues. One possible reason which may explain why social psychology appears to fail to bring the two disciplines closer together is the fact that the field is just another academic specialty, rather than that of practice. Academic concerns seldom necessitate interdisciplinary collaboration the way practitioners in the field are often required to do. Since necessity is said to be the mother of invention, it is only when a real necessity arises that one can expect to see some attitudinal and behavioral change toward collaboration. One of these necessities arises when sociology and psychology practitioners come face-to-face in situations and tasks that are too complex to manage effectively alone. This is where the presence of clinical sociologists becomes an effective bridge between the two disciplines. Both clinical sociologists and clinical psychologists are more likely to participate in social intervention projects than their non-practitioner colleagues. Once they are on the team there is not much option left other than having to adapt to each other's perspectives and approaches. They will have to pay attention as well to take into consideration the intricacies of the psychological aspects of the individual and the sociological dynamics of the complex social context.

Clinical sociology can be to sociology what clinical psychology is to psychology, a parallel which Gouldner pointed out in 1953 when he considered clinical sociology as "the sociological counterpart to clinical psychology" (In Fritz, 1991, p. 21). Just as clinical psychology serves to operationalize psychological concepts and perspectives to be applicable in practice, clinical sociology can do the same for sociology. In order not to be sidelined as redundant or irrelevant to an interdisciplinary team's efforts, clinical sociologists simply have to learn to focus on complementing the efforts and contributions of the clinical psychologists and other social clinicians, such as the social workers, counselors, and so on, rather than working in isolation from the rest of the team.

References

Archibald, W. P. (1976). Psychology, sociology and social psychology: Bad fences make bad neighbours. *The British Journal of Sociology, 27*(2), 115–129.

Auerswald, E. H. (1968). Interdisciplinary versus ecological approach. *Family Processes, 7*(2), 202–215.

Banton, M. (1964). Anthropological perspectives in sociology. *The British Journal of Sociology, 15*, 95–112.

Bates, A. P. (1971). The sociology major in accredited colleges and universities. *The American Sociologist, 6*(3), 243–249.

Berger, P. L. (1963). *Invitation to sociology*. New York: Overlook Press.

Berger, P. L. (1977). *Facing up to modernity: Excursions in society, politics, and religion*. New York: Basic Books.

Billson, J. M. (1994). Society and self: A symbolic interactionist framework for sociological practice. *Clinical Sociology Review, 12*, 115–133.

Bruyn, S. T. (1966). *The human perspective in sociology*. Englewood Cliffs, NJ: Prentice-Hall.

Carr, L. J. (1948). *Situational analysis: An observational approach to introductory sociology*. New York: Harper and Brothers.

Dominelli, L. (1997). *Sociology for social work*. London: Palgrave.

Endleman, R. (1981). *Psyche and society: Explorations in psychoanalytic sociology*. New York: Columbia University Press.

Eversley, D. (1973). *The planner in society*. London: Faber and Faber.

French, D. G. (1956). The behavioural sciences and the professions. *Public Health Reports, 71*(5), 504–510.

Fritz, J. M. (1991). Emergence of American clinical sociology. In H. M. Rebach & J. G. Bruhn (Eds.), *Handbook of clinical sociology* (pp. 17–27). New York: Plenum Press.

Gillin, J. (1954a). Grounds for a science of social man. In J. Gillin (Ed.), *For a science of social man* (pp. 3–13). New York: Macmillan.

Gillin, J. (1954b). The forward view. In J. Gillin (Ed.), *For a science of social man* (pp. 257–276). New York: Macmillan.

Gouldner, A. W. (1956). Explorations in applied social science. *Social Problems, 3*, 169–181.

Heraud, B. J. (1970). *Sociology and social work: Perspectives and problems*. Oxford: Pergamon Press.

Heraud, B. (1979). *Sociology in the professions*. London: Open Books.

Hewitt, J. P. (1991). *Self and society: A symbolic interactionist social psychology*. Boston: Allyn and Bacon.

Homans, G. C. (1987). *Certainties and doubts: Collected papers 1962-1985*. New Brunswick, NJ: Transaction Books.

Horowitz, I. L. (1964). An introduction to the new sociology. In I. L. Horowitz (Ed.), *The new sociology: Essays in social science and social theory in honor of C. Wright Mills* (pp. 3–48). New York: Oxford University Press.

Horowitz, I. L. (1968). *Professing sociology: Studies in the life cycle of social science*. Chicago: Aldine.

Hunt, J. C. (1989). *Psychoanalytic aspects of fieldwork*. Newbury Park, CA: Sage.

Hyman, M. D. (1967). Medicine. In P. F. Lazarsfeld & Sewell et. Al. (Eds.), *The uses of sociology* (pp. 119–155). New York: Basic Books.

Inkeles, A. (1959). Personality and social structure. In R. L. Merton, L. Broom, & L. S. Cottrell (Eds.), *Sociological today: Problems and prospects* (pp. 249–276). New York: Basic Books.

Jary, D., & Jary, J. (1999). *Dictionary of sociology*. Glasgow: HarperCollins.

Lee, A. M. (1978). *Sociology for whom?* New York: Oxford University Press.

Lennard, H. L., & Bernstein, A. (1969). *Patterns in human interaction: An introduction to clinical sociology*. San Francisco: Jossey-Bass.

Lynd, R. S. (1939). *Knowledge for what? The place of social sciences in American culture*. Princeton, NJ: Princeton University Press.

Mannheim, K. (1953). *Essays on sociology and social psychology*. P. Kecskemeti (Ed.). London: Routledge and Kegan Paul.

McDougall, W. (1908). *Introduction to social psychology*. London: Methuen.

Meyer, H. J., Litwak, E., Thomas, E., & Vinter, R. (1967). Social work and social welfare. In P. F. Lazarsfeld, W. H. Sewell, & H. L. Wilensky (Eds.), *The uses of sociology* (pp. 156–190). New York: Basic Books.

Mills, C. W. (1959). *The sociological imagination*. Oxford: Oxford University Press.

Moskowitz, E. S. (2001). *In therapy we trust: America's obsession with self-fulfillment*. Baltimore, MD: Johns Hopkins University Press.

Murdock, G. P. (1954). Sociology and anthropology. In J. Gillin (Ed.), *For a science of social man* (pp. 14–31). New York: Macmillan.

Phillips, D. L. (1973). The Acknowledge of knowledge: The problem of warrant in sociology. *Abandoning Method*. San Francisco: Jossey-Bass.

Roseneil, S. (2015). Pushing at the boundaries of the discipline: Politics, personal life and the psychosocial. In K. Twamley, M. Doidge, & A. Scott (Eds.), *Sociologists' Tales: Contemporary narratives on sociological thought and practice*. Bristol: Policy Press.

Ross, E. A. (1908). *Social psychology*. New York: Macmillan.

Rossi, P. H., & Whyte, W. F. (1983). The applied side of sociology. In H. E. Freeman, R. D. Russell, P. H. Rossi, & W. F. Whyte (Eds.), *Applied sociology* (pp. 5–31). San Francisco: Jossey-Bass.

Smelser, N. J. (2000). Sociological and interdisciplinary adventures: A personal odyssey. *The American Sociologist, 31*(4), 5–33.

Stolte, J. F., Fine, G. A., & Cook, K. S. (2001). Sociological miniaturism: Seeing the big through the small in social psychology. *Annual Review of Sociology, 27*, 387–413.

Swan, L. A. (1984). *The practice of clinical sociology and sociotherapy*. Cambridge, MA: Schenkman.

The Frankfurt Institute for Social Research. (1956). *Aspects of sociology* (trans: Viertel, J.). Boston: Beacon Press.

Turner, S. P., & Turner, J. H. (1990). *The impossible science: An institutional analysis of American sociology*. Newbury Park, CA: Sage.

Wan, A. H. (1988). The role of basic and applied research in developing countries. In *Proceedings of the research utilization seminar, Institute for Development Studies (Sabah) and the Konrad Adeneur Foundation (Germany).*

Wardell, M., & Zajicek, A. M. (1995). Social problems: Pathways for transcending exclusive sociology. *Social Problems, 42*(3), 301–317.

Wirth, L. (1931). Sociology and clinical procedure. *American Journal of Sociology, 37*, 49–66.

Woodroofe, K. (1962). *From charity to social work.* London: Routledge & Kegan Paul.

Znaniecki, F. (1965). *Social relations and social roles.* San Francisco: Chandler.

Part III
The Contributions of Clinical Sociology

Chapter 4
Beyond Research: From Respondents to Clients

The specialty of clinical sociology requires its practitioners to move away from the traditional **researcher–respondent** relations to that of clinical **practitioner–client** relations. Traditionally, research activity has been considered as a sacred and morally desirable sociological activity that is believed to enlighten and benefit society, indirectly and directly. However, very little critical thought is given to exactly how research can bring benefits directly to the respondents or subjects participating in research. A research activity tends to be basically a one-way process whereby respondents are required to supply information that the researcher needs. There is nothing inherent in the research process that requires researchers to reciprocate by providing what the respondent needs. Due to a long-established research tradition in the pursuit of knowledge, researchers are often unaware or are insensitive to what may turn out to be an obviously one-sided exploitative expect of their activities.

This obvious fact, however, has not escaped the radar of several sociologists who had pointed out to the lopsided benefits that research produced. Edwards (1994) directly accused academic researchers of taking information and ideas from those whom they were researching without contributing to the lives of these people in return. In most research or experimental work there is no built-in requirement for sociologists to offer direct help to the immediate situation under study. There does not appear to be much thought given to the idea that researchers are morally bound to help their respondents or subjects. It is simply assumed that the research activity and its findings in themselves are potentially useful and helpful in eventually bringing about positive social changes. The respondents will eventually enjoy the fruits of their contribution in some ways, and at some time in the distant future. The reality that research only benefits the researcher is fairly obvious. Researchers, the authors of this book included, would be able to bid **adieu** to their respondents to present their findings in seminars, reports, books, and articles thus enhancing further their careers, before moving on to their next research project.

There are no ethical rules which require sociologists to be directly involved with their respondents during their research fieldwork, the way other professionals may

© Springer Nature Switzerland AG 2020
P. M. Wan, A. H. Wan, *Clinical Sociology*, Clinical Sociology: Research and Practice, https://doi.org/10.1007/978-3-030-49083-6_4

require. Douglas (1970) remarked that some researchers even conducted several large ongoing research projects simultaneously. This was made possible due to the fact that they could farm out their work to others, namely the paid enumerators and paid interviewers, thus making it less likely for the researchers themselves to come into any direct contact with their respondents, except perhaps for a brief pretesting of questionnaires.

The only social reality that they can get acquainted with will be what the computer generates, far away, physically, psychologically, and socially from the real world and the turmoil of their respondents' daily lives. Some researchers may be present in the field, including those who choose the participant-observation method, but even then some of them may choose to observe their subjects from afar without the respondents being aware that they are being observed or that their movements being recorded. This activity had been described by some critics as a form of **academic voyeurism** (see Humphreys, 1972) or a thief (see Schuster, 2015). Gans (1968) felt that researchers were being dishonest when they deceived the people they studied concerning the true purpose for their study, their true feelings toward their subjects of study, or when they spied on their subjects without the latter's knowledge, awareness or expressed permission.

Going Beyond Research Skills

It will be a gross injustice to academic sociology to accuse it of being totally devoid of practical applicability. Typical sociology students do in fact acquire some skills which may be useful in the workplace, principally the ability to conduct research and fieldwork surveys. At the undergraduate level the students may not be experts in it but they will at least have acquired some notions on how to go about it. Many sociology programs may go out of their way to impart **practical** research skills to their students while others merely expect their students to have a theoretical understanding of the research process in order to graduate. It is hoped that with the long practical experience on the job they will eventually be capable of excelling in this skill. Often the possession of research skills, no matter how rudimentary, becomes the only skill many sociology graduates can boost of having when they are required to contribute to some social problem-solving efforts. What exponents of clinical sociology would argue, however, is that in many nonacademic careers research and fieldwork abilities are simply not sufficient to enable sociology graduates to perform effectively and efficiently. Unfortunately the research abilities form only a small part of the required repertoire of skills that they are expected to possess. Depending on the specific nature of the job specifications and the types of organizations or agencies the sociologists are serving, the whole spectrum of skills required may include those relating to the ability to suggest ways of promoting, managing, and intervening in social situations.

It is not surprising that sociologists in academic and nonacademic careers have acquired the reputation of being researchers since they themselves are likely to flaunt this asset for all others to see. Zetterberg (1962) came to the conclusion, after reviewing the works of his contemporaries, whom he noticed were fond of coming to the invariable conclusion that further research was needed every time some difficult situations were encountered. Hammond (1964) commented on the tendency, as he saw it, for sociologists to move from one research project to another as ends in themselves. According to him, when sociologists were asked for some contribution in a particular problem-solving exercise, they tended to offer the typical response: "We'll have to do more research." Clinard (1966) made a similar observation that when sociologists were asked to propose a practical solution for some social issues they invariably and automatically asked for more research funding. Unfortunately, according to Schuman (1975) non-sociology practitioners in the field were not always impressed with the large amount of sociological research performed since they would contend: "We already know the answers, what we need is action." There appears to be a strong and persistence underlying, although often unstated, assumption that it is not possible, feasible, or even desirable for sociologists to acquire BOTH research AND other practical skills, an assumption that proponents of practical sociology consider as unjustifiable.

Beneficiaries of Research

The researcher or the enumerator intervenes into the lives of the respondents, interrupting the latter's daily routines, probing into their private and personal worlds collecting information, ideas, attitudes, and values which are normally kept with strict confidentiality. Upon obtaining the rich and valuable information, the sociologists then work toward publication in lieu of their promotion with "little chance of making any [real] difference" (Schuster, 2015, p. 19) in the lives of the respondents. The question that is seldom asked is: how does one justify trespassing into the personal and interpersonal, and sometimes even private life-spaces of the respondents without attempting at least to minimally deal with some of their immediate problems and needs.

Any form of research interview and participant-observation is a form of social **intervention**. This may come as a surprise to those who objected to the idea of clinical, or applied sociology, on the ground that sociologists should not be involved in social intervention. Without their realization, every researcher, by their very presence in the field, may already have "intervened" in some aspect of a respondent's life, albeit only temporarily. It is for this reason that Schein (2001) wanted researchers to understand the consequences of their involvement in their subjects in order not to "unwittingly harm" (p. 236) them. In some situations the impact of the researcher's intrusion may be minimal, and the latter may not expect to get anything back in return. However, in situations where respondents are currently facing a dire situation, some attempts to offer direct benefits should at least be attempted as part of the moral responsibility of the researcher. It is possible that some conscientious researchers may make a personal decision to offer some help but usually this is not part and parcel of the role of the researcher **per se**. In fact, such efforts can be seen as breaching the objectivity principle as well as posing as an obstacle to the smooth progress of the research schedule.

The one-sidedness of the benefits of research, in favor of the researcher rather than the respondent, is not always lost on the latter. Several writers had pointed out that in certain cases respondents did experience and expressed a sense of dissatisfaction when their contribution to research efforts did not seem to bring any significant benefit. Lindesmith (1960) wondered how long would it take before what he termed as an academic "Day of Judgment" (p. 273) will finally arrive. This, according to him, would be when "the long-suffering patient" p. 273) respondents, after allowing themselves to be interviewed, observed and recorded, would realize that they were being exploited. At the same time, the sponsors of research might "add up all the money and man-hours expended in pure research, balance it against the results, and wonder whether it has been worth it" (p. 276). Commenting on a public protest toward a research project in the Harlem ghetto in 1968, Josephson (1970) appealed to researchers to always ask the fundamental question of who actually benefited from the research they were conducting. He pointed out that some communities were beginning to realize that survey research was a form of exploitation by researchers "for their gain or for the gain of the institutions and power they serve" (p. 117).

A few years later Vargus (1971) similarly expressed the view that research activity was a form of "an intrusion into people's lives" (p. 241) where the low income or powerless citizens were being treated "like guinea pigs and stepping stones" (p. 241) as researchers built their personal careers. He recounted his personal experience of dealing with the leaders of a community who said that they were tired of being used by professors "to experiment with so they can write books about poor folks" (Vargus, 1971, p. 246). Instead of assuming that researchers had a right to conduct research purely based on the needs of the researcher, he suggested that some sort of social contract should be instituted in order to ensure a **win-win** outcome that would benefit both parties. For him, a failure to do so would only make people less eager to cooperate with the researchers and this would in the long run force sociology to become even more detached and withdrawn from the social issues and problems occurring around them.

Similarly, Deloria (1980) warned social scientists that the community they studied might feel that they were being treated as mere objects as their lives were being **disrupted** by the presence of the researchers. Respondents who resented being **exploited** by researchers might exhibit resistant behavior, sometimes attempting to "psych out and con their questioner" (p. 271) in the interview or to resist the researcher through the responses of "concealment, obfuscation or deception" (Lee, 1993, 133). This resistance was particularly likely when sensitive topics were presented to distrustful respondents and, in response, researchers might even resort to certain **tactics** in order to obtain certain sensitive information from the reluctant respondents, resorting to unethical methods if deemed necessary (Francis, 1992). While the performance of a survey research is a necessary and legitimate academic activity, sociologists can perhaps give a more serious attempt to treat their respondents as **clients** who may be facing some pressing problems that need resolution. Whyte (1979) foresaw that effective work in the future would be conducted by researchers who considered their subjects as "active collaborators in the research process" (p. 65). Wilson (1992) suggested that fieldwork researchers should be more sensitive to the needs of their respondents and that the benefits of research should be gained by all parties during the research **process** itself as much as from the research **product**.

Surely it is not unreasonable to expect that in order to continue to win the confidence of their research subjects sociologists must demonstrate that what they are doing is of value and of direct benefit to them. It seems only logical that sociologists should **walk the talk** since they have always expressed concern with the negative impact of social exclusion, marginality, alienation, anomie, oppression, victimization and so on, on the human condition. A sociologist's continued insistence on doing research solely for the purpose of obtaining data for analysis can create problems especially when they are working alongside other professionals who consider the subject's objective as being important, if not more so.

This contrasting attitude toward applied research is well-illustrated in the following example narrated by Fox (1996) concerning a community AIDS prevention project in the 1990s which targeted drug users on the West Coast of the United States. This project was placed under the leadership of sociologists. In this research, outreach workers were engaged as enumerators for collecting data. While the sociologists assumed that the data would be useful for making policy recommendations on how to improve AIDS prevention programs, the outreach workers expressed the need to provide simultaneously some direct community service to the target group. The sociologist's sole concern with information-gathering in the research made the outreach workers felt as if they were being used as "informants, no better than the police." To the outreach workers ethnography research was "tantamount to surveillance," something which they regarded as antithetical to the interests of the community being studied.

The sociologists insisted that the enumerators should adopt a dispassionate, detached but empathetic posture toward the respondents, focusing only on the particular aspects of the community that the sociologists were interested in. The enumerators, on the other hand, felt the need to focus on helping the respondents to change and improve their disorganized lives as addicts. When specific activities aimed at personally helping the subjects of study were suggested, the sociologists reminded the workers that their task was to help accumulate data and not to be concerned with treatment. The sociologists felt that to do more than this would result in role confusion, undermining, modifying, or compromising the original research objective. Suspicion and distrust later emerged among those who failed to see how they would benefit from a project which only seemed to serve the interests of the researcher.

The nature of researcher–respondent relations is clearly and radically different from that of **practitioner–client** relations. The researcher is supposed to maintain a strict level of detachment and disassociation from his or her subjects. As Ravetz (1971) puts it, the basic researcher chooses to **insulate** themselves "from the moral squalor of ordinary life" making them appear to be "morally detached from reality" (p. 416). This social distance was presumably justified on the grounds that it enabled the researcher to optimize and strictly achieve objectivity throughout the research fieldwork process. Hewitt (1991) felt that because researchers tended to place questionnaires, interviewers, coders, and computer programs between themselves and their respondents, they ended up "several steps removed from real behaving people" (p. 300). The researcher's contact with the real world was thus "fragmentary and brief" where very little insight was obtained pertaining to the subjective meanings respondents attributed to their situation. Theoretically, during research fieldwork, sociologists have the opportunity to meet, interact, and interview the people they study. However, in most cases this does not always happen.

Everyday Sociology

Clinical sociologists enter the world of the everyday lives of ordinary persons. Upon gaining a better understanding of the way people cope and function in their everyday lives, they intervene with the intention of further optimizing the latter's lives. The **sociology of everyday life** or micro-sociology studies people in their natural contexts, their daily functioning based on their conception of social reality. Weigert (1981) pointed out that the sociologist was equipped with what he called a **sociological attitude** a way of looking at reality in a systematic, critical, methodological, metaphorical, and naturalistic manner to arrive at an understanding of how humans construct their view of society and of themselves. This attitude contrasted with what he termed as the **natural attitude** of the average person toward his or her everyday social life in the form of a take-for-granted attitude which prevented them from being able to deal with the more baffling and challenging aspects of everyday life.

Weigert (1981) considered everyday life as the fundamental reality sociologists needed to understand in great depths if they wished to understand society. He warned the sociologist that everyday reality was deceptive because what was assumed to be structured, stable, and unproblematic was in fact something that needed to be constantly reevaluated and reconstructed. Willer (1934) reminded sociologists to develop a **sympathetic understanding** of the state of mind of a person in order to understand behavior, an understanding that could only be attained through direct interpersonal interactions and communication. Perhaps an even more appropriate expression was that of **empathetic understanding** as suggested by Johnson (1996). Sociologists, she wrote, help bring about a "respect for differing standpoints and strategies and outline how certain perspectives can link or clash" (Johnson, 1996, p. 56). According to her only with this understanding could one help to alter and enhance interpersonal and social relationships while avoiding the "harmful, adversarial confrontation or manipulative deception" (Johnson, 1996, p. 56) which may occur in them.

Karp and Yoels (1986) reminded sociologists that they could not afford to neglect the study of everyday life. The writers felt it was unwise to neglect micro-sociology since it provided a deeper understanding of the issues faced by individuals and groups as they struggled to cope with their everyday life challenges. Prus (1997) reiterated a similar point when he asserted that it was the responsibility of the social scientist to understand the day-to-day world in which people found themselves, and then to build "two-way bridges" (p. 3) linking the knowledge that they had acquired to the real everyday existence of the people they claimed to study. A clinical sociological perspective offers clients with a critical analysis and interpretation of everyday life for the purpose of enhancing it.

There is little justification for studying everyday life only to have its findings ending up in some academic journals and textbooks which are irrelevant, inaccessible, and incomprehensible to the ordinary members of the society. The knowledge gained from clinical experiences needs to be made available to the general public in a form that is easily available and useful as a guide on how individuals and groups can cope with their daily life challenges. Sociologists often complain that their contributions to society are not being given due recognition and yet they have not put much efforts to directly address the concerns of everyday life. Sociologists are rarely seen offering specific courses for solving everyday problems. Let us consider the usual "Dear Heart" columns in the popular magazines and the daily newspapers. Many of the problems presented have obvious sociological relevance and yet sociologists do not generally initiate or participate in such columns. Sociologists instead choose to make critical commentaries on current issues aimed at the general public. This fact will be considered by many as adequate proof that sociology is irrelevant to the pressing, intimate, and personal daily dilemmas faced by an ordinary person.

With the development of clinical sociology, this state of apathy is about to change. With sufficient clinical experiences sociologists will be able to develop and offer practical guides to those facing difficult life and social situations. They can be in the form of clinical everyday sociology guide books or sites on the internet that offer an alternative or a complementary perspective to the existing ones. The existing ones available on the shop's bookshelves are provided by popular psychology, self-help, and self-improvement popular literature and resources. Programs and columns in the mass media and the internet will provide opportunities for discussions on how to deal with the daily issues in everyday life from a sociological perspective. Unfortunately, there are sociologists who would argue that offering such guides would amount to degrading sociology. Somehow sociology, in their minds, is meant to deal with bigger and less mundane social issues, not the **trivial** personal and interpersonal ones. They fail to realize that sociology is able to help individuals see how the so-called **trivial** personal issues are linked to larger issues at the organizational, community, societal, and global levels. As an example, helping a person in poverty includes helping him or her to gain knowledge and access to wider social movements and initiatives beyond their immediate physical localities.

One of the objectives of sociological intervention is to sow the seeds of grassroots social movements that are capable of eventually blossoming into bigger ones. To a clinical sociologist, an individual or group should not be perceived as merely that, but rather as beads in the long chain of interlocking social networks. Social movements, after all, begin with the individual person or group. By directly helping small groups of individuals to change, the practitioners are in fact making a significant contribution in the long run. This is because the individuals who become empowered in one situation often tend to develop traits of self-empowerment in many other roles in their lives, in the various social systems in which they participate, including their roles as functional family members, peer group members, workers in an organization, responsible citizens, and so on.

Foote (1975) contended that what might initially appear to be a segmental focus on a particular client or a group of clients targeted for change is in fact something more comprehensive in its impact. By helping a client in one social environment he believed that the sociologist generates a **multiplier** and **ripple** effect which will eventually impact the lives of a much bigger number of people in the long run. To argue that sociology should **not** be relevant for the everyday personal and interpersonal concerns of the average person in the street levels is to argue for an **elitist** view of sociology, as if human anxieties and sufferings should not warrant the attention and contribution from the sociologist. It is the ultimate irony when sociologists who have been traditionally critical of elitism have decided to adopt an elitist stance regarding this matter.

Everyday sociology requires everyday language. Sociology students can recall the anguish they had to endure reading and making sense of famous sociological writings back in their college days. They were not written with the struggling tender sociology rookie in mind. Back in 1954 Lee had already suggested that sociologists should stop from being "in flight from reality" and instead to put in efforts to popularize sociology by writing something for the general public. Of course, writing for the general public would require sociologists to clean up their act and being able to write and express their ideas in a simple language without resorting to unnecessarily abstruse linguistic jargons. Lee (1954) reassured even then that sociology was capable of addressing the broad human concerns and needs as long as these works were written "in simple English" (p. 64). In the following decade Zetterberg (1962) similarly reminded sociologists that other sciences had prepared handbooks to guide their practitioners by offering hands-on knowledge and skills for practice. Sociologists, he argued, should therefore do the same by making sure that these guides were presented in plain everyday language so as not to put off the layman by its technical terminology and roundabout ways of expressing even very simple and basic ideas.

The Client as Person and Social Actor

For many professions the concept of the clientele plays an important central role. For the sociologist this seems to be a relatively novel and alien idea. Traditionally, sociology might have had some difficulties with the use of the term **client** since the term was originally associated closely with that of **patron–client**. When one searches for the meaning of **client** in a sociology dictionary one is directed to look under **patron–client** relationship characterized by an unequal status of the two parties involved in it. Jary and Jary (1999) defined the **patron–client** relationship as one in which "powerful or influential persons provide rewards and services to humbler or weaker persons in return for loyalty and support" (p. 479). In contrast, a social work dictionary defines a **client** as a recipient of a social service, as a **service user** who was either voluntary or involuntary recipients of these services (Thomas & Pierson, 1995). The client in social work tends to be seen as a rather passive recipient of some specified services while in other professions the client is seen more of a problem-solving actor actively seeking advice. In clinical sociology the client should be seen not as someone subservient but rather as an equal with whom the sociologist needs to collaborate to resolve a particular social situation for mutual benefit.

Unlike mainstream sociology which tends to relegate the individual person as trivial and insignificant in comparison to statistical aggregates, clinical sociologists focus on **persons** as **clients** who play a crucial role in clinical interventional efforts. As early as 1939, Lynd expressed his concern with what he saw as the increasing tendency among social scientists to ignore the **person.** The individual, he lamented, was being **dwarfed** and being seen as of insignificant value while social scientists were busy "ploughing their respective research furrows." According to Lynd (1939), whenever sociologists came face-to-face with the individual they were uncertain as to what to make out of the person. Consequently, they simply "shrug their shoulders and pass them off with a sigh of relief to the psychologist to deal with him" (p. 23). By doing so, the sociologist conveniently avoided the need to relate directly in any serious manner with the person's needs and issues.

Throughout the twentieth century, from time to time, sociologists expressed concern with the diminution of the **person** on the sociological landscape. Znaniecki (1965) reminded sociologists that only human individuals and physical objects existed in reality while ideas and concepts were merely "an arbitrary construct of philosophers" (p. 401). Tudor (1976) similarly accused academic sociology of betraying and forsaking the ordinary man while opting instead to focus on the abstract. Fletcher (1975) began his book with a chapter entitled "**Sighting the person"** sadly reflecting on, in his view, how alien the notion of **person** had become for many sociologists. The **person,** Fletcher (1975) explained, needed to be liberated and be put "back into its equations" (p. 82) because, in so doing, he contended that the sociologists would also liberate themselves. As he put it rather succinctly: "A purpose for sociology is the continuous liberation of the person and the liberation of sociology by people."

The **person** is often referred to in sociology as a **social actor** or simply an **actor**. A renowned French sociologist Touraine (1984) expounded for "the return of the actor" (p. 8) by bringing a new focus on social action within sociology after having been somewhat **hidden** by classical sociology. He derided sociology for having degraded into "a discourse that interpreted other discourses, an ideology criticizing other ideologies" (Touraine, 1984, p. 160) while ignoring the need to examine the behavior and situations which social actors needed to deal with. He asserted that the unity of sociological analysis could only be achieved by focusing on the real **subject** of sociology—actors and actions. He wanted his book to "not merely reflect upon the return of the actor" but also as a book that **prepares** for this return. Charon (1992) suggested that sociologists should go on a mission to rescue the **person** by giving a more in-depth focus on it, probing into their world views in order to understand how the person perceives the world.

The emphasis given to the significant role of the social actor is termed as the **actor-oriented approach** (Long, 2001) which focuses on helping social actors to understand and to better deal with events and issues. It recognizes the central role that persons play as active actors interpreting and responding to their subjectively experienced life-worlds. Campbell (1996) believed that multiple actors coexisted and competed within a single context of social heterogeneity. The multiple realities subjectively experienced resulted in contradiction or discontinuity between different "life-worlds" requiring them to negotiate their differences in order to continue coexisting. The sociologist can and should lend a professional hand to this process.

Sociologists sometimes differentiate between looking at the person as an **actor** (**action theory**) with that of looking at it as a **social actor** (**social action theory**). The former focuses on the individual's personal understanding of the subjective meanings and the behavioral responses to them, influenced by, but not dictated, by social influences. The latter focuses on how several individuals or larger groups assign intersubjective or communal, rather than personal, **subjective** meanings. This implies that all meanings are socially, rather than personally, assigned (Campbell, 1996). Simply put, the **social action** perspective emphasizes the influence of the social environment in determining an individual's behavior.

According to Billson (1994) while sociologists accuse psychologists of presenting individuals as "isolated psyches tangled in their internal webs" (p. 130) the traditional sociology perspective of the structural-functionalist kind did not present a much better alternative by considering the individual as being caught in "the morass of their cultures." Both views painted an image of the individual as being caught, trapped, or dictated either by their psyche or by the social structure. It does not take much clinical practice to realize that both explanations are intricately intertwined. No matter how pervasive and dominant are certain aspects of a person's psyche and social context, individuals and groups are capable of finding ways of altering or modifying them to some degree. This means that clinical sociology, together with other practicing disciplines, need to try to find ways of understanding how individuals and groups in society strike a realistic balance between the need to adjust and accommodate to one's environment while at the same time they need to modify parts of the environment which are considered as problematic.

Boudon (1977) chose to support the **action theory** perspective since he did not agree with the conception of the actor as being dictated by the surrounding social forces. The **determinist** paradigm, according to him, was "both useless and costly" (p. 153). By denying the person the faculty of making choices, of decision-making, of creation and innovation, he saw sociologists succumbing to the temptation that was endemic to sociology which he named **sociologism,** a kind of sociological **blindness**. In contrast, Barnes (2000) advocated for the **social action** perspective. He saw the lack of focus on intersubjectivity given by the action perspective as creating a situation "little short of disastrous" (p. 64) to sociological theory. "Individualism," he believed was **false** since human beings were social creatures who functioned as "interdependent social agents, who profoundly affect each other as they interact."

For practitioners, including clinical sociologists, the dichotomy between the two perspectives is not particularly relevant since when dealing with actual behavior, human action is **both** personally determined as well as socially influenced. Clinical sociology places equal importance on both perspectives. Problems or issues experienced by the person are inseparable from the social milieu he or she is in. At the same time the individual person possesses the mental capacity and capability to construct unique personal worldviews as well as the ability of making independent decisions and responses based on his and her own choices.

The focus in clinical sociology on the **person** is somewhat different from the emphasis given by psychologists to the notion of **personality**. The latter focuses on the internal components of an individual, the physical, cognitive, affective, motivational, and behavioral characteristics. The clinical sociologist sees the **person** as "a personality-in-context" with a greater emphasis given to its external relationship within its social context. However, this does not mean that the clinical sociologist can minimize the significance of the internal dynamics of the human **personality** in explaining human social behavior. Inkeles (1959) urged sociologists to understand personality dynamics in order to better understand the nature of personal decision-making and social selection processes. Clinical sociologists can help clients to realize that the so-called purely **psychological** problems are really **psycho-social** in nature. They are not totally internal within the personality structure but rather a result of a combined intricate interaction between internal and external demands and responses. Changing aspects of one's external social environment is as important, if not more so, than merely changing one's internal psychological environment.

In dealing directly with clients, sociologists can finally put into good use the whole subfield of sociology called **micro-sociology**. This subfield delved into the subjective meanings and world views held by the members of a social system. Edwards (1994) asserted that it was through the understanding of the perceptions, actions, and meanings attributed by the person to his or her social environment that one can hope to understand society, as he posed the question: "if we are not learning by comparison from one real-life situation to another, how are we learning?" (p. 286). In the same year, Gove (1994) reminded sociologists that a person's capabilities were affected by both innate biological characteristics as well as by social contexts, rather than by the latter alone. He saw the key components of a theory of human motivation as being a combination of biological, psychological, and social processes, and that sociology was the most appropriate discipline that could help to integrate all these processes, offering a more complete understanding of human behavior. Similarly, Fein (1997) disapproved of sociologists who downplayed the importance of physiological or biological factors in explaining and managing human problems. Fein (1997) insisted that "neither biology nor medicine can automatically be discounted in favor of strictly interpersonal interventions" (p. 41).

By directly dealing with the person, clinical sociologists will in the long run, help to reveal the true human dimensions of social existence. They will help to further enrich the already existing, but hardly thriving, subfield of **sociology of emotion** or what some call **passionate sociology**, as well as other subspecialties relatively neglected within the sociological tradition. The sociology of emotion introduces the concept of **emotion management** as a recognition of the central role that human emotions play in determining the nature of social relationships (Hochschild, 1998). Game and Metcalfe (1996) introduced the idea of **passionate sociology** which they felt celebrated "an immersion in life, a compassionate involvement with the world of others" complementing the mainstream sociological mere "pursuit of idealized abstraction."

Again, although psychologists have already been studying human emotions for a long time they generally tend to restrict their understanding of human emotions as mainly internal components of the personality. This implies that emotions can be changed or modified by conscious internal personal efforts or through the external intervention through therapy and counseling. The clinical sociology approach does not deny the usefulness of the psychological approach but would prefer to see emotions as the results of the impact of the social context, either objectively verifiable or subjectively perceived, on the person.

While psychologists perform therapy directly, the sociologist focuses on the promotion of a healthy social environment through a network of supportive social relationships. Aspects of these external changes are capable of generating some forms of internal therapeutic effect eventually. This approach adopted by clinical sociologist is not intended to invalidate the psychological approach. It merely offers a sociological perspective as a complementary perspective in performing social intervention. It is up to the clients themselves to choose the approach they consider as more appropriate. Clinical sociologists are not in the position to question the validity of an approach that takes into consideration psychobiological aspects that sociologists have chosen to neglect. On the contrary, clinical sociologists will have to familiarize themselves with the micro-level psychobiological aspects of personality dynamics, and the complex mechanics of cognitive, affective, and behavioral change, in order to be able to integrate these micro-elements within the wider macro-elements of the social system. Only then can they approach their clients with confidence armed with a complete arsenal of useful conceptual tools and methodologies.

Working with Values

Applied work, particularly of the clinical nature involves the presence of some clients who claim **ownership** of particular problems requiring inputs from a clinical practitioner. Accusations of **selling-out** to the wishes and demands of their clients are frequently hurled at the sociologists who are accused of transgressing the sacred rule of academic detachment. As early as 1951, Merton and Lerner (1951) issued their warning to social scientists not to surrender their **academic privilege** as true professional social scientists by unwittingly aligning themselves with the interests of

Big Business. They doubted the ability of the practitioners to be able to remain objective and professional in their dealings with their powerful clients since by doing so the former would stand to lose their resources and "the opportunities of getting their findings accepted" by the latter. Similarly, Mills (1959) expressed his fears that the direction, scope, methodology, and outcomes of a research effort would be "expropriated" (p. 106) by the paying clients. He believed that only if social scientists could exercise full control over the means of research could social science be truly autonomous and being able to maintain its credibility as a "publicly responsible enterprise" (p. 106). Berger (1963) shared this general anxiety concerning sociologists becoming too concerned with the practical applicability and consequences of their findings. By doing so, he considered them as automatically having left "the sociological frame of reference" and instead moved into the "realms of values, beliefs and ideas" (p. 19) of the non-sociologists.

Horowitz (1964) went even further to label applied sociology as **sociology for sale** where the sociologists were seen as pawns being manipulated by their pay-masters or research sponsors. In serving the interests of their clients the sociologists were seen as exploiting sociology for the purpose of gaining purely personal interests and greed, or as Spengler (1969) put it, by **hubris.** Spengler (1969) saw the growing trend where social scientists were participating in think tanks funded by wealthy and powerful corporations as the beginning of the emergence of "scientism in the guise of science" (p. 68). He labeled the practicing social scientists as promoting **interventionism** where social scientists discovered that since their wares "command good prices" they must make sales as a means of ensuring that their disciplines continue to flourish. Marshall (1963) was even less civil in his use of words when he warned sociologists not to **prostitute** their services. He warned that by doing so clients may get what they wanted but they would not, in his words "get sociology" (p. 16).

DeMartini (1980) used similarly harsh metaphors to describe the selling of sociological services to clients as being a form of **intellectual prostitution**. Some critics even labeled some forms of applied work as **cow sociology**, accusing the sociologists involved as trying to transform workers into **happy cows** which would benefit the management. The applied sociologists were seen as being powerless to contradict the interests of their powerful clients. Horowitz (1964) referred to this as **establishment sociology** where although in theory any party was able to engage the professional services of the sociologists, in reality the latter were mainly accessible to those possessing great corporate wealth and power.

Waitzkin (1970) regarded some social scientists consultants as having been **co-opted** by those in power. As consultants the social scientists were accused of internalizing the values and goals of their powerful clients without even being conscious of the insidious process. He contended that powerful clients normally merely wanted to create an impression that they were genuinely seeking guidance from the experts. In reality, he asserted, their objective was only to get the experts to justify and to legitimize their predetermined decisions. Allen (1975) was equally pessimistic as to whether the applied sociologists would be able to resist compromising their academic freedom or their intellectual integrity. Their attempts to remain free from the dictates of their clients were more likely to be a **hollow** claim because, in his view, the clients would make sure that their personal interests were directly served by the consultants they hired. Wilson (1992) continued to flog this line of argument by asserting that there would be a constant pressure exerted on the consultant sociologists to justify and validate the actions of their clients. According to him, if the findings of the sociologist did not support the interest of the sponsoring agent, the latter might simply "bury it, rewrite it or bring in a new researcher to do it over again" (p. 184).

The concerns and accusations thrown at the practitioners may not be totally without justification although there are elements of exaggeration. The practitioners of applied work are fully aware of the possibility of manipulation by their clients and the temptations of personal gains which may result in biases and unprofessionalism. Experienced applied sociologists will agree with the assertion that undue pressure and manipulation by clients is capable of affecting the professional and intellectual integrity of applied work. However, the conclusion that practitioners should avoid doing applied work is somewhat opposed to the conclusion forwarded by their critics. While the latter suggests abstinence from applied work as the solution, the former argues that this concern strengthens the argument for making practice as an integral and legitimate part in the training of sociologists. It is argued that those who are not trained to deal with this issue, and who are not constraint by any form of professional ethics, supervision, and control, are more likely to commit grave errors of judgment when dealing with their influential and powerful clients.

Any form of professional work involving the interests and welfare of clients is prone to abuse. This is so obvious to the practitioners of all professions that students are subjected to adequate training and supervision before they are allowed to practice. While the critics of applied work place the blame on the activity itself, the exponents of applied work consider it as the failure of personal self-control and the weakness of the monitoring or supervision mechanisms. Any practitioner in any field or profession is capable of choosing between allowing oneself to be swayed purely by one's client's persuasion and **hubris** or to insulate oneself from influences that are unethical, immoral, or illegal.

Exponents of applied work consider it inappropriate to conclude that all applied work should be avoided. What is even less appropriate is to assume that applied sociologists are somehow less capable of making sound moral and ethical choices than their academic brethren. In reality sociologists are not able to escape from having to deal with **clients** even if they are not involved at all in any form of clinical work. The fellow members of the department where one works, one's academic peers, and one's employers, and one's students and their sponsors, including often their parents, all form part of one's total clientele. In reality, all forms of research involve some issues relating to client relations and consequently the possibility of clients' influence upon one's work. Even those performing so-called **pure** or **academic** research usually have some clients to please and placate. Their clients may be the research funding institutions or the government agencies whom they need to lobby and **sell** their research proposals to. Often the pure researchers have to modify their original research proposals in order to align themselves with the priorities determined by the funding source.

In defense of applied work, Braude (1974) argued that sociologists, like any other professionals, will always have options to choose from when dealing with their clients. If they fear being ethically compromised in a particular situation they can always choose the course of action they see as most the appropriate, taking into consideration the need to safeguard their personal and professional integrity. The solution to the problems associated with client relations will be to prepare sociologists adequately during their training on the ethical and legal aspects of applied work, providing them with clear and specific guidelines on how to deal with the value and behavior dilemmas that can adversely affect their professional performance and integrity. As long as applied work within sociology is treated as a marginal activity that is left purely to the whims and fancies of the individual sociologist, the possibilities for inappropriate and unethical behavior are unlimited. On the other hand, with proper training as well as with the setting up of professional associations to oversee the work of practicing sociologists some form of control can be put into effect.

Closely related to the issue of being manipulated by clients and other forms of what critics allege as value **contamination** occurring in applied work. One of the strongest criticisms against applied work is the accusation that applied work invariably involves value judgments—those of the practitioner and those of the client. Sociology, critics argue, must be value-free. Sociologists, some critics claim, are supposed to be concerned with values and value systems only as subjects for objective scientific analysis. The ideal sociologist is seen as someone who studies society in a detached and objective manner, free from the influences of his or her personal values and those of the subjects. This ideal, it is feared, is threatened when the sociologist turns practitioner. Unlike their critics, the proponents and exponents of applied work do not claim that the practitioners are value-free.

Exponents of applied work do not only admit that values do play an important role in problem-solving and social intervention but they go further to insist that **all** sciences, including basic research and theoretical work, are in fact are intrinsically value-laden. Supporters of applied work argue that even the so-called basic sociologists allow their personal biases and ideological leanings to influence the way they view society. Mills (1959) had pointed out half a century ago that the act of performing sociological research itself was **not** value-free. According to him a research sociologist did more than merely reporting facts when presenting his or her research findings. The presentation of a particular point of view on a social issue in itself, he asserted, implied a particular moral or even political stance as well. Gans (1968) agreed with Mills that the choice of a research topic and the publication of its findings, even if the researcher was not conscious of his or her own ideological leanings, would have certain value biases that were bound to serve the interests of some parties and causes.

Applied sociologists believe that they should recognize, declare, and work with value systems and judgments in an explicit manner as an integral part of dealing with human beings. It is the refusal to be aware and openly acknowledge and deal with one's own value system and how it influences one's work that is the crux of the problem. Alvarez (2001), with some humor, equated the social scientists to **values** as something akin to the relationship of the Victorians to **sex**: "We know they did it. We suspect they liked it. But they had the strange custom of publicly denying both" (p. 4). By declaring one's value orientation and by taking a stand on particular social issues based on one's value system supported by some sociological rationalization the applied worker is not afraid to take a stand. Horowitz (1964) derided sociologists whom he saw as lacking the **moral courage** to make a stand when faced with the need to make ethical choices. According to him, when confronted with such a situation, some sociologists decided "to take the courageous leap to the top of the fence!" (p. 30) claiming themselves to be objective and neutral.

Countering the critics of applied work Phillips (1973) stated that the field of sociology itself was NOT by any stretch of the imagination value-free. To him, pure or basic sociologists were not aware of, or refused to admit, was that even their ideas and decisions were influenced by their personal values, such as when they chose a particular topic of interest to explore; in their choice of the methods and scope of research; and the sources of data they chose to employ. Midgley (2000) reiterated this view by asserting that any form of research, even of the "pure, curiosity-driven" (p. 125) kind, was in fact based on some form of value judgment. This view was further supported by Cohen (1980) who agreed that value judgments play an integral role when one dealt with the social phenomena. Joining the band-wagon, DeMartini (1980) reiterated that it would be "gross self-delusion" (p. 144) for sociologists to believe that their works were value-free just because they rejected applied work. He asserted that at least applied work required sociologists to declare openly the social, political, and moral value implications of their work.

Similarly, Horowitz (1964) saw the social world as one which involved alternative and conflicting systems of values, competing and jostling with one another, each with its own merits and demerits. There were no right or wrong values, according to him, only one needed to make choices as to which value systems to adopt. Warren (1971) even went further to assert that should sociologists, after a full and deliberate consideration of the moral implications of a particular effort, decide that it was best not to condone any particular course of action, they were still making an implicit value judgment. The decision to act or not to act, according to Warren (1971), was actually based on some value choices which one might not consciously be aware of. Simply put, making choices was in itself value-laden.

Acknowledging the need to make value choices does not mean that the practitioners do not adhere to the standards of scientific research and rationality. Etzioni (1965) reminded sociologists not to be confused between being what Max Weber termed as **wert-frei** (free of values) and being **wert-los** (valueless). Sociologists, he explained, needed to be **wert-frei** by ensuring as far as possible that they did not allow their values to influence the way they interpreted their data and the way they conducted their research. However, this did not mean that they should be **wert-los,** existing without any commitment to any value system to guide their actions.

By declaring one's values, the sociologist is at least honest enough not to mislead the public to think that everything that is being said is the truth and nothing but the truth. For this reason the training of applied workers needs to address the issue of how the value systems of the practitioner as well as those of the clients are to be managed. Without proper guidelines, supervision, and control the practitioners may behave in a rather erratic and inconsistent manner with regards to the question of values underlying their work. This is true of any professional activity. Unless practitioners are found to transgress a serious ethical or legal provision, for which they can be blacklisted by their professional association or litigated in court, they should be respected as professionals, like any other trained professionals, capable of making decisions based on their personal value systems and evaluations of particular social issues and situations.

Practice as Intervention

The involvement of a practitioner in a client's problem can be considered a form of **intervention.** Social intervention is defined as an action taken to change a particular situation as well as the behavior of the persons within it through such activities as cajoling, deterring, facilitating, enhancing, and enabling social change (Anderson, 1980). According to Anderson (1980), social intervention took many forms such as through such professional activities as action research, operational research, management science, counseling, community psychology, family therapy, community development, etc. The State also performs social intervention through such action as law legislation, city planning, establishing ethnic relations rules, promoting state propaganda, etc.

Intervention may not appear, at first glance, to be a positive term to use since it does have a somewhat negative connotation. A dictionary defines **intervention** as "any interference in the affairs of others" and yet the use of the term is appropriate, for the lack of a better alternative, because the decision to enter into the social system of others, principally that of the client can be interpreted as **interference** by certain quarters. It is also appropriate to use the term since it does not have the pretentious claim that one is necessarily improving a situation through intervention, unlike other practitioners who claim to be **helping**, giving **treatment,** and performing **therapy** instead of **intervening**.

One can be accused of **interfering** but with the consent of some actors and without contravening the law. When one intervenes one needs to constantly remind oneself to tread carefully and respectfully in the social systems and the lives of others so as not to be accused of trespassing. Even if one is invited by a client to enter it does not necessarily mean that one has the total freedom to do whatever one pleases within the system. Similarly, it does not necessarily mean that everyone else within the system, other than the client, will necessarily benefit from the intervention. On the contrary, what is seen as helping by some members may be considered by as **instigation** by others, especially those who see their interests and reputation threatened by the intervention. Seidman (1983) pointed out that although social intervention might be intended for the purpose of enhancing human and social welfare of those involved he warned practitioners that the outcomes of intervention may fail to achieve this objective, or even worse, it may instead produce the opposite effect.

Considering the serious implications that may arise out of the act of intervention, sociologists should not attempt such efforts without first acquiring the appropriate knowledge and skills to prepare them for the task. Anderson (1980) pointed out that the act of intervention was justifiable based on the assumption that the intervener "knows what he is doing so that he can predict with some success that his action will have some of the desired effect" (p. 9). However in reality, he lamented, many of the theories and evidence on which social interventions had been based had shown to be "simply inadequate, erroneous or irrelevant." Anderson (1980) identified three types of ignorance which could fail to produce the desired outcomes: **substantial ignorance**, when the interveners did not have the necessary criteria for assessing the adequacy and relevance of their knowledge; **methodological ignorance** when they did not realize the inadequacies of their methods; and **critical ignorance** when they failed to take into account the weaknesses that were pointed out by others. It is clear that social intervention is a highly challenging task that requires great care and consideration. More importantly, it requires specific knowledge and skills which have to be acquired through considerable supervised practical training and experience. The goal of clinical sociology training is to inculcate these skills so as to minimize negative outcomes, to avoid the types of ignorance mentioned above, ensuring an effective and efficient intervention.

There are several profiles or postures for clinical sociologists to choose in performing social intervention. Different situations and different phases of a case management process may demand different degrees of **involvement** and **visibility** of the practitioners' role. In some situations they may need to adopt a **high involvement** posture or profile where they visibly play a central and crucial leadership role coordinating and directing the process. In others, they may find it more appropriate to choose a **low involvement** profile where they play, and is seen to play, a marginal role in the process, such as by merely observing or supervising an activity from afar. In some situations the interveners may adopt a **high visibility** posture where they generate considerable publicity and public awareness of their presence. In another situation it may be more appropriate for them to choose a **low visibility** option where they are not constantly or physically present during the client's performance of tasks, or where their involvement is not made obvious to the public.

There are times when they may need to choose from the following combination of involvement–visibility options. Depending on the demands of the situation at hand, clinical sociologists may choose to adopt a **high involvement–high visibility** profile, such as in critical conflict situations where order and control is crucial in ensuring a certain degree of structure and orderliness. A **high involvement–low visibility** profile may be appropriate when some degree of control by the sociologist is needed but the active presence and participation of others need to be given a higher priority. A **low involvement–high visibility** profile is appropriate when the presence of the practitioner is considered important usually for symbolic and ritualistic purposes only. Finally a **low involvement–low visibility** profile is adopted when the practitioner is able to withdraw and eventually terminate the involvement in the intervention effort without adversely affecting the outcome of the situation.

Transforming Clients into Agencies

One of the most divisive controversies in sociological theory, which have been implied earlier on, has been that of **structure versus agency**. The traditional view promoted by the structural-functionalist school of thought was that social structure dominates and constrains the behavior and actions of the individual. This rather extreme view which reduces individuals to mere nonthinking and non-feeling robots or victims of social conditions naturally evokes anti-structural backlash. The exponents of **symbolic interactionism**, as reflected in the ideas of Blummer (1969), highlighted the fact that there were too much variations in human behavior to support the claim that structure dictated behavior. He presented the alternative view that behavior was constructed internally by individuals, not shaped by external stimulus. Goffman (1959), an exponent of **dramaturgical** sociology, believed that it was the dynamic nature of social interactions that shaped the diversity that one saw in human social life, instead of the homogeneity that social structure was expected to produce. Long and Der Ploeg (1994) believed in the paradigm that although social structure exerted an impact from the outside, human behavior was not externally determined. Empowered persons who functioned as **agencies**, as opposed to being mere organisms, have the capacity to interpret and reinterpret their social context and to choose appropriate responses.

In the 1980s the views of prominent sociologists on the **structure–agency** issue indicated a move toward a more accommodative, rather than a conflictive, stand. Giddens (1984), for example, forwarded the idea of **structuration** which effectively linked structure as being complementary to the agency. Social structure was seen as rules and resources that individuals made references to when deciding on appropriate actions to take. In other words, while social structures exerted an influence, the individual was always an active agent who constructed his or her own lives. Giddens (1984) recommended a **hermeneutic** approach in sociology, whereby a practitioner needed to approach closer to a subject under study. It was essential that the way one's social world was interpreted and perceived formed the starting point for achieving sociological understanding. This idea was in line with the clinical sociology practice of understanding how clients perceive their situation before more analytical interpretations are arrived at.

Habermas (1976) also contributed some efforts at linking both sides of the **structure–agency** argument. He differentiated two basic ideas: one was that of **social integration** referring to **life-worlds** of how actors participated in social life, dealing with norms, culture, and action, while the other was that of **system integration**, which dealt with the abstract structural properties of social systems. The former could be seen as representing the **agency** side of the argument while the latter represented the **structure** side of it. Habermas (1976) concluded that both the life-worlds and the systems, in other words, both structure and agency, play equally important roles in helping the sociologist to understand society. In the 1970s Bourdieu introduced the idea of **habitus**, of how identity emerges out of a continuous socialization by society, constantly being shaped, reshaped, and modified by social relations. While **structure** provided inputs into the socialization process, a person was capable of changing and modifying his or her **habitus** especially when personal experiences contradicted it. At the beginning of the New Millenium, Bauman (2000) saw the fluidity, openness, and fragmentation of present-day social life in postmodern society as clearly indicating that social structure was incapable of exerting a homogeneous social behavior as claimed by the traditional structuralists.

Clinical sociologists naturally prefer to straddle both sides of the **structure–agency** debate (Walsh, 1998) rather than leaning on one side of the argument. They willingly concur with the views of Blummer, Goffman, Giddens, Bourdieu, Habermas, and Bauman on the need to stop seeing structure as totally dominating human behavior. Roberts (1991) stated that a useful perspective for the clinical sociologist would be to regard everyone as being both an autonomous actor as well as a **victim** of circumstances, in other words, of being both free and constrained at the same time. Social structures and systems do undoubtedly influence human behavior by motivating and de-motivating, rewarding and punishing, certain behaviors. It is also true that some aspects of social structures and systems are more entrenched and will require more effort and resources to change than others, but they remain potentially changeable nevertheless.

Through clinical intervention the sociologist helps the client to see the perceived social and cultural barriers as in fact merely man-made creatures which are in fact **malleable** to change, despite the fact they usually appear to be "immovable and irrevocable permanent structures." Allen and Kraft (1980) believed that people can and should be taught how to **beat the system**, the title of one of their books. This can be achieved by first understanding the nature of social norms and then to find ways of either functioning within them or bypassing and changing them. He asserted that social norms, if assumed to be unchangeable, will adversely affect the optimal achievement of the human potential. Such an assumption tends to impose a limit on one's creative ability to see the whole range of life choices that one can make. The transformation of clients into active decision-making **agencies** involves helping them to understand and manipulate their social contexts as opposed to merely learning to adapt to them.

The idea held by some sociologists that social structures cannot change has perhaps been based on the expectation that change must occur **in toto** and at a revolutionary pace. To the **revolutionists**, slow incremental changes in social structures, taking generations and perhaps centuries, do not qualify as real change. To them efforts to achieve only minor changes, as those attempted by the social engineers and clinical sociologists, are dismissed as mere "tinkering" with the system, an act which, it is argued, only strengthens and further serves the existing system. Clinical sociologists however believe that any change, no matter how small, is capable of contributing to a gradual evolutionary change that may take generations to manifest itself. Clinical sociologists are in no hurry to change the world. They are content to contribute what they can toward reducing human suffering, even if it is achieved through helping a single client and even it takes many decades or even millenniums to achieve it.

The objective of effective intervention is to facilitate the metamorphosis of a dependent **client** into a self-empowered autonomous **agent** or **agency**. The term **agency** refers to a person who has the capacity to perform voluntary action (Marshall, 1994) by undertaking a certain course of action without being unduly constraint by social structure (Jary & Jary, 1999). In other words, an **agent** is one who possesses **agency** who is capable of actively seeking and processing information as well as being able to monitor and control his or her actions in order to achieve desired goals. The use of the terms **agency** and **agents** is particularly liberating especially when one compares them to the concept of **client** which tends to be negatively defined as someone leaning on or depending on another for help. A dictionary defines an **agent** as a person "that performs an action or brings about a certain result" or as a person "empowered to act for another" (Neufeldt & Guralnik, 1991). Instead of being dependent upon others, an agent is capable of acting independently for self-development, going beyond that, an agent may even act on behalf of others. Giddens (1979) regarded persons as having transformed into agents when they were no longer merely "inert objects of knowledge" but rather as those who were able to "incorporate social theory and research within their own action" (p. 16).

An agent, as envisaged by Long and Der Ploeg (1994), was someone who possessed the capacity "to process social experience and to devise ways of coping with life, even under the most extreme forms of coercion" (p. 66). They regarded **agencies** as knowledgeable and capable social actors who "attempt to solve problems, learn how to intervene in the flow of social events around them, and monitor continuously their own actions, observing how others react to their behavior and taking notes of the various contingent circumstances" (p. 66). The focus given by sociology (the term of **agency** was not used half a century ago) toward the concept of the agency-possessing agent acknowledges the idea of human beings as internally complex creatures "that there is a lot going on inside them, and that what goes on inside them is material to understanding how they act upon what exists outside them" (Barnes, 2000, p. 25) Similarly, Midgley (2000) considered the use of the term **agent** as more appropriate than that of **client**, the former is defined as any individual or group acting with a particular purpose. He held the view that agents are those who have a sense of responsibility whether it is an individual, group, family, organization, or community.

Trower (1984) described an agent as a person who is able to conceive of a wide range of possible and realizable actions as well as having the capacity to abort any particular course of action for another. He regarded an agent as a "watcher, commentator and critic" (p. 61) who was capable of reflection and of integrating an understanding of the agent's past, present, and the intended actions for future goals. In addition, Trower saw an agent as capable of accepting or refusing existing rules and roles that limited one's actions aimed at achieving a wider range of possible future actions. This ability, according to him, distinguished an agent from "cybernetic machines which can only pursue supplied goals" (Trower, 1984, p. 71). In short, the **agent** is capable of freeing himself or herself from the dictates of the social structure to some degree and in some aspects, the structures which some sociologists believe to dictate man's behavior and destiny. The **agent** sees social structure as a man-made reality which is "constructed by man for man" (p. 72) which is capable of being modified over time and incrementally by human action.

The early stages of a practitioner–client relationship is unavoidably characterized by a certain degree of dependency of the client on the practitioner. After all, the practitioner is being engaged exactly for the reason that the client needs help from them. The degree of dependency varies according to the extent of despair that the client experiences—from a relatively low degree of urgency when perhaps a clinical sociologist is engaged to improve an organizational climate or culture in an organization, to a high degree of exasperation and urgency of a client who is contemplating suicide. The practitioner tries to reduce the sense of helplessness or despair by inducing an appropriate degree of confidence in the practitioner's ability to help. As an extreme example, at the early stage a client who is too engrossed or overwrought by a particular problem and lacking the necessary objectivity and the self-confidence to deal with the situation, the professional may even be regarded as a kind of **savior**. Merton (1976) noted that such clients tended to have a high expectancy of the capability of the practitioner, hence the decision to solicit the latter's services tended to be accompanied by "exaggerated hopes and exaggerated fears." Such a client has a profound desire to know where he or she stands **vis-à-vis** the problem at hand, desperately wanting to obtain a definite and firm **diagnosis** and **prognosis** as quickly as possible.

The state of anxiety faced by such clients might make them, according to Merton (1976), easily feel uneasy and hostile toward the practitioners, even those who are doing their utmost to help. Some clients may experience some degree of ambivalence toward them. On the one hand, they realize that they need help while at the same time they feel that the disclosure of their innermost feelings and personal privacy makes them vulnerable to negative judgment by others, or even perhaps resulting in some legal jeopardy. The clinical sociologist should realize that this initial over-dependency is an understandable phenomenon which is only a temporary situation that can be gradually transformed by the use of appropriate methods of empowering the client (Capelle, 1979).

Critics of the clinical professions warn of the possibility that clients, being relatively weak and venerable, are totally at the mercy of the more powerful professionals. Dominelli (1997), a social worker, agreed that some professionals sometimes treated their clients in an unprofessional manner by encouraging or expecting clients to become passive and dependent, while the professionals assumed the active and dominating role. This happened despite the professionals' claim to cherish client self-determination as an important value and goal of helping. Most traditional social work methodologies, according to her, were still based on the idea of social workers as the expert professionals who had the right to maintain control and impose their definition of the client's needs. As a result many clients felt disempowered and unhappy with the services they received when these services failed to meet their real needs. Rosengren (1970) agreed that the professional–client relations tended to be asymmetrical in nature since the client had to submit to the authority of the professional with an expectation of the latter being capable of "responsible and effective performance" (p. 39). Lee (1988) advised sociologists to adopt non-manipulative and nonexploitative approaches so as to gain and maintain the trust of their clients. He was confident of the ability of sociologists to do so because he had personally observed how several sociologists of his generation had already successfully developed some forms of individual and group self-help therapeutic programs that empowered clients to help each other rather than depending excessively on the professionals.

The transformation from a client into an agent is obviously not an easy task to achieve. This is the challenge that clinical sociologists should be trained to face. This task can only be achieved gradually and gingerly since exposing vulnerable clients to excessive challenges may be counterproductive, unduly exposing the still dependent clients to the possibilities of failures, rattling their self-confidence and leaving them even worse off. A practitioner needs to move at the pace that is appropriate for the client while at the same time trying to accelerate the process whenever possible. Hall (1990) considered clinical sociology as capable of bringing about an **identity empowerment** of its clients by helping to change the latter's self-perceptions and worldviews until they see themselves as active agents in society.

Empowered clients will be capable of liberating themselves from dysfunctional social relationships; of identifying new life goals; and of strengthening their sense of personal identity and independence. Rebach and Bruhn (1991) emphasized the need for clinical sociologists to envision their clients being free from a current state of dependency on others being transformed from a state of passivity and reactivity into one that was prepared to face any life challenges. They wanted clinical sociologists to ensure that their clients were not "passive responders to situations" (p. 6) but instead they should be "actively, creatively construct and reconstruct themselves and reality" (p. 6). Ideally speaking, clinical sociologists as intervenors should provide models for agents to emulate. This means that the empowered client will, in turn, be capable eventually of performing as intervenors in their own life-situations, independent of the sociologists. Briefly, it is the **client** that approaches for help, but it is an **agent** that terminates the help.

References

Allen, V. L. (1975). *Social analysis: A Marxist critique and alternative*. London: Longman.

Allen, R. F., & Kraft, C. (1980). *Beat the system: A way to create more human environments*. New York: McGraw-Hill.

Alvarez, R. (2001). The social problem as an enterprise: Values as a defining factor. *Social Problems, 48*(1), 3–10.

Anderson, D. C. (1980). The ignorance of social intervention: A polemical introduction. In D. C. Anderson (Ed.), *The ignorance of social intervention* (pp. 9–20). London: Croom Helm.

Barnes, B. (2000). *Understanding agency: Social theory and responsible action*. London: Sage.

Bauman, Z. (2000). *Liquid modernity*. Cambridge: Polity Press.
Berger, P. L. (1963). *Invitation to sociology*. New York: Overlook Press.
Billson, J. M. (1994). Society and self: A symbolic interactionist framework for sociological practice. *Clinical Sociology Review, 12*, 115–133.
Blummer, H. (1969). *Symbolic interactionism: Perspective and method*. Englewood Cliffs, NJ: Prentice-Hall.
Boudon, R. (1977). The logic of relative frustration. In: *The unintended consequences of social action*. London: Palgrave Macmillan.
Braude, L. (1974). *A sense of sociology*. New York: Praeger.
Campbell, C. (1996). *The myth of social action*. Cambridge, UK: Cambridge University Press.
Capelle, R. G. (1979). *Changing human system*. Toronto, ON: International Human System Institute.
Charon, J. M. (1992). *Ten questions: A sociological perspective*. Belmont, CA: Wadsworth.
Clinard, M. (1966). The sociologist's quest for respectability. *The Sociological Quarterly, 7*(4), 399–412.
Cohen, B. P. (1980). *Developing sociological knowledge: Theory and method*. Englewood Cliffs, NJ: Prentice-Hall.
Deloria, L. V. J. (1980). Our new research society: Some warnings for social scientists. *Social Problems, 27*(3), 265–271.
Demartini, J. R. (1980). Constraints to the development of curricula in applied sociology. *The American Sociologist, 15*(3), 138–145.
Dominelli, L. (1997). *Sociology for social work*. London: Palgrave.
Douglas, J. D. (1970). The relevance of sociology. In J. J. Douglas (Ed.), *The relevance of sociology* (pp. 185–233). New York: Appleton-Century-Crofts.
Edwards, M. (1994). Rethinking social development: The search for 'relevance'. In D. Booth (Ed.), *Rethinking social development: Theory, research and practice* (pp. 279–297). Essex: Longman.
Etzioni, A. (1965). Social analysis as a sociological vocation. *The American Journal of Sociology, 70*, 317–323.
Fein, M. L. (1997). Clinical sociology and the individual client. *Clinical Sociology Review, 15*, 40–50.
Fletcher, C. (1975). *The person in the sight of sociology*. London: Routledge and Kegan Paul.
Foote, N. N. (1975). Putting sociologists to work. In N. J. Demerath, O. Larsen, & K. F. Schuessler (Eds.), *Social policy and sociology* (pp. 321–338). New York: Academic Press.
Fox, K. J. (1996). The margins of the underdog sociology: Implications for the "west coast aids project". *Social Problems, 43*(4), 363–386.
Francis, E. (1992). Qualitative research: Collecting life histories. In S. Devereux & J. Hoddinott (Eds.), *Fieldwork in developing countries* (pp. 86–101). New York: Harvester Wheatsheaf.
Game, A., & Metcalfe, A. (1996). *Passionate sociology*. London: Sage.
Gans, H. J. (1968). The participant-observer as a human being: Observations on the personal aspects of field work. In H. S. Becker et al. (Eds.), *Institutions and the person: Papers presented to Everett C. Hughes* (pp. 300–317). Chicago: Aldine.
Giddens, A. (1979). *Central problems in social theory: Action, structure and contradiction in social analysis*. London: Macmillan.
Giddens, A. (1984). *The constitution of society: Outline of the theory of structuration*. Berkeley, CA: University of California Press.
Goffman, E. (1959). *The presentation of self in everyday life*. New York: Doubleday.
Gove, W. R. (1994). Why we do what we do: A biopsychosocial theory. *Social Forces, 73*(2), 363–394.
Habermas, J. (1976). *Legitimation crisis*. London: Heinemann.
Hall, C. M. (1990). Identity empowerment through clinical sociology. *Clinical Sociology Review, 8*, 69–86.
Hammond, P. E. (Ed.). (1964). *Sociologist at work*. New York: Basic Books.

Hewitt, J. P. (1991). *Self and society: A symbolic interactionist social psychology*. Boston: Allyn and Bacon.
Hochschild, A. R. (1998). The sociology of emotion as a way of seeing. In G. Bendelow & S. J. Williams (Eds.), *Emotions in social life* (pp. 3–15). London: Routledge.
Horowitz, I. L. (1964). An introduction to the new sociology. In I. L. Horowitz (Ed.), *The new sociology: Essays in social science and social theory in honor of C. Wright Mills* (pp. 3–48). New York: Oxford University Press.
Humphreys, L. (1972). Tearoom trade: Impersonal sex in public places. In W. Feigelman (Ed.), *Sociology full circle: Contemporary readings on society* (pp. 259–276). New York: Praeger.
Inkeles, A. (1959). Personality and social structure. In R. L. Merton, L. Broom, & L. S. Cottrell (Eds.), *Sociological today: Problems and prospects* (pp. 249–276). New York: Basic Books.
Jary, D., & Jary, J. (1999). *Dictionary of sociology*. Glasgow: HarperCollins.
Johnson, B. C. (1996). Socioemotional understanding and recreation. *Clinical Sociology Review, 14* (1), 44–61.
Josephson, E. (1970). Resistance to community surveys. *Social Problems, 18*(1), 117–129.
Karp, D. A., & Yoels, W. C. (1986). *Sociology and everyday life*. Itasca, IL: F. E. Peacock.
Lee, A. M. (1954). Sociologists in an integrating society: Significance and satisfaction in sociological work. *Social Problems, 2*(1), 57–66.
Lee, A. M. (1988). *Sociology for people*. New York: Syracuse University Press.
Lee, R. M. (1993). *Doing research on sensitive topics*. London: Sage.
Lindesmith, A. R. (1960). Social problems and sociological theory. Reproduced in A. B. Shostak (Ed.) (1966) *Sociology in action: Case studies in social problems and directed social change* (pp. 270–275). Homewood, IL: Dorsey Press.
Long, N. (2001). *Development sociology actor perspectives*. London: Routledge.
Long, N., & Der Ploeg, J. D. V. (1994). Heterogeneity, actor and structure: Towards a reconstitution of the concept of structure. In D. Booth (Ed.), *Rethinking social development: Theory, research and practice* (pp. 62–89). Essex: Longman.
Lynd, R. S. (1939). *Knowledge for what? The place of social sciences in American culture*. Princeton, NJ: Princeton University Press.
Marshall, T. H. (1963). *Sociology at the crossroads: And other essays*. London: Heinemann.
Marshall, G. (1994). *Oxford concise dictionary of sociology*. Oxford: Oxford University Press.
Merton, R. K. (1976). *Sociological ambivalence and other essays*. New York: Free Press.
Merton, R. K., & Lerner, D. (1951). Social scientists and research policy. In D. Lerner & H. D. Lasswell (Eds.), *The policy sciences* (pp. 282–307). Stanford, CA: Stanford University Press.
Midgley, G. (2000). *Systemic intervention: Philosophy, methodology, and practice*. New York: Kluwer/Plenum Publishers.
Mills, C. W. (1959). *The sociological imagination*. Oxford: Oxford University Press.
Neufeldt, V., & Guralnik, D. B. (1991). *Webster's new world dictionary*. New York: Prentice-Hall.
Phillips, D. L. (1973). *Abandoning method*. San Francisco: Jossey-Bass.
Prus, R. (1997). *Subcultural mosaics and intersubjective realities*. Albany, NY: State University of New York Press.
Ravetz, J. R. (1971). *Scientific knowledge and its social problems*. Oxford: Clarendon Press.
Rebach, H. M., & Bruhn, J. G. (Eds.). (1991). *Handbook of clinical sociology* (pp. 81–97). New York: Plenum Press.
Roberts, L. W. (1991). Clinical sociology with individuals and families. In H. M. Rebach & J. G. Bruhn (Eds) (1991). *Handbook of clinical sociology* (pp. 143–163). New York: Plenum Press.
Rosengren, W. R. (Ed.). (1970). *Organizations and clients. Essays in the sociology of service*. Columbus, OH: Merrill.
Schein, E. H. (2001). Clinical inquiry/research. In P. Reason & H. Bradbury (Eds.), *Handbook of action research: Participative inquiry and practice* (pp. 228–237). London: Sage.
Schuman, H. (1975). Race relations: Some policy implications, proximate and remote, of a negative finding. In N. J. Demerath, O. Larsen, & K. F. Schuessler (Eds.), *Social policy and sociology* (pp. 37–44). New York: Academic Press.

Schuster, L. (2015). The sociologist as voyeur. In K. Twamley, M. Doidge, & A. Scott (Eds.), *Sociologists' Tales: Contemporary narratives on sociological thought and practice*. Bristol: Policy Press.
Seidman, E. (1983). Unexamined premises of social problem solving. In E. Seidman (Ed.), *Handbook of social intervention* (pp. 48–67). Beverly Hills, CA: Sage.
Spengler, J. J. (1969). Is social science ready? In N. J. Demerath, O. Larsen, & K. F. Schuessler (Eds.), *Social policy and sociology* (pp. 54–73). New York: Academic Press.
Thomas, M., & Pierson, J. (Eds.). (1995). *Dictionary of social work*. London: Collins Educational.
Touraine, A. (1984). *Le retour de l'acteur: Essai de sociologie*. Paris: Librairie artheme fayard. Translated in English by M. Godzich (1988). Return of the actor. Minneapolis, MN: University of Minnesota.
Trower, P. (Ed.). (1984). *Radical approaches to social skills training*. London: Croom Helm.
Tudor, A. (1976). Misunderstanding everyday life. *Sociological Review, 24*(3), 479–503.
Vargus, B. S. (1971). On sociological exploitation: Why the guinea pig sometimes bites. *Social Problems, 19*(2), 238–248.
Waitzkin, H. (1970). Truth's search for power: The dilemmas of the social sciences. In J. D. Douglas (Ed.), *The relevance of sociology*. New York: Meredith.
Walsh, D. F. (1998). Structure/agency. In C. Jenks (Ed.), *Core sociological dichotomies* (pp. 8–33). London: Sage.
Warren, R. L. (1971). *Social change and human purpose: Toward understanding and action*. Chicago: Rand McNally College Publishing Company.
Weigert, A. J. (1981). *Sociology of everyday life*. New York: Longman.
Whyte, W. F. (1979). On making the most of participant observation. *The American Sociologist, 14* (1), 56–66.
Willer, W. (1934). Insight and scientific method. *American Journal of Sociology, XL*(3), 285–297.
Wilson, K. (1992). Thinking about the ethics of fieldwork. In S. Devereux & J. Hoddinott (Eds.), *Fieldwork in developing countries* (pp. 179–199). New York: Harvester Wheatsheaf.
Zetterberg, F. (1962). *Social theory and social practice*. New York: Bedminster Press.
Znaniecki, F. (1965). *Social relations and social roles*. San Francisco: Chandler.

Chapter 5
Case Management

Whether dealing with a personal, organizational, or with a wider social issue or problem the clinical sociologist is said to be dealing with **cases**. In his renowned article on **clinical sociology**, Wirth (1931) recommended what he termed as the **case method** as the main approach in clinical sociology. He identified three main characteristics of this approach. The **first** characteristic was the presence of a person or persons presenting a specific problem to be solved. A **case** involved a request or representation by a particular client or clients who labeled a situation as problematic and requiring help for its resolution. The **second** characteristic was that the problem required an interdisciplinary and cooperative effort involving a number of specialists. In other words, clinical sociologists did not necessarily need to have all the resources to deal with a case on their own, except in simple cases. The **third** characteristic was that the efforts were aimed at achieving some form of **therapeutic** outcomes, aimed at achieving some positive or desired effects on the clients.

The idea of using the **case method** as suggested by Wirth (1931) had been generally accepted by several clinical sociologists after him. Rebach and Bruhn (1991), for example, described the work of a clinical sociologist as that of bringing about a planned positive social change on a **case-by-case** basis based on the principles and methods of scientific sociology. The use of the term **case** represents a radically different approach from that which mainstream sociologists have become familiar with. Sociologists often use the term **case** in a different sense—to refer to a respondent who is included in a research survey. For example, a sample of 100 respondents is referred to as equivalent to 100 cases. As pointed out by Platt (1992) the term **case** in survey research was used not to refer to a whole person but rather only to a particular variable or a collection of variables concerning the person selected as a respondent. These variables were measured as statistics to be generated and manipulated and "treated as though they had an autonomous existence" by the researcher. In other words, the traditional researcher is not interested in the respondent as a whole person but rather with specific selected aspects of him or her. The **person** is often considered to be significant only as statistics for sociological studies. In traditional survey, research cases are significant only when seen in aggregates.

© Springer Nature Switzerland AG 2020

P. M. Wan, A. H. Wan, *Clinical Sociology*, Clinical Sociology: Research and Practice, https://doi.org/10.1007/978-3-030-49083-6_5

The uniqueness of individual cases is drowned in the statistics of averages, probabilities, and standard deviations.

Allen (1975) defined a **case** as a **situation** that contains a problem. Lofland (1976) described a **situation** as consisting of a collection of people, objects, and ideas and spaces occurring within a specific time period, all of which needed to be taken into account in order to understand and to intervene in it. In other words, a situation is a unique combination of objectively real and subjectively perceived conditions existing at a given time which provided the social and physical context within which people acted. Berenson (1981) believed that one might choose to understand a situation at a superficial level by merely describing the observable facts and enumerating a sequence of events. Alternatively, one might choose to delve into the more complex levels by understanding the deeper "motives, desires, ways of coping, intentions, moral or religious attitudes, beliefs and reactions" of the people involved in it. By adopting the latter approach a clinical sociologist would be able to obtain a more complete and accurate understanding of how persons in a particular situation perceived it, providing the practitioner with the crucial data upon which one could perform the task of constructing, analyzing, and solving the case.

Another use of the term **case** which sociologists are familiar with is through the use of the term **case study**. A **case study** involved an inductive approach toward examining a social phenomenon where a highly complex and dynamic phenomenon was studied within its social context with considerable depth. The phenomenon under investigation in a case study represented experiences and interactions of its actors where meanings and symbols which were not normally captured in traditional sample research were considered to be of great significance. The proponents of the case study method believe that the study of cases has contributed significantly to the development of sociological theories in the past. From these in-depth case studies, comparisons between them generate new theories, hypothesis, and concepts which further contributed to the enrichment of sociological understanding of social phenomena.

Critics of the case approach is concerned that, by focusing on specific cases, the sociologist will not be able to relate the cases to the wider social phenomenon. Mills (1943) expressed this concern when he stated that the case approach is more appropriate for certain professionals—such as for the judges, social workers, and social pathologists—because their occupational training had **incapacitated** them from going beyond the involvement in a series of cases and situations. The main cause of a negative evaluation of the case approach is probably due to the impression that a case invariably involves only a single client or a small social situation, such as a single individual, family, group, or community. On the contrary, for the clinical sociologist, a case does not necessarily involve such small and limited situations. A case may include any potentially problematic situation, ranging from small concrete situations to broader abstract global social issues that need some form of intervention. As an example, a global endeavor to promote world peace may hypothetically be initiated by an international organization which includes the involvement of clinical sociologists together with other professionals from many different countries and regional organizations working together to achieve a specified goal. This can be considered as a case. It may require more resources and a much longer time frame but as long as it is constructed as a case, with clear and measurable objectives, a clinical sociologist should treat it like any other case.

A clinical sociologist who is looking for a case to construct may adopt a **deductive** approach by looking at a particular macro-level phenomenon and then decides to focus on a more limited and manageable subcomponent of the phenomenon Alternatively, the sociologist may decide on an inductive approach where he or she begins by identifying a specific problem occurring at personal and interpersonal levels. Upon a realization that the problem is shared by a larger community, the practitioner may decide to construct a case at a higher and more inclusive level, such as dealing with an organization or a community faced with the problem. Znaniecki (1965) favored the inductive approach, where instead of starting with what was supposed to be the dominant, most inclusive system, sociologists began with a comparative study of various relatively small and simple systems. Later they could move on to examine it within the context of much larger and more complex supra-systems. He saw the need to start with the most basic social system, that of the interaction and cooperation between two interdependent individuals, and then to proceed investigating the various kinds of more inclusive social systems within which the core social system was located. Regardless of which approach one chooses, what is important for the clinical sociologist is the awareness of the need to consider all levels of social reality as possible and feasible levels for intervention.

Some practitioners may use the concept of **target group** as synonymous with that of **client's system**. Warren (1971) identified the various parties that could be identified within the target system. This included an **inviter**, the client who approached the practitioner for the latter's involvement; the **target group** that the client may represent; the **donor** system which was composed of persons who defined and provided the resources needed to solve a problem; the **administrative** system composed of persons who were placed in charge of the administration of a problem-solving program; the **delivery** system consisting of those who interacted directly with the recipients of particular services offered by the donor system; and finally the **recipients** of those services. The final component, according to Warren (1971), tended to be seen purely as passive receivers of the services. They tended to be relatively ignored and were seldom involved in the process of problem-solving itself, and yet they might even be labeled as the **main problem** by other parties.

The critical search for an inkling of "the bigger picture" makes the clinical sociologists more tentative in their response to a request for intervention by a particular client or interest group. This "bigger picture" is what one can regard as the **case**, and the efforts at visualizing and constructing it can be considered as the process of **encasement.** This process is not simply one where professionals define cases as how their clients see or want them to be. To the clinical sociologists, the process of encasement itself is problematic rather than automatic because there are many possible scenarios to wrestle with. The **first scenario** is fairly straight forward where sociologists consider the situation as one of a genuine **client with case**. In this uncomplicated typical situation where they decided that the concerns of the client are substantive, legitimate, genuine, and resolvable with the help of some form of sociological intervention. In the **client with case** scenario the clinical sociologist may respond to a client's request for help.

In a **second scenario**, the practitioner may be dealing with a **client without case** situation where, after exploring the concerns of the client the clinical sociologist comes to the conclusion that there is no clear or definite situation to be resolved, or that it is not the kind of issue that the practitioner feels is solvable or worthy of intervention. In a **third scenario**, the practitioner deals with a **case without client** situation where the sociologist personally encases a situation as problematic in which he or she initiates some form of intervention although no particular party has directly for help. In the remaining **fourth scenario**, the practitioner deals with a **no client, no case** situation where the sociologist performs other types of community activities, not strictly speaking that of a clinical sociologist, since it does not involve neither the presence of a case nor the presence of any client. The importance of the fourth scenario should not be underestimated since it is often through this scenario that they come in contact with their potential clients.

It is seldom adequate or effective for the clinical sociologist to deal only with a single client in trying to resolve a problem. Even if the party which approaches for help is made up of only a single person, it does not mean that the practitioner needs to work with only that single client. According to the systemic perspective, what initially appears to be a purely personal problem almost always involves or affects many other significant individuals and groups within the client's social system. The systemic practitioner needs to deal with the whole **client system** rather than merely focusing on the single client. The **client system**, according to Rebach (Rebach, 1991a–c), included others within the client's social network, including the family members, coworkers, adversaries, employees, service providers, or anyone else that one might need to be taken into consideration for the purpose of intervention. He and his coauthor, in a latter source, further described a client system as referring to "those co-actors who participate in the problem, they may be the ones who define it as a problem, and may be involved in the planning or participating in the intervention. They may be the ones to change or be affected by change" (Bruhn & Rebach, 1996, p. 19).

Midgley (2000) considered the participation of a variety of **stakeholders** in problem-solving as essential since they would bring different insights and criticisms to bear on the case at hand. The concept of client's system is important since it alerts the practitioner that while he or she may be dealing directly with one client, there are other people who are affected by the intervention. These people may respond in ways that may help or hinder the achievement of the desired objective. By working with the client's system the sociologist can avoid the tendency to focus solely on the client's perspective, as if it exists in isolation from the wider client's system. This is an important and unique contribution clinical sociologists can make toward improving social well-being which other more traditional **therapeutic** and **treatment** approaches tend to neglect.

Too often social intervention is performed as a knee-jerk response to a particular situation without working through the various stages needed by the manager to identify the issue and to ensure that the intervention achieves its goals. A practitioner's involvement in a case should be seen as an effort to manage effectively a particular situation, not merely to intervene in it. This means that the main function of clinical sociologists is that of **case management** and their main role is that of a **case manager**. Case management can be seen as a systemic and systematic attempt to solve a particular issue, situation, challenge, problem, conflict, or crisis. The term **case management** has also been used by other professionals but with somewhat different meanings and approaches. Social workers use the term to refer to efforts at coordinating, integrating, and allocating resources, usually in managed care situations, to help their clients to obtain some specific services. Summers (2001) considered the case management carried out by social workers as involving the identification of the needs of each client to ensure the adoption of the most efficient manner of utilizing resources and the provision of services. According to her, the primary purpose of case management was to improve the quality of life for the client, preventing the problem faced by the client "from growing worse and costing more to remedy in the future" (p. 46).

In order to perform **case management** effectively, a clinical sociologist needs to possess the relevant micro-skills, such as the interpersonal skills of establishing rapport, listening, probing, confronting, focusing, assessing, monitoring, researching, guiding, training, making referrals, supervising, evaluating, and finally terminating the relationship with the client. Although these skills are utilized by many professionals, over time clinical sociologists may be able to contribute their own unique approaches based on sociological principles that focus on factors and perspectives neglected by others. As a model, the sociologist may be able to impart the above skills to all actors in a social situation, not only their principle clients, such as parents, peers, community leaders, counselors, teachers, doctors, nurses, lawyers, politicians, policemen, managers, religious leaders, government officers, and anyone else who themselves need to manage difficult situations. This management function involves complex multi-level and multi-role action-oriented purposive activities that need to be executed. As a management process it involves the task of steering through the full problem-solving cycle, including the tasks of problem identification, goal setting, planning, strategizing, intervention, controlling and performing evaluation, and obtaining feedback.

Social Activism

For those who are critical of what they see as the clinical sociologist selling their principles, bodies, and souls to the highest bidder, they can be assured that this needs not be the case. Clinical sociologists do not necessarily need clients in order to make their contribution to society. While the first two scenarios listed above placed clinical sociologists as **passive** invitees by clients as initiators to perform intervention, in the third scenario the sociologists are **the** initiators of the intervention. Here, clinical sociologists function as **social activists** who are sufficiently concerned with a particular social issue or situation to initiate social intervention to prevent what they see as an undesirable situation from worsening, without waiting to be engaged by clients to do so. They need not be approached or sponsored by any particular group or stakeholder in order to perform what they see as a moral and professional responsibility as clinical sociologists.

These sociologists may construct a case, or on a wider scale, a **cause,** by self-initiating some action toward achieving particular goals which they themselves set. Without a legal contract to fulfill, as social activists, the clinical sociologist's involvement does not have to begin with a request from specific clients, nor it is dictated by them. They see themselves as promoting social causes based on particular humanistic concerns. They may eventually incorporate specific persons or groups of persons who may eventually play the role of clients voluntarily although they are the ones who initiate the case initially. In this situation the sociologist is not appointed as consultants to the clients.

Perhaps more typically, clinical sociologists may initially play the role of **consultants** who are formally and contractually appointed by specific parties to achieve particular and specific objectives. The role of the consultant is clearly documented in formal contracts signed and recognized as legal documents, or in the form of less formal **memoranda of understanding** prepared by their clients and agreed upon by the consultants. After finishing their consultancies the **consultants** can turn into **social activists** should they decide to pursue the same particular case or issue based on their personal commitments or interests. Similarly **social activists** may turn into **consultants** once they choose to work for a specific client interested in the case they had initiated. Capable clinical sociologists can perhaps even play both roles as consultants and as social activists concurrently or simultaneously. This dual role is not necessarily problematic if they are able to demonstrate and convince the client that their social activism does not interfere, but rather enhances further, their obligations as consultants.

In order to ensure that practitioners do not end up putting sociology, or worse still putting themselves, up **for sale**, they need to seek and maintain a healthy balance between their roles as paid consultants and that of social activists. They may earn their living by performing consultancies which are not contrary to the basic values of their professions while at the same time they are able to self-initiate cases for the purpose of social intervention on a ***pro bono*** basis. The latter is performed based on the conviction that sociologists have a moral obligation to act and intervene for the purpose of improving social life and reducing human suffering, without waiting for clients to commission them to do the work. This double role will help to diminish somewhat the accusation often made toward professionals that they are only interested in living off the suffering and misery of their clients. In many cases, clients are simply too poor to pay for the services of a clinical sociologist, or for that matter that of any other practitioners. For this reason it is important that a certain amount of **pro bono** work is performed by clinicians who offer help to clients who are disfranchised, alienated, marginalized, and excluded by mainstream society.

Debating "Sociology Proper"

There are all sorts of justification offered as justifications for not wanting to change the main scope or focus of sociology, for not incorporating applied and clinical skills beyond that of research fieldwork skills, and for refusing to accept applied and clinical work as part and parcel of "sociology proper." One of the rationales is the claim that applied work is unscientific in nature and therefore it does not deserve to constitute as part of **sociology proper**. It has often been argued that sociology must maintain its so-called original **purity**, a science based on the philosophy of **positivism–empiricism** which studies and analyzes a subject or field in an objective and detached manner. Social intervention, it is claimed, would only contaminate the objectivity and the detachment that one is expected to observe. The **purists** would remind us that the founder fathers of sociology embraced **positivism** as the most scientific basis of the discipline, and therefore any movement away from this tradition will be unacceptable.

Sociologists, they believe, should be dedicated to the sole task of seeking knowledge without needing to think of its immediate applicability. Applied work, it is argued, should be performed by others, or for that matter by anybody else **but** sociologists. Sociologists can of course apply sociological ideas, but only in their capacity as ordinary citizens, not as sociologists. Queen (1941) wrote as early as in 1941 that sociologists considered the efforts to achieve social changes as merely **extracurricular** activities, and that the twin roles of sociologists **qua** sociologists and sociologist **qua** citizens should be separated. Odum (1951) similarly agreed that applied work should be considered as **borderline sociology** rather than as sociology proper. A decade later Lindesmith (1960) suggested to sociologists to concentrate on **sociological problems** rather than **social problems**. Focusing on the former, he felt, could be done in a dispassionate, objective, and impartial manner, focusing on "what things are" and not with "what ought to be." Arguing along the same lines, Hauser (1971) believed that since the mission of the sociologist was to contribute to sociological knowledge the sociologist should not succumb to "the temptation to turn activist" (p. 438). Bernard (1973) likewise wanted sociologists to limit their role to that of promoting an understanding of community issues, and not to go beyond it.

Sociologists should, it was argued, only present the information and analysis of a particular phenomenon or situation, after which others, principally policy-makers, would "have to carry the ball from there." The general drift of the argument presented by the **purists** is that applying sociological findings is not a legitimate concern of sociologists. Let us consider further Bernard's (1973) suggestion that sociologists should let others "to carry the ball." In the first place, why would any other practitioner be interested in taking over from where the sociologist leaves off especially when in the first place they can perform both the analysis AND the application by themselves without having to rely on the sociologist? If they decide to take the **ball** from the sociologist, how would the latter transfer his or her experiences, knowledge, and understanding in its entirety to the **ball-handler** who will need the details to be able to perform intervention? Why is it not conceivable that another sociologist, not the one who performs the research or the analysis, but one who is trained to intervene, let us say, a clinical sociologist, be the one to "carry the ball"?

These are important questions that are left unanswered by those who advocate that sociologists should not go "all the way." Heraud (1979) questioned the wisdom of allowing someone else, usually one who is less informed than sociologists, to finish the job. He does not agree that sociologists should allow others, including their clients, to "do their own sociology" (p. 17). Those who advocate the **hands-off** policy make the assumption that by merely obtaining data and providing analysis by the sociologist anyone will be able to decide on the appropriate action to take. It is of course rather convenient for sociologists to **pass the buck** to someone else to deal with the rather messy and risky part of problem-solving while they focus on the comparatively **safer** and **cleaner** task of gathering and analyzing information. Sociologists then can lean back and relax as soon as they have submitted their final report, not having to be concerned with how it is to be utilized by its consumers. Should the inheritors and implementers fail to achieve the desired objectives sociologists can always disclaim any responsibility for this failure. In fact, as it sometimes happens, they may even join the critics in blaming the implementers for not properly utilizing the information and analyses provided.

Clinard (1966) noted that some sociologists considered colleagues who were involved in applied work as being involved in **degrading** work, not only **sullying** their own professional reputation but, even worse, tarnishing the reputation of the discipline with their **substandard** work. Rossi (1980) reiterated this view with his observation that applied work during his time was clearly rated as being below that of basic or academic sociology in the hierarchy of "preference, prestige, and esteem" (p. 889). According to him, many sociologists seemed to have an ambivalence toward applied work because it was considered as not being worthy of "our best efforts and our best minds." What criteria were used to judge the work done as **substandard** were not always clearly stated or proven by the critics.

Clinard (1966) himself disagreed with this negative evaluation of applied work. He argued that social scientists in the other disciplines had consistently proven that being involved in applied work did not tantamount to either endangering their personal and professional reputations as scientists or did it tarnish the image of their disciplines. Similarly, another sociologist, Olsen (1981) pointed out that the pursuit of pure science unaccompanied by a concern for its applied relevance was, in his view, intellectually and morally indefensible. He predicted that the public would **not** continue to tolerate or support a field of study that did not demonstrate its usefulness for enhancing the welfare of the society. The supporters of applied work respond to the allegation that applied work is invariably substandard or unscientific by counterarguing that so-called academic work in fact does not always abide by the scientific standards that sociologists have set for themselves. Rossi and Whyte (1983) made the assertion that many articles appearing in scholarly journals were in fact based on **flimsy evidence** and that the research designs and methodologies were often questionable. Another exponent of applied sociology, Rossi (1980) also offered support for this argument by pointing out that applied work often demanded even greater technical skills than did basic research.

The reality is that an applied sociologist is even less able to perform substandard work for the simple reason that their work is invariably exposed to public scrutiny. Members of the general public and potentially critical clients observe the work of the clinical sociologists and they can be far more ruthless and merciless than the civil and guarded criticism made by one's academic peers and students. In major controversial applied work the social scientist will need to ensure that the quality of his or her work is beyond reproach to avoid a public outcry. A piece of work published in journals and books may not lend itself to such public exposure since its readers tend to be those who are not immediately impacted by a particular policy recommendation or social action. Furthermore, the consumers of academic sociology often do not have the means to verify the accuracy and the authenticity of the data presented in basic academic work. Whatever criticisms made tend to be mainly limited to the more obvious methodological and analytical faults and errors rather than the important substantive ones which only the researcher, the enumerators, and the client can vouch for their accuracy. In contrast, clients and the general public are able to detect and point out every flaw or inaccuracy should they be committed by their practitioners.

If applied work is considered as not being a legitimate part of **sociology proper**, or of being substandard in quality, its practitioners will naturally experience difficulties in gaining recognition for their work, which is essential for the purpose of career advancement especially within the academic world. Clinard (1966) speculated that some sociologists stayed away from applied work due to the fear that their involvement would not receive as much professional recognition as the academic work performed by their colleagues. According to Morrissey and Steadman (1977) becoming a practicing sociologist could **perish** due to what they viewed as a lack of occupational support and academic recognition of such activities. Berk (1981) was convinced that the discipline's **gatekeepers** tended to discriminate against applied sociological work. Work that did not have the usual academic content and which did not fit in easily into the usual theoretical discourse, polemics and controversies were seen as less worthy of being published. He also noted that some academic departments tended to consider applied experience as inadmissible for promotion purposes while some job openings explicitly stated that only basic researchers needed to apply.

The belief that sociology should as far as possible emulate the **pure** natural sciences, and that scientists should only be concerned with the acquisition of knowledge, not in its application, has never been unanimously accepted by the whole sociology community. Its critics, although relatively small in number, have always been vocal. They counterargue that sociology can never be a pure science because it deals with human behavior and therefore should not be equated with the study of the physical and biological phenomena. They believe that as a social science sociology has to develop its own scientific philosophy and methodology.

The sociological method does not necessarily have to be restricted to that of **positivism–empiricism** which tends to be translated narrowly as the performance of empirical research for the sole purpose of seeking and promoting **enlightenment**. Furthermore the claim often made that scientists are usually not motivated by the desire to apply, is highly contentious. While scientists may be superficially pictured as dedicated lone researchers in their laboratories detached from the concerns of the real world, they are in fact motivated by the pursuit of knowledge that can be directly or eventually applicable toward enhancing the quality of the human condition. The final test of the validity of their scientific research findings lies very much in their usefulness in real-life application. The pressing needs for research funding and the desire to improve the quality of human life motivate many scientists to continue to be involved in applied work while remaining as **bona fide** scientists. The applied natural sciences demonstrate clearly how the two wings of the same discipline are considered as being equally legitimate and complementary to each other.

The Maturing of Sociology

The underlying perspective that the **raison d'etre** of sociology has been and still is for the purpose of improving society is seldom openly questioned in recent sociological literature. Although a considerable number of sociologists do believe that practical sociology has a definite potential in the distant future but they tend to cling to the idea that sociology is still a relatively young science. They insist that sociology will need more time to grow before it can be tested in the field of social intervention. Lazarsfeld and Rosenberg (1955) who later became an outstanding exponent of applied sociology was initially cautious with the idea of applying sociology. He pointed out in 1955 that the natural sciences required about 250 years beginning with the ideas of Galileo up to the beginning of the industrial revolution before they could claim to have helped transform the world. He, therefore, cautioned that "if we expect from it quick solutions to the world's problems, if we demand of it nothing but immediately practical results, we will just corrupt its natural course" (In Mills, 1959, p. 100).

Lazarsfeld's and Rosenberg (1955) referral to Galileo was unfortunate since he overlooked the fact that practically all fields of applied science, such as medicine and the like, matured **through** practice instead of practice **after** achieving maturity. Still, over a decade later Waitzkin (1970) made the assertion that only when the social sciences eventually reached a state of **maturity** somewhere in the future that its discoveries would be capable of improving society, but not until then. Exhibiting the same level of over-cautiousness, Merton (1976) remarked that the applied sociologists of his time were guilty of undertaking substandard investigations and of making **off-the-cuff pronouncements** which were to him **of questionable validity**. He realized that the public wanted sociological solutions to social problems, but he felt that the demand then exceeded the capacity of sociologists to deliver. Consequently he advised sociologists to avoid making what he saw as premature responses which would be mere "nominal approximations to the genuine article" (Merton, 1976, 113).

Fernandez (1975) talked of the **great promise** sociology made that one day, when sociology became sufficiently developed, it would help members of the society to bring about **radical yet peaceful** planned social change. To many sociologists, the delivery of this promise had been long overdue. Some sociologists had expressed surprise that society had been lenient and patient with their discipline, giving it the whole of the last century to explore fully its potentials. The argument that sociology will only be ready for application when basic sociology has accumulated sufficient knowledge is based on a questionable assumption. It was the unfounded assumption that theoretical knowledge could make the magical leap into the world of practice, that accumulated knowledge could be easily and directly transformed or translated into action. Berelson (1966) clearly disagreed with this assumption. He pointed out that the nature of applied work was basically different from that of basic knowledge. This meant that applied sociological work could not evolve merely as a **spill-off** from basic sociology. The basic and the applied, he wrote, had **different masters** and so it is hard to "simultaneously to serve both well" (p. 18).

Zetterberg (1962) considered the descriptive knowledge accumulated by basic sociologists as of limited use for practitioners. It was not always very helpful, he asserted, in helping practitioners to choose an appropriate course of action, no matter how much of it was accumulated or how orderly and systematic its collection had been carried out. Exponents of applied work emphasize upon the principle that while the development of theory and practice of a discipline needs to be seen as having different trajectories, both are capable of developing simultaneously, independently but complementing each other. Instead of a linear theory of knowledge development, with basic knowledge preceding application, sociologists need to adopt a lateral view where different concurrent strands within a discipline develop independently of one another but are mutually reinforcing.

Not all sociologists agreed with the argument that sociology was **not ready** to apply. As early as 1941, Argow (1941) reproached sociologists for giving evasive answers when asked to apply sociological knowledge. He was dissatisfied with the rationale given by sociologists of his time that sociology was just at the point of **forging the tools** which one day, in some distant future, would be fully developed. In the following decade, Young (1955) unhappily noted that sociologists were still claiming that the discipline was still **youthful** and that it had only managed then to acquire "a small store of useful knowledge" (p. 644). He summarized the other reasons given for the lack of **readiness** on the part of the discipline to apply. He saw a lack of effective liaison between sociology with the other established professions; that applied sociology would be considered as a departure from the **normal** career expected of sociologists; and that the sociology taught then was a poor preparation for a career in applied work. Podgorecki and Los (1979) argued that sociology was ready and able even in the late 1970s to produce more than mere superficial **one-dimensional** or **black-or-white** pictures of society. Similarly, Gouldner (1965) disagreed with sociologists who held the view that basic sociological knowledge should first reach a stage of maturity before attempts at application could be made. He considered it as a **bad advice** that should be discarded.

The question that should be posed back to those who claim that sociology was not yet ready would be: When would it be ready? Unfortunately none of those who posed the immaturity argument is prepared to speculate or at least give some indication as to when sociology will be considered as sufficiently **matured**. The general argument that there must be a certain measurable quantum of sociological knowledge before the application can be attempted is hard to fathom. The sociologists have been kept busy for more than a century accumulating massive amounts of sociological knowledge, analysis, and endless theoretical polemics. The claim that sociology is **still young** appears to be nothing more than an excuse to delay the inevitable. The authors of this book, as well as most readers who are familiar with family intervention activities, are able to see the parallel between this assertion with those parents who refuse to acknowledge their children's independence on the ground that the latter are not **matured** even though, in some cases, the children are already in their adulthood.

Some sociologists are also fond of making claims that sociology was still in a state of **poverty**, or in a state of **crisis**. For clinical sociologists the response to these allegations is an obvious one. The field of clinical sociology can help sociology to overcome both the **poverty** and **crisis** allegations simultaneously by enabling sociology to be directly applicable while at the same time helping to strengthen its approaches, fine-tune its methodologies, and sharping its tools. Instead of arguing that sociologists need to first overcome its so-called poverty, internal crisis, or immaturity before attempting to apply, it is more rational to argue that only through actual application can sociology ever hope to overcome its internal shortcomings. Sutherland (1947) believed that the social scientist will have to wait "for an eternity" (p. 1) if they expect theoretical knowledge to reach some imaginary ideal state of completion before embarking on social intervention. Similarly, Lundberg (1961) argued that instead of waiting "for the social sciences to develop" (p. 143) one should harvest and enjoy the "fruits of science" (p. 143) while it was in the process of development. Science, he asserted, was a growth or learning process in a continuous process of development, not a "sudden revelation" of its final products. Znaniecki (1969) supported this line of argument, asserting that it was through practical applicability that the ultimate practical and theoretical value of a science could be tested.

Zetterberg (1962) reminded sociologists that social problems were **crying** for solutions and therefore it cannot wait for social sciences to take their own sweet time to develop solutions. However imperfect they may be, Zetterberg (1962) believed that social science practitioners and consultants needed to utilize whatever knowledge and understanding that they had already possessed to offer help in dealing with difficult social situations. All societies, he wrote, must learn to deal with "exigencies and emergencies." Sociological practitioners should emulate others in the fields of medicine and engineering who developed their practice by applying whatever knowledge and skills they possessed, no matter how inadequate and tentative they might initially be. Until today, the medical profession is still experimenting with treatments, able to deal only with symptoms of many diseases, rather than curing the diseases, but it does not throw up its arms in exasperation and concluded that "we are not ready."

Horowitz (1968) offered further support to this view giving the example of how the Chicago School of Sociology developed. It was not, he explained, out of some abstract theorizing but rather with a commissioned research project to find out ways on how to reduce urban crime rate. That effort helped to spurt a phenomenal development of the sociological approach toward societal problem-solving. The message these writers wished to make was clear. Knowledge and skills did not have to be perfected for it to be applicable, rather it could be useful when applied while it was being developed. It followed that any alleged ineffectiveness and defectiveness of some practices should not be used as a justification for not intervening. Rather, it should be used as the basis for finding better and more effective means of intervention.

Some exponents of applied work believe that all the talk about sociology as not being ready, or the argument that sociology needs to be totally value-free, are mere rationalizations that disguise a more deep motivation and fear to take risks and to face challenges. Horowitz (1964) had earlier criticized what he saw as a lack of **moral courage** to take a stand on social issues. Stuart Queen (1941) had simply concluded that the sociologists in the 1940s did not have the confidence to face the social crises and emergencies; the solution therefore was not to respond to the social demands that the society expected of them. Although Queen (1941) agreed that sociologists should refrain from being involved in **unnecessary** controversies he disagreed that they should not try to avoid risk-taking altogether. He did not wish to see, on the one extreme, sociologists hiding away in a safe ivory tower spending their time "playing with concepts."

On the other extreme, he did not want them adopting the **Jehovah Complex** of trying to save the world. Wirth (1939), the most prominent exponent of clinical sociology in the Pre-Second World War period, derided some of his contemporaries for trying to play it **safe** by turning away from the problems of the world to focus on the problems of science. This interest in science, he asserted, was not due so much to a genuine interest in science as such. Rather, it was because the sociologists lacked the confidence to handle the situation. He considered it an irony that the sociologists, the very individuals who were supposed to be most intimately involved with society, were the very ones who tried to distance themselves as far away from the actual problems of society as they possibly could. A contemporary of Wirth, Argow (1941) believed that by becoming overcautious and overconcerned with safety sociologists would eventually be invisible, dispensable, forgotten, and ignored by society. Writing in the early 1940s Argow (1941) remarked that what hurt the sociologist's ears most was not the criticisms but rather "the increasing thunder of silence" as the work of sociologists failed to stimulate inquiries and interests from others in the society.

The call for sociologists to learn to take risks for the sake of improving social conditions began to be heard by supporters of applied sociology in the succeeding decades following the 1940s. In the 1960s Horowitz (1964) warned sociologists not to slide into **cynical apathy** toward social problems and issues on the pretext of practicing professional **exclusivity**. He appealed to them not to lose sight of the main reason why sociology was conceived in the first place which was to create a better society. He implored sociologists to stop trying to be safe by adopting a **mechanical** approach toward studying society, but instead to exhibit "adventurism, fighting spirit, and even insecurity" which would be conducive for promoting the growth of sociology. Etzioni (1965) urged sociologists not to fear being involved in controversial and risk-taking activities just because of some **misadventures** that might have been committed by some early applied sociologists. Sociologists should not, Etzioni (1965) advised, overreact to criticisms by becoming overcautious and adopting a **restrictive interpretation** of their discipline in order to remain within a safe and low-risk domain.

While some sociologists advise their more adventurous colleagues not to drag sociology as a profession into the **heat** of the political arena (Hauser, 1970) others hold a more supportive stand as sociology approached the New Millennium. Hewitt (1991) pleaded to sociologists and social psychologists not to hold the social world "at arm's length" (p. 319). Wilson (1993) warned that sociology would be **ignored** by the policy-makers and the media if they try to "play it safe" (p. 6) all the time, a view that echoed the concerns of Argow (1941) five decades earlier. Wilson wanted sociologists to focus on **social** issues rather than merely on **sociological** ones. By focusing on the latter, sociology, he feared, will become less attractive to students and that it will be more difficult for the discipline to justify its continued existence or in trying to obtain funding support from relevant agencies.

Sociology needs to develop a better theoretical, methodological, and ethical framework to guide and supervise sociological practice. Those who have been involved in applied work realize that practitioners need to be better trained and supervised. None of the criticisms of applied work is considered as a valid excuse not to apply. On the contrary, sociology is seen as potentially having more to lose in the long run by not learning and maturing through applied activities, including learning from the occasional failures or other shortcomings. If sociology is said to lack the appropriate tools and instruments to enable them to perform applied work effectively, then the conclusion to arrive at is to allocate more resources and priority toward developing them. It will be a more logical and rational response than that of avoidance.

According to Whyte (1979), intervention work always involves risk-taking but applying an appropriate style or approach in intervention to a particular situation the risks can be calculated and minimized. Sociological theories and application needs to go through a process of **trial-and-error** and **self-correction**, while taking into consideration the feedback offered by clients, critics, and skeptics. Some degree of risk-taking and public criticism is not only unavoidable but is desirable. Social controversies are the direct consequence of being actively involved in explaining social issues, in recommending policy choices and in suggesting behavioral changes for the purpose of social enhancement.

Complement and Compliment

Clearly applied sociology in general and clinical sociology in particular has much to contribute to the discipline of sociology itself. By venturing into the highly challenging and exciting world of clinical practice while at the same time maintaining its umbilical cord with sociology, this specialty is both a **complement** and a **compliment** to sociology. Clinical sociology **complements** the efforts and achievements of other sociologists by widening the scope of the discipline while the existing core mainstream sociological concerns and activities continue to flourish. The genesis of clinical sociology is analogous to the putting in place of one of the final missing pieces of the sociological puzzle. The clinical sociology piece of the puzzle helps to complete the picture showcasing sociology as possessing a complete repertoire of roles in society, a whole continuum of approaches ranging from the purely theoretical at the one end to the highly challenging applied approaches at the other end.

With the development of a clinical arm, sociology becomes more complete, successfully striking a healthy balance between the acquisition of knowledge and understanding with the acquisition and application of skills to deal with social reality. As indicated earlier, the two wings of sociology are perhaps analogous to the two wings of a bird, which when working in tandem, enable sociology to trust forward to fly confidently high into the sky. The two wings remain different and separate but both are equally important for the optimal performance of the discipline as a totality. As sociology becomes complete, the career options open to sociologists are significantly increased, providing a wider range of choices on how sociologists can contribute to society. They no longer need to limit their choices of employment mainly to that of teaching and researching. They no longer need to be constantly apologetic, uncomfortable, and inapt when requested to perform social intervention of any kind. They no longer need to pass this task to others to perform, others who are unlikely to be equipped with a systemic sociological perspective and approach to fill what in effect are sociologists' shoes.

As a **compliment** to sociology this clinical specialty is capable of enhancing the overall image and status of its parent discipline. The genesis of the specialty is capable of elevating the parent discipline to a new status and a higher level of credibility **vis-à-vis** other disciplines and in the eyes of the public. Sociologists are no longer seen as an awkward adolescent lacking the social skills and self-confidence to face the challenging world of adulthood with confidence. After studying how other professions have managed to elevate their status in society, due simply to their willingness to take risks and face challenges without flinching, sociologists will come to realize that they can emulate the success of others. They will come to the realization that other disciplines had entered the field of practice in the past with even less resources and capabilities than what sociology now possesses. The existing sociological knowledge accumulated over the past century is potentially capable of being transformed into practical approaches and tools for intervention. Some of the world sociologists need not merely continue to do more of the same that is to continue accumulating knowledge and data without regard as to how the newly acquired information can be made applicable to the world of practice. The born-again sociologists will soon realize that no matter how established certain ideas are within the sociological tradition, they are of little value to problem-solving efforts if they are not translated and transformed into specific application tools and methods.

Through practice, sociologists will come to the inevitable conclusion that ideas and theories are **heuristics**—tools that may or may not be useful or applicable in specific cases—rather than seeing them as different forms of social reality. It is very rare that only one particular sociological perspective is capable of explaining all aspects of a particular case. A clinical worker needs to adopt a flexible and eclectic frame of mind when approaching a particular situation, with respect to all potential perspectives and approaches, within and without the discipline, as potentially valuable inputs. The more experienced and confident a practitioner is, the more likely for this intellectual openness to occur, and the lesser the need to cling to exclusivity. Inkeles (1959) considered the quest for disciplinary purity when sociologists tried to defend their territory against the encroachment by the "barbaric heathen invaders" (p. 29) from the other disciplines as a reflection of **intellectual insecurity**. Straus (1987) agreed that **eclectism** was essential because of the pragmatic nature of clinical work. It required the clinician to put aside rigid adherence to so-called theoretical purity and the neat categorizations which theoretical analysts were particularly fond of.

Podgorecki and Los (1979) were confident that through direct practice the various perspectives in sociology could be synthesized and this would eventually result in the blurring of the divisions between them and consequently minimize the conflict, competition, and polemics they tended to produce. Roger A. Straus (1987) believed that the mature clinical sociologist would, out of the accumulated experience of using particular perspectives in dealing with specific cases, arrive at a "full cognizance of the overarching ecological frame of social life" (p. 77).

All this talk of **eclectism** and **common wisdom** shared by experienced practitioners however does not exclude the possibility that sociologists are able to develop in the future their own newly formulated effective and efficient methods of intervention inspired by a particular school of thought within sociology. The schools of Marxism, functionalism, feminism, symbolic interactionism, humanism, etc. within sociology may want to develop their own unique clinical approaches without having to consider the perspectives of other disciplines. Good luck to them! It is too early in the development of clinical sociology to exclude the possibility that a particular perspective might predominate utilizing its own exclusive appropriate tools for intervention without the need for **eclectism**.

Cases as Data

A potential contribution that clinical sociology is capable of delivering to its parent discipline will be the wealth of case management data containing valuable, detailed, and intricate knowledge of specific cases of human behavior and the outcomes of social intervention. Although each case is invariably unique, an accumulation of case studies material will reveal valuable insights into common social dynamics which normal statistical research and analysis is unable to furnish. The accumulation of recorded cases constitutes a data-bank that can generate interesting hypotheses to be for validity by the sociologists who prefer research over clinical work. Wirth (1931) and other clinical sociologists were convinced that sociology as a science would be enhanced by the materials accumulated through case studies.

Scientific sociology, Wirth (1931) asserted, like any other sciences, stands to gain rather than lose by coming into close contact with real human problems. According to him through its contact with the problems of everyday life sociologists could test out hypotheses and theories inspired through the "patient accumulation and assimilation of the cases that actual human experience offers." In fact Wirth (1931) considered the analysis of cases as a method that came close to that of a carefully controlled observation, generally considered by researchers as the ideal scientific method. Lee (1955) had long recognized the fact that clinical studies were capable of contributing to the growth of **sociological wisdom** gained through the intimate knowledge gained from studying the effects of social intervention on problematic social situations. Clinard (1963) felt that sociologists who avoided performing **social action** missed a very important scientific opportunity to test their points of view and knowledge which would otherwise be merely assumed to be appropriate or valid, but remained untested.

Becker (1970) saw the case study approach of the practitioners as capable of making a **double** contribution to sociological theory. On the one hand, it helped toward a comprehensive understanding of the phenomenon under study while, on the other, it generated general theoretical generalizations and hypotheses concerning the social structure and its processes. The fields of medicine and psychology clearly showed how case studies helped to forge a healthy symbiosis between theory and practice. The effectiveness of the interventional efforts of clinical psychology, for example, helped to validate and upgrade theoretical knowledge and this in turn contributed to the refinement of the existing theories of human behavior within the parent discipline of psychology (Bellack & Hersen, 1980). Becker (1970) suggested that sociologists could systematically gather all the cases that had been studied and after taking into consideration the effects of the various variables and influences, they could undertake comparative studies of cases to arrive at new hypotheses concerning the phenomenon under study.

Lazarsfeld and Reitz (1975) pointed out that the study of concrete and circumscribed practical problem areas had in fact always contributed significantly to the accumulation of knowledge and theory-building. Even if the practitioners seemed to overemphasize the immediate objective of solving clients' problems, such efforts could be simultaneously used as a testing ground for sociological theories and assumptions, to see how valid and applicable the theoretical underpinnings of the discipline were. Straus (1987) agreed that practice was the ultimate corrective test for theory because it forced sociologists to face the flaws and biases inherent in their simplistic theories about the real world. Practice would make sociologists realize that all theories were "incomplete maps of overwhelming complex territories" (Straus,

1987, p. 77). Zorbaugh (1992) similarly considered case records accumulated by a clinician as "a mine of living material" (p. 20) on how social and cultural factors influenced the development of the person in his or her social environment.

Bridging Dichotomies

A **dichotomy**, according to a dictionary, is a "division into two parts, groups or classes, especially when these are sharply distinguished or opposed" (Neufeldt & Guralnik, 1991). Wiese (1932) frowned upon sociologists who he saw as exploiting the "aesthetic satisfaction of cheap, facile simplification, the deceitful pseudo-clarity of polar opposites" (p. 82) which, he asserted, were mistaken for social reality. He asserted that the world was not dualistic, but manifold and that all the elements interacted in a constant process of change where "here it unites, there it divides." The development of clinical sociology is capable of bringing sociologists beyond the other dualistic and dichotomous mode of thinking, the situation which had for a long time divided the sociology community and had left students baffled and exasperated for a considerable part of their academic lives.

The conceptual dichotomies which academicians are particularly fond of imparting to their students included theory versus practice; structure versus agency; continuity versus change; quantitative versus qualitative; normal versus pathological; culture versus nature; relativism versus absolutism; functional versus conflict; micro versus macro; sociology as art versus sociology as science; and numerous others. Although the polarized dichotomies listed above may facilitate academic debates concerning the relative strengths and weaknesses of the opposing approaches, Jenks (1998) pointed out that such thinking also tended to promote and exaggerate imaginary antagonisms and conflicts. A newly recruited clinical sociologist, upon entering a real-live highly complex problematic situation, has to acclimatize to a different way of seeing things, instead as opposing to that of complementarity.

Sociologists who are not able to see the complementarity of the so-called conflictive sociological ideas will find it hard to perform clinical work where oversimplistic and often erroneous "black-and-white" assumptions tend to generate problems rather than solving them. Midgley (2000), among many others, advocated for **theoretical pluralism,** promoting the idea of theoretical diversity as a way of enriching understanding by accepting ideas and approaches which appeared superficially to be incompatible. Clinical sociologists have to be able at one level to see all concepts and perspectives as being part of an integrated body of knowledge composing of components that are interdependent, overlapping, and mutually complementary. Maruyama (1966) considered dichotomous thinking as a product of what he termed as mental **mono-polarization,** the tendency to depend on a "one right theory, one truth" (p. 133) perspective. As a solution to this tendency, Seidman (1983) suggested the opposite process of **de-mono-polarization** which was more appreciative of alternative ways of thinking.

Macro-, Meso- and Micro-sociology

One of the sociological dichotomies which have kept many sociologists arguing for a long time is that of the **micro-level versus macro-level** sociology. Macro-sociology has traditionally provided the holistic theories and perspectives of society, of dealing with "the wider structures, interdependent social institutions, global and historical processes of social life" (Marshall, 1994). It analyzes how the external structural constraints and opportunities influence the nature of social relations (Blau, 1990). Micro-sociology, on the other hand, dealt with how individuals within a particular system perceive, construct as well as subjectively assign meanings to human actions and interactions (Mouzelis, 1995). With the focus on individual interaction and communication, **micro-sociology** uses important concepts such as that of social exchange, social reciprocity, roles, **verstehen**, beliefs, motives, rationality, and the dynamic processes of interpersonal relations, represented by such perspectives as phenomenology, symbolic interactionism, and ethnomethodology.

Berger and Luckmann (1966) presented a **phenomenological** perspective that described how, at the micro-sociological level, individuals constructed and defined their realities, influenced, but not totally determined, by group processes. Individuals were seen as far from being the passive responders to situations that macro-sociologists assumed. According to another micro-sociological perspective, the **dramaturgical** approach (Goffman, 1959), individuals were seen as actively playing, choosing and changing their roles, again influenced but not totally dictated by the social systems within which they functioned.

The development of micro-sociology is partly a response against the mainstream predominance of macro-sociological theories in sociology. The latter tends to de-emphasize the significance of the **person** while overestimating the significance of social structures in determining behavior. According to Adler, Adler, and Fontana (1987) macro-sociology applies a **mono-causal gloss** on social reality, depicting the individual as an overly passive and helpless **tabula rasa** at the mercy of the societal pressures for conformity, or as a **homo economicus** whose behavior was conditioned by class membership. They felt that such a view failed to reflect the true complexity of social existence where persons might respond differently to their social environment.

Clinical sociology can contribute toward narrowing this divide through the adoption of the comprehensive systemic perspective discussed earlier in this book. Micro-sociology gets the boost that it needs from clinical sociologists since when directly dealing with the personal and interpersonal levels of social existence, clinical sociologists come close to what Adler et al. (1987) referred to as **every-day-life sociologists**. These are sociologists who study people in their natural context, their everyday social world. In other words, through the micro-sociology perspective, sociology comes closer to the conception of social reality as perceived by individual persons in their day-to-day living contexts. Some sociologists suggest closing the gap between the macro and micro levels by developing an intermediate level of **meso-sociology** which focuses on the group, kinship, organizations and agencies, communities and social networks levels of social existence (Bruhn & Rebach, 1996). In line with the meso-level approach, Merton (1949) argued that sociologists should focus on reachable and measurable aspects of social lives rather than emphasizing on remote aspects to develop grand theories. These empirical studies in turn would enable sociologists to derive middle range theories to explain social phenomena and upon the development of various middle range theories, a "unified theory" will be developed (p. 448).

Others, however, feel that adding another level to mediate the alleged gap will only confuse further the situation. Instead, they suggest that efforts should be made to move away from a dichotomous frame of mind on the subject altogether, abandoning the idea of macro- and micro-level sociologies as distinct entities. Ritzer (1981) reminded overzealous sociologists that the world was not really divided into different **levels**—these so-called **levels** are merely convenient heuristic devices invented by social scientists. Turner (1991) agreed there had been too much agonizing over the question of whether the alleged gap really existed. Instead he advised sociologists to emulate other disciplines, such as the field of economics where the micro and macro levels coexisted and complemented each other without the need to "hurl insults at one another" (p. 588). He, however, agreed with the usage of **the micro–meso–macro** distinctions but only as **conceptual handles** of reality, not to be confused with reality itself which would always be **seamless and continuous** in nature.

Marshall (1994) advised that it was not appropriate to exaggerate the alleged gap since he saw much sociological research as being indistinguishable as far as whether they represented macro- or micro-level sociology. He gave the example of Max Weber who was often characterized as a **micro-sociologist** concerned with social action, while his works in fact equally dealt with the analysis of broad historical processes and comparative structures, the concerns of macro-sociologists. Similarly, he pointed out to the works of Talcott Parsons who was considered a **macro-sociologist**, renowned for his elaborate attempts to promote grand theories, and yet Parsons incorporated a focus on action and interpersonal interactions in his overall theory of society. Edwards (1994) agreed with the idea that two levels of society coexisting in a symbiotic relationship. For that reason, he argued, it was meaningless to assume that a people-centered view of micro-sociology entailed the need to ignore the influence of social structures that macro-sociology emphasized.

Supporting this general line of argument, Mouzelis (1995) suggested that the **micro–macro distinction** should be seen merely as points along a continuum of "more or less" (p. 155) rather than "either/or" (p. 155). The students of society, then, will be able to move with ease from one level of analysis to the next, such as moving from a lesser to a more encompassing social system. Bruhn and Rebach (1996) placed the levels on a **continuum** which they considered as more useful for the students of sociology than the usual dichotomy. The **macro end of the continuum** studied large social units on the societal and intersocietal levels, comprising of national or world economic, social, media, religious, education, social welfare, and science systems, while at **the micro end of the continuum** are located the small social units, such as the couples, dyads, and families and the individual social actor.

By creating a nexus between the so-called two levels of sociological analysis the conceptual boundaries constructed by sociologists in the past becomes fluid. The clinician is then able to incorporate effectively the subjectively perceived worlds of real-life individuals and groups in real-life situations, the focus of micro-sociology, with the overarching social structures of the macro-sociologists.

References

Adler, P. A., Adler, P., & Fontana, A. (1987). Everyday life sociology. *Annual Review of Sociology, 13*(1), 217–235.

Allen, V. L. (1975). *Social analysis: A Marxist critique and alternative*. London: Longman.

Argow, W. W. (1941). The practical application of sociology. *American Sociological Review, 6*(1), 37–44. Arts and Becker, 1990.

Becker, H. S. (1970). *Sociological work*. New Brunswick, NJ: Transaction Books.

Bellack, A. S., & Hersen, M. (1980). *Introduction to clinical psychology*. New York: Oxford University Press.

Berelson, B. (1966). Sociology in action: In population and in general. In A. B. Shostak (Ed.), *Sociology in action: Case studies in social problems and directed social change* (pp. 15–21). Homewood, IL: Dorsey Press.

Berenson, F. M. (1981). *Understanding persons: Personal and impersonal relationships*. New York: St Martin's Press.

Berger, P. L., & Luckmann, T. (1966). *The social construction of reality: A treatise in the sociology of knowledge*. London: Penguin Books.

Berk, R. A. (1981). On the compatibility of applied and basic sociological research: An effort in marriage counselling. *The American Sociologist, 16*(4), 204–211.

Bernard, J. (1973). *The sociology of community*. Glenview, IL: Scott, Foresman.

Blau, P. M. (1990). Microprocess and macrostructure. In K. S. Cook (Ed.), *Social exchange theory*. Newbury Park, CA: Sage.

Bruhn, J. G., & Rebach, H. M. (1996). *Clinical sociology: An agenda for action*. New York: Plenum Press.

Clinard, M. B. (1963). The sociologist and social change in underdeveloped countries. *Social Problems, 10*(3), 207–219.

Clinard, M. (1966). The sociologist's quest for respectability. *The Sociological Quarterly, 7*(4), 399–412.

Edwards, M. (1994). Rethinking social development: The search for 'relevance'. In D. Booth (Ed.), *Rethinking social development: Theory, research and practice* (pp. 279–297). Essex: Longman.

Etzioni, A. (1965). Social analysis as a sociological vocation. *The American Journal of Sociology, 70*, 317–323.

Fernandez, R. (1975). *The promise of sociology*. New York: Praeger.

Goffman, E. (1959). *The presentation of self in everyday life*. New York: Doubleday.

Gouldner, A. W. (1965). *Enter Plato: Classical Greece and the origins of social theory*. New York: Basic Books.

Hauser, P. M. (1970). On "action and sociology" by James W. Loewen. *Sociological Inquiry, 40*(1), 109.

Hauser, P. (1971). On actionism in the craft of sociology. In J. D. Colfax & J. F. Roach (Eds.), *Radical sociology* (pp. 425–439). New York: Basic Books.

Heraud, B. (1979). *Sociology in the professions*. London: Open Books.

Horowitz, I. L. (1964). An introduction to the new sociology. In I. L. Horowitz (Ed.), *The new sociology: Essays in social science and social theory in honor of C. Wright Mills* (pp. 3–48). New York: Oxford University Press.

Horowitz, I. L. (1968). *Professing sociology: Studies in the life cycle of social science*. Chicago: Aldine.
Inkeles, A. (1959). Personality and social structure. In R. L. Merton, L. Broom, & L. S. Cottrell (Eds.), *Sociological today: Problems and prospects* (pp. 249–276). New York: Basic Books.
Jenks, C. (1998). *Core sociological dichotomies*. London: Sage.
Lazarsfeld, P. F., & Reitz, J. G. (1975). *An introduction to applied sociology*. New York: Elsevier.
Lazarsfeld, P. F., & Rosenberg, M. (Eds.). (1955). *The language of social research*. Glencoe, IL: The Free Press.
Lee, A. M. (1955). The clinical study of society. *American Sociological Review, 20*(6), 648–653.
Lindesmith, A. R. (1960). Social problems and sociological theory. Reproduced in A. B. Shostak (Ed.) (1966), *Sociology in action: Case studies in social problems and directed social change* (pp. 270–275). Homewood, IL: Dorsey Press.
Lofland, J. (1976). *Doing social life*. New York: Wiley.
Lundberg, G. A. (1961). *Can science save us?* New York: Longmans, Greens.
Marshall, G. (1994). *Oxford concise dictionary of sociology*. Oxford: Oxford University Press.
Maruyama, M. (1966). Monopolarization, family, and individuality. *Psychiatric Quarterly, 40*, 133–149.
Merton, R. K. (1949). On sociological theories of the middle range. *Social Theory and Social Structure*. New York: Free Press.
Merton, R. K. (1976). *Sociological ambivalence and other essays*. New York: Free Press.
Midgley, G. (2000). *Systemic intervention: Philosophy, methodology, and practice*. New York: Kluwer/Plenum.
Mills, C. W. (1943). The professional ideology of social pathologists. *American Journal of Sociology, 49*(2), 165–180.
Mills, C. W. (1959). *The sociological imagination*. Oxford: Oxford University Press.
Morrissey, J. P., & Steadman, H. J. (1977). Practice or perish? Some overlooked career contingencies for sociologists in nonacademic settings. *The American Sociologist, 12*(4), 154–162.
Mouzelis, N. (1995). *Sociological theory: What went wrong? Diagnosis and remedies*. London: Routledge.
Neufeldt, V., & Guralnik, D. B. (1991). *Webster's new world dictionary*. New York: Prentice-Hall.
Odum, H. W. (1951). *American sociology: The story of sociology in the United States through 1950*. New York: Longmans, Green.
Olsen, M. E. (1981). Epilogue: The future of applied sociology. In M. E. Olsen & M. Micklin (Eds.), *Handbook of applied sociology* (pp. 561–581). New York: Praeger.
Platt, J. (1992). Cases of cases. . .of cases. In C. C. Ragin & H. S. Becker (Eds.), *What is a case? Exploring the foundations of social inquiry* (pp. 21–52). Cambridge: Cambridge University Press.
Podgorecki, A., & Los, M. (1979). *Multi-dimensional sociology*. London: Routledge and Kegan Paul.
Queen, S. A. (1941). Sociologists in the present crisis. *Social Forces, 20*(1), 1–7.
Rebach, H. M. (1991a). Clinical sociology: Defining the field. In H. M. Rebach & J. G. Bruhn (Eds.), *Handbook of clinical sociology* (pp. 49–64). New York: Plenum Press.
Rebach, H. M. (1991b). Communication and relationships with clients. In H. M. Rebach & J. G. Bruhn (Eds.), *Handbook of clinical sociology* (pp. 81–97). New York: Plenum Press.
Rebach, H. M. (1991c). Intervention in clinical sociology. In H. M. Rebach & J. G. Bruhn (Eds.), *Handbook of clinical sociology* (pp. 49–64). New York: Plenum Press.
Rebach, H. M., & Bruhn, J. G. (Eds.). (1991). *Handbook of clinical sociology*. New York: Plenum Press.
Ritzer, G. (1981). *Toward an integrated sociological paradigm*. Boston: Allyn and Bacon.
Rossi, P. H. (1980). The presidential address: The challenge and opportunities of applied social research. *American Sociological Review, 45*, 889–904.

Rossi, P. H., & Whyte, W. F. (1983). The applied side of sociology. In H. E. Freeman, R. D. Russell, P. H. Rossi, & W. F. Whyte (Eds.), *Applied sociology* (pp. 5–31). San Francisco: Jossey-Bass.

Seidman, E. (1983). Unexamined premises of social problem solving. In E. Seidman (Ed.), *Handbook of social intervention* (pp. 48–67). Beverly Hills, CA: Sage.

Straus, R. A. (1987). The theoretical base of clinical sociology: Root metaphors and key principles. *Clinical Sociology Review, 5*, 65–82.

Summers, N. (2001). *Fundamentals of case management practice: Exercises and readings.* Belmont, CA: Wadsworth Thomson Learning.

Sutherland, E. H. (1947). *Principles of criminology*. Philadelphia: J.B. Lippincott.

Turner, J. H. (1991). *The structure of sociological theory*. Belmont, CA: Wadsworth.

Waitzkin, H. (1970). Truth's search for power: The dilemmas of the social sciences. In J. D. Douglas (Ed.), *The relevance of sociology*. New York: Meredith.

Warren, R. L. (1971). *Social change and human purpose: Toward understanding and action.* Chicago: Rand McNally College Publishing Company.

Whyte, W. F. (1979). On making the most of participant observation. *The American Sociologist, 14* (1), 56–66.

Wiese, L. V. (1932). *Systemic sociology : On the basis of the beziehungslehre and gebildelehre, adapted and amplified by Howard Becker*. New York: Wiley.

Wirth, L. (1931). Sociology and clinical procedure. *American Journal of Sociology, 37*, 49–66. Reprinted in *Clinical Sociology Review, 1*, 7–22, 1982, entitled 'clinical sociology'

Wirth, L. (1939). Social interaction: The problem of the individual and the group. *The American Journal of Sociology, XLIV*(6), 965–979.

Young, D. (1955). Sociology and the practicing professions. *American Sociological Review, 20*(6), 641–648.

Zetterberg, F. (1962). *Social theory and social practice*. New York: Bedminster Press.

Znaniecki, F. (1965). *Social relations and social roles*. San Francisco: Chandler.

Znaniecki, F. (1969). *Florian Znaniecki on humanistic sociology*. R. Bierstedt (Ed.). Chicago: University of Chicago Press.

Zorbaugh, H. (1992). Sociology in the clinic. *Clinical Sociology Review, 10*, 16–20.

Chapter 6
Attracting the Clinically Inclined

Sociologists have pointed out an insidious trend that they saw as posing a major threat to the future development of sociology. This threat was in the form of an increasing encroachment of other disciplines, as well as the birth of applied specialties, into what used to be the **traditional hunting grounds** for sociologists. As early as the 1940s Argow (1941) expressed his concern, as several others during his time, with the trend whereby young sociologists were turning their backs "on their doddering old parent" (p. 38) as they chose the applied fields such as the fields of social work and social research. Three decades later sociologists were still noticing how applied courses were considered by students as being more attractive than the basic ones. Some writers described what they saw in the 1960s and 1970s as a process of the **balkanisation** of sociology. This was in the form of sociological programs having developed independently of, and with little interaction and communication with, mainstream sociology (Arts & Becker, 1990). Collins (1982) saw sociology as gradually losing its public impact because of its reluctance to be involved in social action, making it a discipline that **lacks excitement** and was not capable of attracting the most motivated students. He warned of the impending fragmentation process whereby emerging specialties in sociological-related fields were gradually drifting away from sociology. He believed that one way of stopping this fragmentation process would be for sociologists to become more involved in several of these new specialties themselves.

The process of attrition underwent by sociology continued to worry the sociologists in the 1990s. Turner and Turner (1990) were concerned with what they saw an increasing number of what used to be mainstream sociological areas of studies being offered by other departments instead. According to them sociology had by then already lost much of its monopoly on social issues and problems. They foresaw that unless sociologists gain a grip of this reality sociology would end up as a residual social science which would continue to shrink as new programs competing for sociology students continued to proliferate. The specialties which were historically part of sociology, but which had by then successfully established their own separate programs in non-sociology departments, included that of criminology, gerontology,

© Springer Nature Switzerland AG 2020

P. M. Wan, A. H. Wan, *Clinical Sociology*, Clinical Sociology: Research and Practice, https://doi.org/10.1007/978-3-030-49083-6_6

family studies, urban studies, culture studies, gender studies, ethnic studies, organizational studies, social work, opinion polling, market research, and many others.

Using the newly emergent field of criminology as an illustration, Akers (1992) reminded sociologists how this area of concern was initially an integral part of the sociology discipline. Sadly, by the beginning of 1990s it was being offered by a large number of universities and colleges throughout the United States as separate specific degrees in law enforcement, criminology, and criminal justice. The writer explained that the obvious explanation for this split from sociology was the fact that criminology needed to develop as an **applied** field, not as an **academic** one. The applied-shy sociology departments, instead of allowing criminology to grow as an applied specialty within the bosom of sociology, chose instead to criticize criminology for being **too applied** for it to qualify as real sociology. These voices of concerned sociologists went largely unheeded. It was probably brushed aside by some as mere voices of **prophets of doom**. Most sociologists and their departments remained indifferent or even antagonistic toward the idea of applied sociology. As a consequence, those who were passionately interested in it had no option but to look for alternative careers to pursue outside the confines of the sociological discipline.

As has been frequently emphasized throughout this book, the main contribution of clinical sociology to the discipline of sociology is to provide it with a clinical arm. If mainstream sociology does not welcome it with open arms, is it possible that clinical sociology will be another addition to the list of cases of attrition that had been inflicting sociology? This may not seem to be a likely scenario due to the retention of the word **sociology** in its label. Labels do seem to play matter in determining the future direction of a new specialty—whether it will remain as part of its original discipline or whether it will gradually drift away and eventually become divorced from it. Just look at how social work, criminology, social psychology, and many others which do not appear to share any part of their parent's DNA, have completely been disassociated from the discipline of sociology. The only danger of clinical sociology becoming a totally separate entity will be the consequence of it being totally rejected by mainstream sociology. Berk (1981) had argued that one of the logical responses to a rejection by its parent discipline would be for it to seek **divorce** from sociology, something which be, according to Berk (1981), as a **divorce made in heaven**.

A final blow will be when the name of clinical sociology is changed to something else, with the word "sociology" being replaced, With such a divorce, traditional sociology can then distance itself from practical work while the practicing renegades will choose some other career designation. Clinical sociologists can consider themselves as **social clinicians** or social **technologists**, etc., no longer considering themselves, or being considered by others, as sociologists. As long as "sociology" is retained in their designation, clinical sociology will remain as an integral part of the sociology discipline. Berk (1981), however, was not in favor of the hypothetical **divorce** because he believed that both parties would be losers. He saw the basic and the applied as needing each other in order to thrive. Addressing those who were reluctant to accept applied specialties as part of legitimate sociology, he suggested that instead of contemplating divorce it was not too late for a **marriage**

reconciliation of sorts in order to enable both arms of sociology to coexist **productively**, if not **blissfully**, under one roof.

Social Clinics

The services offered by clinical sociologists can be made available to the general public in many ways. Mention has been made regarding **everyday sociology** literature and other resources, either in soft or hard copies, which offer guides to the general public on how to cope with difficult social situations. Added to this are radio and television programs and newspaper columns that respond to direct public calls for assistance manned by clinical sociologists in addition to the existing ones already in place. To complement this further, there is a definite necessity for some form of direct face-to-face interaction. Practitioners and the client or clients need to meet to discuss particular problematic personal and social issues with the objective of helping the latter to overcome them.

Face-to-face interaction and dialogue are important for establishing rapport and interpersonal trust which less direct interaction methods of interaction, such as through the web and the mass media, may not be as appropriate or as effective. This service can be provided by setting up what some sociologists have suggested in the past referred to as **social clinics**. Although the use of the term **clinical** in clinical sociology does not necessarily imply the idea of establishing a physical structure some practitioners may choose to supplement their activities by offering their services through the establishment of physical facilities along the lines of community centers known to the community as **social clinics**. Through the application of the clinical sociology approach, alongside the psychological or psychiatric ones, the clinical sociologist will be able to offer refreshing alternatives and complementary nonpathological approaches toward dealing with personal and social issues. Clients are regarded as normal persons needing to optimize their social functioning, rather than as **sick** or **deviant** patients needing treatment and therapy. Rooms for various forms of social support group meetings and social mediation sessions should be made available in these social clinics. Like their clinical psychologist counterpart, clinical sociologists can set up social clinics in universities, schools, mental health centers and clinics, hospitals, business and industrial sites, government offices, labor union premises, prisons, or even in their own private clinics.

While clinical sociologists **do not** have to offer their services in a clinic (Swan, 1984), Wirth and few others did not want them to exclude this as an **option**. The clinics can be manned by a team of professionals and volunteers with clinical sociologists as team members. Zorbaugh (1992), for example, recounted his experience of working in a **sociological clinic**, set up in 1926 under a New York University project. Based on this practical experience, he advised sociologists that such a clinic was potentially viable as long as it emphasized the provision of direct services to help clients solve their problems instead of doing what sociologists were most prone to do, conducting research or data-collection activities. The latter approach, he learned the hard way, was likely to lead to failure. He assured sociologists that through the provision of direct problem-solving services they would be able to accumulate in the long run **the fruits of research**. He also echoed what Wirth (1982) had voiced decades earlier that it would be a **fruitless** undertaking to set up a purely and wholly sociological clinic since clinics should ideally be interdisciplinary in approach. The interdisciplinary clinic would, in Wirth's (1982) opinion, provide for the meeting of minds participated by professionals trained in sociology, medicine, psychiatry, psychology, and caseworker (social work). Despite the discussion on the need to set up or participate in clinic settings, this is not a prerequisite for offering clinical services. The closed-door private and confidential encounters between practitioners and clients as practiced by some may be necessary in some exceptional cases, but the sociological approach should not simply emulate these practices.

Not many problem-resolution and intervention need to be done privately or confidentially since the sociological approach involves the mobilization of social support for those needing help. Sociologists should operate within a natural social environment as far as it is possible and appropriate. To clinical sociologists, the **society in its totality is their clinic**, and every citizen its **potential client**. Outreach work is crucial since clinical sociologists do not only react to difficult situations but are proactively seeking signs of impending problems for early intervention for the benefit of public interests.

The authors' own experience of setting up a 3-year experimental social clinic in Malaysia, named **The Pintas Project**, involved the offering of 4 service components. The first was the **Promotional or Developmental Service**. In this component, activities were directed toward promoting a positive and healthy development at the individual, family, group, organizational, community, or in the wider society. The second component was the **Preventive Service** component where the activities focused on analyzing and identify potentially disruptive social issues, trend, and behavior of specific individuals and social groups or special social categories with the objective of performing proactive action. The third component was the **Crisis Intervention** Service which focused on the need for harm reduction and crisis management, mainly due to the failure of the earlier two phases, aimed at reducing personal and social chaos and re-establishing some form of social order. Finally, there was the **Rehabilitation Service** component which helped to re-establish or normalize the individual or group to the point where every individual or group can achieve optimal social functioning.

Sociology in Developing Countries

The need for sociologists to be directly involved in intervening for social change is especially crucial and critical in the developing societies of the **third world**. Especially in the poorer and more remote areas of these countries, the number of trained professionals, including social scientists, are very limited if they at all exist.

This is in contrast to industrialized societies where there are many more trained professionals and practitioners who can perform the various tasks of resolving social issues. In the economically advanced societies, the sociologists are probably more justified in choosing to avoid being directly involved on the grounds that others can act as their proxies. The situation is radically different in the lesser endowed third world countries. Inadequate resources in these countries make it morally unjustifiable for sociologists to isolate themselves in their ivory towers, far from the immediate problems faced by the populace.

Sociologists in poor and remote communities, if they do exist may be one of very few trained social scientists available and they are usually teaching in the local institute of high learning or universities. There is a very limited number of trained psychologists, social workers, counselors or psychiatrists, and other practitioners who can serve a small fraction of the total needs of the local community. In the towns, because of poverty, a fast-changing urban population and a turbulent past social history there is a tremendous need for social intervention, mediation, and conciliation. Sociologists living in such communities clearly have a moral obligation to be involved in some form of practice to help resolve personal, family, organizational, or community issues and problems rather than merely teaching theory and research methodology. The specific problems which the members of the local community and the authorities face include poverty, illnesses, neighborhood disputes, ethnic conflicts, addictions, corruption, family violence, and crimes, to name the major ones. Without professional intervention, the alternative is lawlessness that can lead to arbitrary police response or the kind of expensive, lengthy, and inaccessible litigation in the courts which ordinary do not have the resources to resort to.

Many native-born sociologists working in developing countries are already highly receptive to the idea that sociology should serve the immediate and pressing needs of their societies. They expressed through their writings the need for sociology to be made more relevant in helping to bring about social change. Starting with the South Asian region, Mohan (1975) suggested that sociologists in India should be able to help their fellow Indians to deal with the impact of the tremendous rate of social change encroaching upon their daily lives. He felt that the rapid rate of societal transformation could potentially damage **the personality structures** of the ordinary Indians unless sociologists, among others, offered some help to prepare them to adapt to such changes. According to him, the younger generation of sociologists could perform a great service to the country by widening the horizons of the people's mind-sets, preparing them for the inevitability of social change. He believed that the slow progress or growth of sociology in his country was attributed to such weaknesses as the lack of clarity as to the proper scope of sociology as reflected in its course offerings. He asserted that there was a clear lack of consensus as to what the professional role of the sociologist should be.

All these weaknesses, he believed, tended to discourage students from pursuing their higher studies in the discipline. It was essential, he felt, for students in a relatively poor country to be able to see the concrete role and career implications of their training. He believed that in a relatively poor country like India students needed to be convinced of the returns on their considerable financial investment by choosing careers that were relevant to the immediate needs and problems of their society. Similarly, Damle (1976) wrote on the need for sociology to be more relevant to what he termed as the **Indian question** which basically referred to the serious social issues and problems faced by the Indian society. He felt that sociology needed to identify and diagnose "the soft spots" (p. 99) in the society in order to resolve those problems and issues.

Similarly, in neighboring Pakistan, some sociologists expressed their desire to see sociologists doing more to directly deal with the social problems and the human misery and suffering. Gardezi (1975) noted that the graduate students in Pakistan were generally interested in studying social problems as could be seen in their choice of thesis topics, such as the topics of crime, poverty, population increase, educational standard deterioration, low status of women, and urban vices. He saw ample opportunities for sociologists to contribute toward solving social problems since they were often engaged in applied and action research on a large scale, usually sponsored by governmental agencies. These, however, are basic academic research rather than applied research. He believed that sociologists could not continue ignoring the practical significance of sociological work, especially where there was so much human suffering generated by the endemic conflicts and inequalities within the society. Despite the obvious need to seriously reflect on the basic question of "sociology for what?" (p. 418) he lamented the fact that many Pakistani sociologists had not overtly brought up this question the way their colleagues in the more industrialized society would have done.

Sociologists in the Southeast Asian region were similarly becoming vocal on the need for sociologists to address directly the social conditions within their respective societies. Tjondronegoro (1995) noted the fact that sociology in Indonesia had not been an active element in policy formulation. He attributed this in part to the tendency for sociologists themselves to avoid facing problems that were deemed to have **sensitive** social implications. They did not respond to the obvious situations requiring social intervention for the simple reason that their training had favored research activities and other academic pursuits. Consequently, he felt that the Indonesian government tended to rely upon law enforcement agencies to resolve social conflicts rather than bringing the sociologists into such efforts. He believed that such a move was unlikely to offer long-term solutions toward creating harmonious social relations. At the same time, it was only logical for the government not to engage sociologists if the latter were not sufficiently equipped and competent to deal with such highly challenging tasks.

Writing on the role of social scientists in Malaysia Muijzenberg (1995) noted that some sociologists were involved in some forms of **social engineering** efforts, such as in helping to promote and direct noneconomic processes toward economic growth; offering social criticism or reflexive action; and being involved in social activism based on social scientific insights and practices. Nordholt and Visser (1995) made a general comment that very few social scientists and government officials in Southeast Asia seemed to possess sufficient social skills and political will to communicate and collaborate with each other. The writers also asserted that since the complexity and variability of social action required social scientists to study the actual context of everyday life, there should logically be a link between academic education and the ability to translate theoretical issues and concepts into "actual social practice" (p. 147).

A feeling of dissatisfaction with the current performance of sociology is also felt on the African continent. Commenting on the development of sociology in Egypt, Hegazy (1975) felt that it was unforgivable for sociology to continue giving an undue emphasis to theoretical and academic knowledge alone while failing to provide professional training to its students. He believed that the neglect shown toward the need to acquire professional skills was one of the major causes for a lack of job opportunities for the increasing number of sociology graduates. There was little point of arousing public interest in sociology, he argued, if sociologists themselves failed to take a more active role in society, going beyond the traditional role of solely conducting research. He realized that the mere performance of research was not an effective means of becoming involved in social change. Oftentimes, research findings were either totally ignored or were not utilized fully due to what he termed as "administrative turnover and bureaucratic rigidity" (p. 386).

Magubane (2000), a prominent African sociologist, similarly criticized what he saw as the superficiality of acquired knowledge which did not go beyond the superficial attempt to "unmask the pretentious from the real" (p. 23). He criticized the accumulation of a vast and growing mass of research monographs that dealt with highly specialized topics which somehow tended to be "as dry as dust" (p. 25). All this work, he argued, contributed little more than making social scientists into individuals who knew "more and more about less and less," echoing an almost similar comment made by Manis (1976) a few years earlier.

All the criticisms directed at sociology in developing societies can be largely corrected through a concerted effort to get the specialty of clinical sociology to be included in the sociology programs in these countries. Such programs will prepare sociologists to become practitioners, capable of going beyond the limitations of survey research and policy research to delve into problematic social situations equipped with the appropriate skills to respond effectively to them. Developing countries do not have the luxury of waiting for the sociologists of the developed industrialized world to seriously and systematically implement clinical sociology programs within their ivory towers. It may be necessary for developing countries to take the lead in implementing such programs. For too long the sociology developed in the more advanced Western societies seemed oblivious to the pressing issues faced by sociology and sociologists in the economically developing and underdeveloped societies.

Student Encounter with Sociology

Basic sociology courses are offered, and presumably will continue to be offered, to all students pursuing academic disciplines across the board in the institutes of high learning as elective and services courses. Sociology courses offered appear to be popular because they tend to address the challenging social issues of the day. Courses on issues such as gender, family life, ethnicity, crime, poverty, social class, and aging are a fresh change for students from courses that are primarily high-tech with low-human touch in their contents. These courses focus on many aspects of the topic, including why policies fail with the local government being blamed for it, but it does not prepare the students to undertake an intervention initiative. When offered as service courses that students are required to take as part of their graduation requirement, the future of sociology appears to be relatively safe with its firm hold on this captive audience.

What is of concern, however, is whether the current and future number of students choosing sociology as a **major** will be sufficient to ensure that sociology will not only merely survive, but thrive as well. The question that one needs to ask: Is becoming a sociologist an attractive career option? For those who freely choose to do sociology, are their expectations of sociology adequately met? It is important to understand what is the initial motivation that moved students and their financial sponsors to choose sociology as their choice? For many students who freely choose to become sociologists, this choice is almost invariably based on some degree of interest and passion not only to comprehend the intricacies of the social life, but also the expectation of being able to utilize the knowledge and expertise gained for the betterment of society, in whatever shape or form. As for the authors of this book, coming from a relatively young, socially and culturally heterogeneous postcolonial nation, Malaysia, social challenges were seen as insurmountable obstacles to national unity and economic advancement.

By choosing to pursue sociology, theoretically, one can potentially be an asset to society by applying what one has learned to good and fruitful use upon graduation. Many writers and teachers of sociology would concur with this basic motivation for choosing sociology. They have noted the great interests shown by students towards topics that are related to the major social problems of the day. For students in general, especially for students in and from developing countries their choice of courses and specializations goes beyond merely wanting to "understand society." Even in the early 1940s, Argow (1941) noted how students of social science seemed eager to want to learn what could be done about the "ominous pyramiding of problems" within society. He felt that the average student was not necessarily interested in some drastic and revolutionary social action propagated by the radical sociologists. They were interested rather in the more modest and definite actions that could help reduce what they saw as increasingly deteriorating social conditions around them. One example was illustrated in the effort done by sociology students in Humboldt Park Chicago where Batey Urbano, a Puerto Rican/Latino cultural center was set up. This center serves as a platform for Puerto Rican/Latino to watch and perform their creative cultural expression in addition to "encourages and empowers young people to struggle for self-determination and to reach out in solidarity to other marginalized communities" (Flores-González & Rodríguez-Muiz, 2011, p. 65).

Berger (1963) noted that the sociology students gave their reasons for majoring in sociology as "because I like to work with people," "would rather deal with people than with things," "do something for people," "help people," "do work that is useful for the community," and so on (pp. 1–2). Alfred McClung Lee (1973) noticed that his sociology students were excited to learn from sociologists who had had experiences in applied work. They were asking questions concerning the exciting and challenging risks, consequences, and tensions as sociologists became involved directly in real human drama. According to him, sociology students were asking such questions as: "Can we really use the stuff we're getting? Does it work when you try it out 'in life'?" (p. 28). The single clear message that one gets upon asking students of their expectations from learning sociology, is the idea that sociology will help them to deal with social issues and problems.

Similarly, Turner and Turner (1990) believed that very few undergraduate students had any interest in the theoretical or methodological issues of sociology. Instead, their interests were mainly focused on such topics such as crime, juvenile delinquency, family problems, and the like, which the students felt were more relevant to their everyday lives. Similarly, a study by Wan (2016) with 259 senior sociology students in Malaysia showed that the majority of the students believed that the main role of sociologists was not merely to teach more people to become sociologists. They did not want sociologists to continue studying and researching society, creating and presenting theories, statistics, and predicting aspects of the future. Rather, they expected to be able to assist the communities in which they lived, as advocators and intermediaries, through such efforts as in attitudes and behavioral change, and to help the government and other concerned bodies to find and implement viable and effective actions to deal with social problems (Wan, 2016).

Argow (1941) noted that although there was an increasing popularity of academic courses dealing with social problems among sociology students, the departments chose to ignore this demand and refused to move along with the changing trend. They preferred instead to maintain a posture he described, somewhat derogative, as **suspended animation**. He lamented the fact that the students were being made to accept the paths of **theoretical purity** based on the ideological leanings of their professors. Argow (1941) was convinced that academic knowledge and principles developed in sociology should instead be put to good use by applying them in the **clinical arena** in the form of highly technical therapeutic practices. Such a move, he believed would help to convince prospective students that sociology was a discipline of high potentiality. Instead, he regretted, it was being regarded by many students merely as an interesting **snap elective** to add to their credits requirements.

Students totally expect to begin their sociology courses with an exposure to basic concepts, theories, and perspectives concerning society and the institutions within it. However, what becomes tedious is when their courses do not seem to go beyond the prolonged and endless polemics regarding different and conflicting theories, which the founders and the succeeding generations of sociology professors and writers love to dwell upon. The endless focus on what appears to be rather trivial academic polemics and sociological generalities and abstractions can be very disorienting for students who crave for hands-on experience in handling social situations. The few students who patiently continue to pursue sociology at the graduate level soon realize that they were learning "more of the same" with an additional research-based thesis that they have to complete. Research, statistics-gathering coupled with an occasional case study is probably the only exposure they gained from their course.

Some sociology professors may go beyond basic research skills to ensure that their students perform some other practical tasks through community placements or in projects dealing with specific target groups to ensure their students understand the practical implications of what they have learned (i.e., Joseph, 2011). However, this usually constitutes a co-curriculum activity rather than being an integral part of the core curriculum. It is unrealistic to expect the students to make sense of the abstract concepts and theories without providing them with sufficient opportunities to operationalize and apply them to specific everyday situations. Students need to be able to see the linkage between theory and practice before they can make any meaningful evaluations of the validity and usefulness of concepts and perspectives. Sociology seems to stop before action can even start. The follow-up to research is to carry out more research. The follow-up to academic polemics is more academic polemics.

There are some **matured** students, such as social and community workers, who had had some practical experience in dealing with social issues before enrolling in a sociology course, they naturally hold the expectation that sociology will provide an additional insight on how to perform their job upon graduation. They know that, upon graduation, they will be expected to put sociology into practice. For these experienced mature students, an obvious disconnect and neglect of the relationship between theory and practice are particularly disconcerting. If the twain should never meet, what is the point of learning sociology, they may ask themselves. To offset this deficit, they may enroll in other additional non-sociology courses and training packages. However, they will soon discover that the approaches adopted by these other professions may be at odds with the basic tenants of sociology. For example, while **social peer pressure** and influence are considered crucial for changing social behavior in sociology, other professions may choose to focus solely on the individual client or their immediate social context as the prime and sole mover of social change.

In the late 1950s, Mills (1959) came to the rescue of students struggling then with what he saw as abstruse language and the lack of "intelligibility" of Talcott Parsons' writings. He decided, with tongue in cheek, to "translating into English" some of Parson's ideas, which obviously were already written in English, albeit one that was not easily comprehensible. He posed the question: were sociological writings "merely a confused verbiage or is there...something there?" (p. 27). Mills (1959) wanted to see a link established between sociologists who **observe without thinking** and those who **think without observing**. He implored those who developed grand theories to get down from the **higher generalities** to approach the concrete problems occurring in their historical and structural contexts, rather than to flaunt "arbitrary and certainly endless elaboration of distinctions" (p. 28), which failed to help the attainment of a better and more sensible understanding of the social reality.

The criticisms that Mills (1959) made of sociological writings is still very much what puzzle many students today. Many present-day students have to struggle, especially those with English, and, may I add, French, as a second language, just to be able to make sense of the abstruse and esoteric ideas forwarded. The idea of writers such as Pierre Bourdieu, Jurgen Habermas, Jean Baudrillard, Lyotard, Zygmunt Bauman, and Michel Foucault as far as the fresh students are concerned are not sufficiently well-elaborated, illustrated, or operationalized. Although not widely acknowledged, even some sociology professors themselves may secretly have problems comprehending some of these writings with sufficient clarity. This is sometimes reflected in the way they respond to students' inquiries; the way some problematic topics are glossed over or are conveniently skipped. Some professors may even openly admit to students the vagueness and irrelevance of some of those ideas.

Public Expectation of Sociology Graduates

Unlike the sociology professors who are already gainfully employed within academia, the student's future career is usually far from certain. While the former may insist that students only need to focus only on gaining knowledge, and not to be too concerned with the question of future employment, most students cannot afford this luxury. In 1941, Argow (1941) expressed his disagreement with those who retorted that it was not the job of sociologists to "peddle his services on the open market" (p. 37). And therefore they need not be concerned with equipping students with specific skills for the job market. He was convinced that such a response failed to satisfy students who could not afford to pursue a university education that merely contributed to their personal **character development**. They desperately needed to ensure that their educational investment would produce some form of tangible dividends as well.

Most students are realistic enough to realize that they cannot all end up with careers as academicians and researchers, which the main knowledge and skills that they have acquired in their present sociological training appear to prepare them for. For the students who expect to acquire some applied skills, by the time they graduate they will discover to their dismay that sociology is not what they expected. The only major skill they may acquire might be some basic research methods and basic statistics which actually formed only a very small portion of their whole sociology curriculum. They learn much less statistics than a statistics or mathematics graduate does, as well as exposure to practical research methodology skills.

Some sociologists had expressed their concern concerning this inherent deficit in sociological training. As early as 1941 Queen expressed disapproval of the discipline's tendency to produce **sociological sociologists**, graduates who were familiar with theories but were unequipped with what he termed as **social technology**. In early 1960s Sibley (1963) made an observation that sociology graduates of his time were generally unable to compete with other social science graduates. The latter, he noticed, did not hesitate to offer answers to social problems even though they held rather naïve and simplistic conceptions of society. He argued that sociology students would be in a better position to impress their prospective employers if only they were better prepared and adequately trained to offer appropriate practical solutions to social problems. Morrissey and Steadman (1977) similarly agreed that sociologists should acquire the appropriate techniques for practice that will make them more **salable** in public and private job markets. Laue (1978) warned that the society will not continue to tolerate the failure of sociology unless it became more involved in what he termed **constructive action**. Unless sociologists did more than merely talking and writing about society, he cautioned, the job market would force many graduate sociology programs to atrophy or extinction. Another sociologist, Lee (1978), expressed his fears that without proper training sociologists might fail to abide by some scientific or professional standards as they offered their **social nostrums** to their clients.

The concern with the fate of sociology graduates who needed to enter the **non-academic** job market continued to vex many sociologists throughout the 1980s. They realized that many students were eager to enter this market but somehow the actual sociology curriculum that they covered was slow to respond to this need. The exponents of applied sociology noticed the trend whereby students tended to choose courses that were applied in nature when compared to the more theoretical ones. In the 1960s, when sociology graduates in the United States were asked whether they were satisfied with their doctoral training in sociology, those who were **not** satisfied gave the following reasons: sociology lacked substance or scientific rigor or both, and that employment opportunities were better for those with non-sociology degrees (Sibley, 1963).

It was relatively true that the number of sociology graduates employed in nonacademic positions appeared to be low when compared to psychology and economic graduates. In the later 1970s, Morrissey and Steadman (1977) wanted sociology departments to adequately prepare their graduates to seek employment or be employed outside the academia. They were concerned that should the departments fail to make the necessary reassessments and adjustments in sociology programs, the graduates would be in for a nasty **reality shock** Weber and McCall (1978) agreed that since the market for sociologists within the academic institutions was becoming increasingly limited, sociology departments should instead produce graduates who could be gainfully employed due to the skills they possessed in dealing directly with social issues and problems.

By the 1980s Bradshaw and McPherron (1980) were alarmed at what they saw as the declining numbers of enrollment of sociology majors, while courses in the human services, criminal justice, and social work were increasing in popularity. At this point in time, the writers were constantly pointing out to the need to equip sociology graduates for the nonacademic employment market. Baum and Bourner (1981), for example, reported that sociology graduates in the United Kingdom appeared to fare worse when trying to enter the labor market than the graduates from other disciplines. Brennan (1982) similarly wrote that because sociology in Britain had not developed a professional identity outside teaching and academic research, unlike some other social science disciplines, the graduates had to pay **a heavy professional cost** for failing to enter the nonacademic job market. He implored that it was time for more interests to be shown in the graduate labor market so as to ensure that sociologists would gain a fair share of the nonacademic job market. However, such pleas appeared to fall on deaf ears.

The apologists for the existing system loves to repeat the same **mantras**. The university is **not** the **University of Life** that covers one's whole life span upon. Within such a short time span, it is argued, it is only possible for university education to provide a **general exposure** to a particular field of knowledge. It is unrealistic to expect the formal education system to provide anything more than that. Students should be contented with whatever the system provides. The university's role is not to prepare them for the job market. The academic world in general does not subscribe to a **utilitarian** view of education. The acquisition of knowledge is a **desirable end in itself**. Members of the general public, especially in developing countries, are baffled as to why most academic disciplines often choose to be detached from the immediate and pressing daily concerns confronting people in their daily lives. The world of academia, as envisaged primarily by Western societies, appears to exist within its own artificially created world of reality and priorities. The justification often given for this **nonchalance** is that the world of academia needs to detach itself in order to objectively study and contemplate society. Presumably, this **sabbatical** from society will eventually bear fruit when academicians are finally able to impart their accumulated knowledge and understanding of social realities to the general public. This is not unlike the wise ancient **guru** who finally emerges from the cave where he hibernated and meditated to finally share his newly discovered secrets concerning human society.

The wider society, the students and their families, their financiers, and their employers, view the situation rather differently. Those who shoulder the financial burden of educational sponsorship have to assume that university education would be capable of achieving more. A tremendous amount of scare resources that a society continue to allocate to its formal education system needs a stronger justification than that. Society in general expects the elaborate system of formal education to offer definite, direct, and tangible benefits to society. It is certainly unreasonable to expect society to make sociology and sociologists an **exception** to this rule. Society does not envision graduates as being good at what they do but they do expect them to be equipped with the basic tools to at least start doing it and being able to learn more upon graduation.

In the mid-1950s, an early warning was issued by Young (1955) when he reminded sociologists that society expected them to **earn their keep**, and that the ultimate judge of the continued existence of sociology was society itself, not the members of the sociology profession. Sociologists have always claimed that although they do not directly apply their findings, they are making indirect contributions toward improving society. Young (1955), however, dismissed this claim because he believed that sociologists had contributed little of practical value to the practitioners, including those in the fields of social work, law, and health services. Lindesmith (1960) argued that sociologists were taking risks when they chose **not** to be involved in social problems. By artificially differentiating their **civic** from their **scientific** responsibilities, they inadvertently commit a **sin** by neglecting social problems rather than being involved in resolving them. The exponents of sociological practice warn that the society which has traditionally supported the existence of the sociology discipline will in the future become increasingly impatient with the discipline's inability to deal with the society's pressing problems. Selby and Tilley (1975) pointed out that academics in effect killed students' interests in the practical applications of sociological knowledge by the very nature of most sociology courses. They issued a warning: "Sociology does not exist in a vacuum. It is funded and developed in both research and teaching through public policy and public resources, which could be allocated elsewhere" (Selby & Tilley, 1975).

Unfortunately, the financial implications of a declining number of sociology majors as well as a general societal concern concerning the employability of sociology graduates do not particularly concern many academics. Many academicians, particularly those in public universities, are seldom too concerned with the financial performance of their departments' academic programs. Most universities do not require academicians, sociologists included, to be directly involved or at least held responsible, with how their courses are marketed. The very idea that academics should even give a thought to what some consider as **mundane commercial issues**, such as addressing the needs of the employment market or constantly reviewing their training programs from the financial point-of-view as compared to a purely academic one, would be deemed to undermine the **sanctity** of academia. It is argued that academicians need not be concerned with **customer service**, it is the job for others within the administrative structure to keep institution financially afloat. Academic institutions are generally built upon a dualistic structure that effectively separates the roles of the academics from those of their nonacademic or administrative counterparts. With an exception of a few academicians who are entrusted with some administrative roles, the vast majority are supposed to focus almost solely on their roles as teachers and researchers. The task of determining the extent university education is relevant to employability within the job market might possibly be considered critical for some disciplines and professions, but it does not seem to apply to the field of sociology.

Talking about the different situations graduate sociologists are likely to find themselves in, let's begin with several possible scenarios involving sociologists in nonacademic employment. In the **first scenario**, the graduate is offered a job in public institutions where he or she is expected to deal with some **problematic** family situations. The employer decides on employing a sociology graduate based on the belief that a sociological perspective would be useful and relevant in resolving family and other social issues beyond merely providing financial, psychological, or emotional support. In the **second scenario**, the graduate is offered a job in a non-government institution that is concerned with interethnic tensions and conflicts within an urban community. The graduate is offered the job because the employer notices that the student has undertaken several sociology papers related to urban society, ethnic relations, and social deviance. In the **third scenario**, the graduate is offered to work in a private enterprise that faces several human resource problems.

The graduate is expected to be able to find ways of promoting a better organizational climate to deal with some **problematic** employees. In the **fourth scenario**, the graduate is posted in a local authority where he or she is expected to contribute a sociological perspective to a proposed local development plan with the objective of enhancing the quality of social life and minimizing the negative effects of social dislocation as a result of a squatter resettlement project.

In all the above scenarios, to what extent do sociology graduates have at least some inkling of how to approach the above tasks? If they have not been previously exposed to some rudimentary guidelines and protocols on what to look for when approaching a particular social situation before performing social intervention, they would be overwhelmed by the situation they are in. This is so much more complex than the weeping adolescent pouring out his or her heart in a counselor's room, or a worried woman with her sick and aging mother discussing nursing home needs with a social worker. They would be lucky if they can rely upon and learn from some seniors who had some previous experience in the field. It is almost certain that their training as sociologists has not prepared them to even know where to start when faced with the above scenarios. Could they look for resources prepared by and for sociologists in the Internet or the library for some useful resources and practical guidelines? The probable answer is a dismal "no." Chances are, they will need to resort to resources and guidelines that are provided by other disciplines and professions. Without some form of exposure to some form of theoretical if not practical interventional sociology, their performance will be that of **muddling through** as they go through a long and probably hazardous and costly **trial-and-error** learning process. Sadly, they have to learn from other disciplines and professions, utilizing their approaches, not from those who can provide sociological approaches to be applied in those scenarios.

The graduates may try to justify their unpreparedness by repeating to themselves what sociology professors had been saying all along: "This is not **really** a sociologist's job." It would, however, not be so simple to explain to their employers that a sociologist's job is not to apply, and that managing social problem should be delegated to non-sociologists, such as the psychologists, counselors, social workers, and numerous other professionals. The baffled employer will ask the obvious question: "What, then, exactly does a sociologist do?" The safest answer will be: "We do research. No problem can be solved without first conducting research. This is what we are good at." Assuming that the employers were sufficiently impressed with the answer and allow the sociology graduates to conduct some form of research, then what will be their next role after presenting an analysis of the findings? The employers naturally expect the sociologists to know what next to do.

Unfortunately, there is no logical or natural connection between research findings and guidelines for action. What may appear to be rational inferences derived from research findings may, in fact, be un-implementable due to specific social, political, moral, legal, and economic implications. The graduates may provide an additional excuse that any undergraduate training is naturally too basic to be adequately applied to real-life situations. What if the sociologists are be allowed to pursue postgraduate studies with the employers' expectation that they would then be equipped with the necessary practical skills. Would this significantly improve the situation? The employers will be in for a disappointment to discover that no amount of postgraduate sociology is likely to equip sociologists with even the most rudimentary guidelines and skills on how to conduct social intervention programs. Even if, as it is usually the situation, the sociologists are part of a bigger team of professionals jointly performing the task at hand, they are still expected to contribute sociological inputs to the intervention process beyond merely presenting research findings.

The above scenarios are not mere hypothetical situations. Many sociology graduates, the authors of this book included, do in fact find themselves in very similar situations, oblivious to the sociology professors who remain behind the ivory towers. Of course, the graduates can try to downplay their sociology pedigree and masquerade as general administrators or holding some other management positions. They may simply abandon sociology totally to pursue some other more practical-oriented professions and training programs. Many other disciplines and professions, such as those of clinical psychology, social work, counseling and management, provide training guides, and practical hands-on training programs within their respective disciplines. Should the sociologist approach the library or their previous professors for help they will generally be frustrated by the lack of concrete suggestions on how to deal with the specific and concrete problems at hand. They would have better luck if they leave the sociology section of the library to see what other disciplines and professions have to offer to help them to perform their tasks.

The hypothesis presented here is that sociology graduates are generally not well-prepared for nonacademic employment unless they are employed purely in the capacity as a researcher. And yet, it was noted by Riley Jr. (1967) that by the 1060s an estimated 1 out of 4 sociologists in the United States were already holding posts at various levels in the public and private **nonacademic** sectors. The sad reality is that they end up doing all kinds of tasks, its just that **they do not do sociology**. Riley stated that he saw a certain lack of clarity and ambiguity among sociologists toward their role, identity, and status in their workplace. He saw sociologists experiencing an **identity crisis** which made them feel **awkward** when working with other professionals. He remarked that employers were generally uncertain as to how to classify or assign sociologists within the organizational structure other than to place them in a **special project office**, or to give them some other marginal roles within the organization.

The Need for Curriculum Change

Many sociologists themselves are critical, sometimes rather brutally, of the non-practicality of much sociological discourse which students are subjected to. Writing in 1941, recounting his personal experiences during World War 1, Queen (1941) noticed that most sociologists, including himself, encountered difficulties when performing as sociologists even when undertaking seemingly simple tasks. He attributed this to the failure and weakness of the kind of training that sociologists of his generation were exposed to. He felt that much of the training then was relatively devoid of useful or relevant information. He strongly accused some sociology professors of "offering their audience polysyllabic substitutes" instead of what he considered as "real information," of resorting to "a camouflage of pseudo-profundity" (p. 211) in order to conceal their personal limitations and their lack of specific application techniques and skills.

Marshall (1963) found it necessary to remind sociologists that their concepts should be "made for use, not for show" (p. 14). He described some sociologists as ostensibly enjoying a sense of power by, as he put it, "tying the student's brain into knots but often failing to disentangle it again, leaving students in a state of confusion" (p. 14). The tendency to impress students with profound and esoteric writings, intentionally or otherwise, is not new to sociology. Sibley (1963) described sociology in the 1960s as being in **a state of confusion** due to its lack of a clear sense of value commitment or goals. The result, as he saw it, was that students suffered from **anomie** as they became bewildered by the preoccupations of their sociology professors with the latter's own personal inclinations, unable to offer the answers to societal problems. In 1970s Tarter (1973) expressed his wish that sociologists were trained as **social technologists** because he considered the abandoning of the clinical task to others, in particular the social workers, as an unacceptable option. He objected to the idea of relegating this important task to a discipline that to him was "even less scientifically adept and far more politically encumbered than our own" (p. 154). He believed that sociologists needed to go beyond merely recommending programs aimed at what he described as **mental manipulation**. Based on the **reinforcement theory** of human behavior, the task of the social technologist, he explained, was to identify the reinforcing stimuli in social environments, to create new reinforcements where needed, and to demonstrate how best to establish the appropriate reinforcement contingencies to change social behavior.

Rhoades (1980) stated that students had enrolled in sociology courses in large numbers during the preceding decade because they were expecting to find knowledge and skills that would help them to solve the existential problems facing them and their society. He noted that the students found the courses they took failed to give them **a sense of progression** as students of society. These courses, he asserted, were scholastic in nature focusing on the learning of theories, concepts, perspectives, and facts, rather than providing them with the skills and methods of applying them to the problems of the society. The curriculum, Rhoades (1980) concluded was **dysfunctional** both for the discipline as well as for the profession. Two decades later, Odeix, Korgen, and Carmen (2001) echoed the same concern. They noticed how sociology courses that were applied in nature were more popular than the more theoretical ones, and that doctoral students preferred to specialize in the more applied subfields of the discipline. This, they felt clearly indicated the increasing interest in applied sociology, probably due to the ever-increasing opportunities available for sociologists to be employed in the nonacademic sectors.

By 1996 Bruhn and Rebach were still pointing out to the fact that mainstream sociologists choose to merely observe and comment on the process of social change, adopting a **hands-off** stand instead of being actively involved as participants and agents of social change. As a result, they feared that sociology would continue to lose its attractiveness to students who wanted to have more **hands-on** experience.

From the 1980s up to the present, many sociologists continued to voice out almost the same criticisms as their predecessors had done for many preceding decades. Bailey (1980) continued to lament the fact that sociological theory courses were being taught **as ends in themselves** or as **arenas for the practice of style** rather than as a means toward a better understanding of society. He felt that it was **depressing** for students to realize that sociology does not seem to be interested in bringing about some change in the troubled world. Sociology appeared to continue neglecting the important task of helping its students to see the connection between theory and practice, a state of apathy and disconnect that effectively reduced the extent of personal satisfaction enjoyed by the students. "Sociology fails its students," wrote Bailey (1980), "not because of the way it was taught, but because what was taught was devoid of practical application" (p. 11). Similarly, Anderson (1980) made rather stinging remarks to express his displeasure with the sociology that continued to fail to produce what he considered as practical knowledge. He described sociology as a discipline which

> reacts to its own state in a language of immodest achievement, confusing the writing of the program with the performance of the play, in volatile oscillation between the indicative, the subjunctive and the imperative; concerned to use data to show perspectives and ideologies rather than for its own properties; rearranging and selecting that data according to its perspectives and ideologies, even distorting its own systems into simplistic phantasies; erecting levels of generality without any procedures for movement from one level to another (pp. 11–12).

For clinical sociologists who are aware of the dynamic forces that influence how one's **habitus** and general world-views develop, it is too simplistic to accuse academicians of being deliberately anti-change. It is simply due to the reality that the demands of the academic **vis-à-vis** that of the nonacademic realms are radically different. The larger world **out there** poses challenges that are oblivious to the average academician unless one has had some personal experience of working within it. Furthermore, the exact nature of the challenges faced by sociologists in specific job-situations has seldom been seriously researched. This lack of research and exploration only prolongs the illusion that all is well on the sociology front, and that its graduates are adequately equipped with the necessary tools to function as sociologists no matter in which situations they find themselves. Clinard (1966) believed that sociologists were secretly insecure about their inability to undertake social action despite their "verbiage and claims" (p. 246) that sociology should be placed on an equal footing as other sciences. In the 1960s,

Generally speaking, academic sociologists do not approve of others giving ideas on what and how they should teach, on the assumed grounds that they know best. At the same time, there is often very little motivation for academicians to introduce any innovation into their curriculum unless there is some external pressure to do so, or when there are some immediate tangible personal gains to be had. Like any other profession, academic sociologists can be very set in their ways, teaching the same courses in the same way often using the same old references, year in and year out. It is ironical that the very institution which is supposed to prepare the younger generations to deal with the changing social world is often the one that is highly resistant to change. Of course, changes do occur in sociology's curriculum from time to time. It is just that many of these changes tend to be based on the academician's changing personal interests and the department's internal need, such as due to staffing and logistic considerations. The changes are rarely made in response to the needs of the students or as a response to structural changes occurring in the outside world. In order to justify the **status quo**, the mainstream sociology academicians may choose to see the problem as emanating, not from their own weaknesses rather on **the public ignorance of what sociology** is all about. For example, Green, Klug, Neider, and Salem (1980) believed that it would be a **folly** to change the existing sociology's curriculum.

The problem, as they saw it, was with the employers' **ignorance** of sociology. It is the public that needs changing, not the sociologist. This, they suggested, could be done through such programs as the placement of sociology students in internships in agencies, not in academia, a strategy they termed as **subversion from within**. This strategy, however, did not consider the possibility that the public image of sociology was in fact be based on reality—that sociologists had failed to demonstrate their specific abilities and skills in dealing with challenging public issues. Furthermore, the use of the term **subversion**, unfortunately, reflected a lack of genuineness to correct a serious weakness inflicting sociology of their time. Anderson (1980) did not agree that the general public should be blamed for sociology's predicament. He berated the tendency for sociologists to offer what he termed as **relativistic initiations**, talking of what they **could** see, what **should** be done, **whom** to blame, **how** bad the situation was, and so on, but failing to follow through to actually change the situation for the better.

Despite such critical observations made by sociologists themselves, the universities continue to show very little interest in monitoring and remedying the situation. The graduates, in the meantime, have to learn to make the most of their difficult situations, learning and acquiring new skills by observing and acquiring from others the appropriate skills they need. However, emulating how others perform their tasks is not a satisfactory option for sociologists. Sociology, with its broader, comprehensive, and holistic understanding of society possesses special and unique approaches and perspectives that are needed to complement and supplement other approaches. It is indeed a pitiable state of affairs and a valuable loss to society when sociology misses the opportunity to improve human and societal conditions simply because their graduates choose to merely emulate what others are already doing. It is like watching an incomplete jigsaw puzzle being assembled without a missing piece—the sociological piece.

The general reluctance on the part of many sociologists to introduce some elements of social action or applied sociology in their curriculum and training continued to vex many writers throughout the 1970s. Lachenmeyer (1971) recalled vividly his own experience as an undergraduate major in sociology. He remembered experiencing "a vague intellectual strain" (p. v) when trying to relate what was being taught in sociology courses with the events he observed happening around him.

While he was impressed with the great contributors to sociology, he was perplexed by the failure of sociological knowledge to help students like himself better understand actual human behavior. He found his training focused on statistical and methodological issues, which he found to be too divorced from reality enable him to deal effectively with real-life situations.

Lee (1973) concurred with this assessment and wanted the usual academic sociology courses or textbooks to stop ignoring the problems facing by the individuals in society. Instead, he suggested that they should incorporate what he described as the "magnification of the individual, to what society can become, and to how to help change society" (p. 38) into the sociology curriculum. An often passionate and sharp critic of nonpractical sociology Lee (1973) went even further to regard sociologists who did not play a part in resolving society's problems as constituting "a part of the society's problem" (p. 38), reflecting the popular current adage among management gurus that "if one is not part of the solution, one is part of the problem" (p. 38). By refusing to become involved, Lee (1973) felt that sociologists were in fact condoning the existing **social equilibrium** or the **status quo**. He wanted to impress upon the fact that inaction and non-involvement was not necessarily a virtue. What was inferred by Lee's comment was that the failure to be involved in problem-solving efforts could be equated with an inherent or intrinsic support for the present state of social inadequacies, inequalities, injustice, and so on. By not intervening in situations where the clients were struggling with dilemmas and problems, sociologists were giving the message that sociology was not at all concerned with human discomfort and misery. Two years later, Tarter (1973) expressed his regret with the fact that the graduate training in sociology in his time was focused almost entirely on research techniques while neglecting to give equal emphasis on the acquisition of other techniques that would reflect the practicability of sociological principles.

Some sociologists go further to warn that the need for change will not only benefits the students. Even sociology professors need to be prepared to hold nonacademic careers since the opportunities for pursuing academic careers are not guaranteed for life. In 1976, a long-suffering, Anonymous (1976), sociologist reflected on his long period of unemployment after having served a long tenure in academia. He was shocked to discover that despite possessing a PhD and having had an extensive teaching and research experience as well as having produced academic publications he was unable to obtain employment inside or outside the academia. He came to the bitter conclusion that sociologists were not in demand in the outside world because of their own fault. They were not able to demonstrate their ability to deal with the magnitude of social problems existing around them. He, therefore, suggested that there should be more sociologists who were trained in the applied arena, what he termed as **extension sociologists**, who were capable of working with various public and private agencies involved in solving social problems. Later in the decade, Heraud (1979) agreed that sociologists usually appeared to be **uncomfortable** when approached for ideas and help in specific problem-solving situations. He attributed this to the fact that most sociologists lived in a protected world of the academic institutions that restricted their roles to that of a teacher and researcher.

References

Akers, R. L. (1992). Linking sociology and its specialties: The case of criminology. *Social Forces, 71*(1), 1–16.

Anderson, D. C. (1980). The ignorance of social intervention: A polemical introduction. In D. C. Anderson (Ed.), *The ignorance of social intervention* (pp. 9–20). London: Croom Helm.

Anonymous. (1976). Reflections of an unemployed sociologist. *The American Sociologist, 11*(4), 193–198.

Argow, W. W. (1941). The practical application of sociology. *American Sociological Review, 6*(1), 37–44.

Arts, W. A., & Becker, H. A. (1990). Strategies for future achievement in sociology. In C. G. A. Bryant & H. A. Becker (Eds.), *What has sociology achieved?* (pp. 238–247). London: Macmillan Press.

Bailey, J. (1980). *Ideas and intervention: Social theory for practice*. London: Routledge and Kegan Paul.

Baum, A., & Bourner, T. (1981). Initial employment experiences of sociology graduates in the UK, 1976-78. *The Sociological Review, 29*(2), 339–360.

Berger, P. L. (1963). *Invitation to sociology*. New York: The Overlook Press.

Berk, R. A. (1981). On the compatibility of applied and basic sociological research: An effort in marriage counselling. *The American Sociologist, 16*(4), 204–211.

Bradshaw, T. K., & McPherron, S. M. (1980). Issues and resources in undergraduate sociology curriculum. *The American Sociologist, 15*(1), 6–21.

Brennan, J. (1982). Sociologists and employment. *The Sociological Review, 30*(4), 647–667.

Bruhn, J. G., & Rebach, H. M. (1996). *Clinical sociology: An agenda for action*. New York: Plenum Press.

Clinard, M. (1966). The sociologist's quest for respectability. *The Sociological Quarterly, 7*(4), 399–412.

Collins, R. (1982). *Sociological insight: An introduction to nonobvious sociology*. New York: Oxford University Press.

Damle, Y. B. (1976). Sociology. In S. C. Dube (Ed.), *Social science and social realities: Role of the social sciences in contemporary India* (pp. 103–114). Shimla: Indian Institute of Advanced Study.

Flores-González, N., & Rodríguez-Muiz, M. (2011). Youth culture, identity, and resistance: Participatory action research in a Puerto Rican Barrio. In K. O. Korgen, J. M. White, & S. K. White (Eds.), *Sociologists in action: Sociology, social change and social justice*. Thousand Oaks, CA: Pine Forge Press.

Gardezi, H. N. (1975). Contemporary sociology in Pakistan and Bangladesh. In R. P. Mohan & D. Martindale (Eds.), *Handbook of contemporary developments in world sociology: Contributions in sociology no. 17* (pp. 413–422). Westport, CT: Greenwood Press.

Green, C. S., Klug, H. G., Neider, L. A., & Salem, R. G. (1980). Careers and the undergraduate curriculum: An integrated program. *The American Sociologist, 15*(1), 30–39.

Hegazy, E. (1975). Contemporary sociology in Egypt. In R. P. Mohan & D. Martindale (Eds.), *Handbook of contemporary developments in world sociology: Contributions in sociology no. 17* (pp. 379–390). Westport, CT: Praeger.

Heraud, B. (1979). *Sociology in the professions*. London: Open Books.

Joseph, C. (2011). Sociology: Promise and potential through praxis. In K. O. Korgen, J. M. White, & S. K. White (Eds.), *Sociologists in action: Sociology, social change and social justice*. Thousand Oaks, CA: Pine Forge Press.

Lachenmeyer, C. W. (1971). *The language of sociology*. New York: Columbia University Press.

Laue, J. H. (1978). Advocacy and sociology. In G. H. Weber & G. J. McCall (Eds.), *Social scientists as advocates: Views from the applied disciplines* (pp. 167–200). Beverly Hills, CA: Sage.

Lee, A. M. (1973). *Toward humanist sociology*. Englewood Cliffs, NJ: Prentice-Hall.

Lee, A. M. (1978). *Sociology for whom?* New York: Oxford University Press.

Lindesmith, A. R. (1960). Social problems and sociological theory. Reproduced in A. B. Shostak (Ed.) (1966), *Sociology in action: Case studies in social problems and directed social change* (pp. 270–275). Homewood, IL: The Dorsey Press.

Magubane, B. (2000). *African sociology: Towards a critical perspective: The collected essays of Bernard Makhosezwe Magubane*. Trenton, NJ: African World Press.

Manis, J. G. (1976). *Analyzing social problems*. New York: Praeger Publishers.

Marshall, T. H. (1963). *Sociology at the crossroads: And other essays*. London: Heinemann.

Mills, C. W. (1959). *The sociological imagination*. Oxford: Oxford University Press.

Mohan, R. P. (1975). Contemporary sociology in India. In R. P. Mohan & D. Martindale (Eds.), *Handbook of contemporary developments in world sociology: Contributions in sociology* (pp. 423–438). Westport, CT: Greenwood Press.

Morrissey, J. P., & Steadman, H. J. (1977). Practice or perish? Some overlooked career contingencies for sociologists in nonacademic settings. *The American Sociologist, 12*(4), 154–162.

Muijzenberg, O. D. V. D. (1995). Social science in Malaysia and Indonesia. In N. S. Nordholt & L. Visser (Eds.), *Social science in Southeast Asia: From particularism to universalism* (pp. 121–132). Amsterdam: Vu University Press.

Nordholt, N. S., & Visser, L. (1995). Reflections on the construction of knowledge in Southeast Asia: Some concluding remarks. In N. S. Nordholt & L. Visser (Eds.), *Social science in Southeast Asia from particularism to universalism* (pp. 145–151). Amsterdam: Vu University Press.

Odeix, P. M., Korgen, K. O., & Carmen, A. D. (2001). Recent trends in faculty employment in sociology. *The American Sociologist, 32*(4), 98–106.

Queen, S. A. (1941). Sociologists in the present crisis. *Social Forces, 20*(1), 1–7.

Rhoades, L. J. (1980). Undergraduate sociology curriculum: A proposal. *The American Sociologist, 15*(1), 21–29.

Riley Jr., J. W. (1967). The sociologist in the nonecademic setting. In P. Lazarsfeld, W. H. Sewell, & H. L. Wilensky (Eds.), *The uses of sociology* (pp. 789–805). New York: Basic Books, Inc.

Selby, J., & Tilley, N. (1975). An apt sociology for polytechnics. *Higher Education Review, 8*(2), 38–52.

Sibley, E. (1963). *The education of sociologists in the United States*. New York: Russell Sage Foundation.

Swan, L. A. (1984). *The practice of clinical sociology and sociotherapy*. Cambridge, MA: Schenkman Publishing Company.

Tarter, D. E. (1973). Heeding skinner's call: Toward the development of a social technology. *The American Sociologist, 8*(4), 153–158.

Tjondronegoro, S. M. P. (1995). Indonesia's social science agenda: A personal view. In N. S. Nordholt & L. Visser (Eds.), *Social science in Southeast Asia: From particularism to universalism* (pp. 59–77). Amsterdam: Vu University Press.

Turner, S. P., & Turner, J. H. (1990). *The impossible science: An institutional analysis of American sociology*. Newbury Park, CA: Sage.

Wan, P. M. (2016). The role of sociology and sociologists: Aspirations and perceptions of sociology students in Malaysia. *Southeast Asian Social Science Review, 1*(1), 79–99. Selangor: PSSM.

Weber, G. H., & McCall, G. J. (Eds.). (1978). *Social scientists as advocates: Views from the applied disciplines*. Beverly Hills, CA: Sage.

Wirth, L. (1982). Clinical sociology: Sociology and clinical procedure. *Clinical Sociology Review, 1*(1), 7–22.

Young, D. (1955). Sociology and the practicing professions. *American Sociological Review, 20*(6), 641–648.

Zorbaugh, H. (1992). Sociology in the clinic. *Clinical Sociology Review, 10*, 16–20.

Chapter 7
Where Do We Go from Here? Conclusion

Against the background of a long-established tradition of being relatively free from the need to respond to the practical needs of the wider society, why should there be any need to review the existing role of sociology? For many traditionalists, sociology is alive and well, well-entrenched as a legitimate, and essential social science discipline that no educational institution can do without. It will continue to provide at least some basic service courses for many science and social science students. Why fix it if it is not broken? After all, society has come to accept sociology as an **academic** discipline devoted to the study and analysis of social institutions and social behavior. That in itself justifies its existence and the public funding it receives. It is the role of other professions to fully utilize and transform the knowledge, which has been so meticulously assembled and analyzed by sociologists into something that can be directly relevant and instrumental for resolving social issues. Sociologists themselves do not have to do this.

All these pleas for a more practical sociology remained unheeded among the mainstream community of sociologists. Clearly, with the exception of some committed applied sociologists, the situation for the vast majority of sociology programs remained basically unchanged as the discipline entered the new Millennium. Proponents of a more applied, practical, and clinical sociology, however, were undeterred. They remain convinced that sociology has always been capable of offering and delivering what society expects of them. They want to prove that a better balance between the two wings of their discipline, the pure and the applied, is not only crucial and feasible but that its seeds had been sown and its shoots have taken roots. What they are waiting for is for it to bear the fruits that many concerned sociologists had been dreaming about for decades. They are no longer talking about the **coulds** and the **shoulds** of sociology but rather on the **whats**, **when**, and most importantly the **hows** of practical sociological intervention.

Kasarda (1975) recommended that modifications be made in graduate training to enable students to perform the linkage between theory, research, and social policy. Students, he suggested, should be allowed to select a practical problem for the purpose of making diagnoses and solving problems as are required in other

© Springer Nature Switzerland AG 2020

P. M. Wan, A. H. Wan, *Clinical Sociology*, Clinical Sociology: Research and Practice, https://doi.org/10.1007/978-3-030-49083-6_7

professional training programs. The students were also suggested to undergo internships in selected institutions that will expose them to the practical and real problems typically faced by those involved in policy and program formulation and implementation. Schein (2001) wanted graduate education at both the doctoral and masters levels to provide the skills to sociology students on "how to be helpful" (p. 236) instead of making a **sacred cow** out of the research paradigm which, in his view, produce neither the valid knowledge nor the help which is needed for problem-solving. He suggested that sociology graduate students be placed in organizations early in their graduate training not for the purpose of performing research but in order to work on specific practical problem-solving activities.

The need for specialized clinical skills naturally requires the development of clinical curriculums that are capable of producing the desired practitioners. Several sociologists had offered their suggestions on what competencies should be included to overcome the shortcomings of present-day sociology curriculums. Woolf Jr. and Bishop (1980) suggested a Competency-Based Education (CBE) program for students, centering on the concept of teaching specific demonstrable abilities and skills rather than merely delivering particular substantive contents. The 8 major outcomes or competencies they suggested included effective communication ability, analytical capability, problem-solving ability, valuing in a decision-making context, effective social interaction, effectiveness in individual/environment relationship, responsible involvement in the contemporary world, and aesthetic responsiveness. In order to ensure that the CBE program did not merely serve the existing technological system, they suggested that within it should be included critical and theoretical inquiry, which should remain central to academic sociology. Swan (1984) agreed that the idea of sociologists playing a clinical role will not be realized until specially formulated programs are designed to equip students with the necessary clinical competencies. Bradshaw and McPherron (1980) wanted a new curriculum that was more structured and hierarchical than the usual loose form of the sociology curriculum of their period.

The curriculum should start from the simpler basic skills moving toward more complex and demanding ones. They criticized the existing programs then which they felt did not have a clear notion of an entry point into the discipline and a lack of a structured sequence whereby the mastery at one level of knowledge and skills proceeded to the other higher levels. They believed that the failure to structure the curriculum worked against the sociology departments. The lack of a clearly constructed and holistic training sequence would render the curriculum incomplete, inconsistent, or disrupted. Hall (1996) suggested some forms of supervised service-learning opportunities for sociology students which would enable the students to acquire a deeper "experiential and theoretical understanding" (p. 147) of themselves and of the society they need to deal with.

A pertinent question arises as to whether clinical sociology should be introduced at the undergraduate or at the graduate level. At the undergraduate level, an exposure to the idea of clinical work can be incrementally incorporated into the basic sociology courses. Including it within the existing theory and research methodology courses may be a good start in view of the considerable time and resources required before totally new courses on the specialty can be offered. Some sociologists suggest that clinical training will be more appropriately introduced at the graduate-level program although they do not exclude the idea that undergraduates should already be exposed to some aspects of clinical practice. Marshall (1963) wanted sociology departments to ensure that an undergraduate was equipped with both theory **and** techniques and not merely attended university to "enlarge the contents of his mind" (p. 42). This, he felt, will produce more well-rounded and confident students who would have acquired something tangible that could be applied.

Any initial step to expose students to any basic skills in social intervention at any level will be welcomed regardless of whether it is done at the undergraduate or the graduate level. Many students with their typical fresh and youthful idealism want **to make a difference** by being involved in activities that they see as helping to improve the social conditions of their society. Some sociologists may argue that there is already too much demand made by the present curriculum upon the students' time and energy that anything additional will only pose an additional burden on the latter. This argument is little more than a convenient rationalization for maintaining the **status quo** of the present sociology curriculum. The assumption is that existing courses in sociology are already adequate or even perfect. Anything new must be in the form of **new additional** courses while existing ones should be left changed. However, it does not have to be that way. It is possible, with some efforts and clear thinking, to incorporate the applied and clinical elements within the existing curriculum.

There is little danger of overloading the existing curriculum because some degree of rationalization of the existing courses is required. If a process of prudent **pruning** to reduce redundancy, irrelevance, and repetitiveness existing within the current curriculum is undertaken there will be ample room for incorporating practical sociology theories and practice without overburdening it. Those sociologists who are not aware of how **unintelligible** and **unreasonable** much of the contents of the sociology curriculum appear to the students have obviously not bothered to seek honest feedback from their students. In addition to the restructuring of the existing curriculums, new courses in practical sociology can be offered as additional electives to the existing ones. Instead of imposing them upon all sociology students, these courses only need to be made a requirement for students interested in pursuing the applied and clinical specialties. What is important is that students who intend to seek nonacademic sociological careers have an equal option and opportunity to learn the relevant skills and techniques as their colleagues who are interested in pursuing academic ones.

The general public too has a crucial role to play in promoting clinical sociology. The stakeholders of university education, including the general public, need to constantly review the role and performance of all disciplines, including that of sociology. As taxpayers supporting the cost of university education, the public have the right to expect a greater contribution from sociology. The shareholders of private universities should also expect more concerted and innovative efforts to be put in by the sociology departments to attract more students. Politicians have a right to ensure that the allocation of public funds for sociology is fully justified. Sussman

(1966) reminded the academic world not to make decisions and choices based solely on internal considerations of its individual disciplines while ignoring changes occurring in its external environment, the general public. Academicians, he asserted, had generally always been more concerned with their colleagues' evaluation of their work than they were with their students' feedbacks. In fact students' evaluation of sociology programs and the performance of their professors in many universities were either non-existent or inconsequential. In contrast, in clinical work, the evaluation and feedback provided by clients or consumers played a crucial role in determining the outcomes of clinical intervention.

Although many sociologists, like other academicians, feel that the effectiveness of their performance should not be assessed in terms of "in dollars and cents," it is not totally unreasonable for the taxpaying public to want to see an optimal utilization of the public funds. Tertiary education needs to mean more than the usual accumulation of academic credit hours, with proper course sequencing based on some clear academic and practical objectives. Howery (1983) advocated that university administrators should be concerned not only with the overall enrollment trends but also with the need to ensure that each department can justify its existence by taking into consideration the needs and interests of the society it is supposed to serve. Laue (1978) wanted sociology departments to introduce more innovative curriculums and to reject its **business-as-usual** attitude toward sociology and its students. The authorities, he felt, need to be able to respond convincingly to the usual argument that tertiary education should not be concerned with "fitting students to the job market." This argument that has remained relatively unchallenged in most academic circles has effectively insulated the world of academia from the concerns, realities, and expectations of the outside world.

In order to prepare students to perform clinical tasks, it is important that interdisciplinary collaboration is instituted early on in their training program. It will be unrealistic to expect students who have not been exposed to such cooperation to feel comfortable or competent doing so once they are already on their jobs. They may either choose to distance themselves from other members of an interdisciplinary team or, on the other extreme, they may end up adopting **in toto** the perspectives and approaches of other professionals to the point that their unique sociological approaches are abandoned. In order to inculcate a more moderate response, sociology students should be prepared through actual practice with the ways of effective **esprit de corps** bonding with other interdisciplinary team members. Young (1955) pointed out that when sociologists were working closely with other practitioners they served as **living links** between the different disciplines. Practitioners often found themselves oblivious to the disciplinary divisions as they work together to find an effective means of dealing with and solving the challenging and pressing common problem facing them. Undoubtedly, the academic departments should incorporate interdisciplinary cooperation activities as an essential part of graduate training. Rossi and Whyte (1983) had warned of the failure of academic sociology departments to make it their policy to institute interdisciplinary training. They left it to the individual sociologist to explore and be acquainted with the approaches and practices of other practitioners.

In order to rectify this situation, Kasarda (1975) advised sociology departments on the need to conduct interdisciplinary workshops regularly, providing the opportunity for graduate students and faculty members of the various disciplines "to interact on particular issues to identify critical problems, evaluate means of social intervention, and assess the probability of achieving given objectives through specific programs of action" (p. 53). Similarly, Dowdall and Pinchoff (1994) implored sociologists to play down the idea of the exclusivity of their disciplinary identity in order to participate effectively in interdisciplinary teams. They saw the mainstream training of sociologists as having the tendency to lead students to just the opposite direction. At the same time, students need to be reminded and demonstrated, that while they need to be part of a bigger team, it is important that they do not totally disregard and respect disciplinary boundaries by trespassing and belittling them.

It is possible that other professionals may not be ready to work alongside clinical sociologists, as **the new kid on the block**. Bruhn and Rebach (1996) offered an advice to **budding** clinical sociologists that they do not need to defend their stand against critics as long as they are totally convinced of the importance, significance, and validity of their professional contribution to society. Being eventually accepted by other practitioners would be a strong motivation for clinical sociologists to continue proving themselves to others. Bruhn and Rebach (1996) reiterated that it was up to the clinical sociologists themselves to sharpen the image of their discipline, which no doubt would require considerable "time, experience, persistence, and an ability to make changes and accommodate new needs" (p. 222).

Clearly, there are no quick fixes toward achieving this. Instead of adopting a combative stand toward other practitioners, it was essential that sociologists adopted a diplomatic approach of respecting and regarding others positively in a spirit of collaboration. Smelser (2000) felt that his personal experiences of being involved in interdisciplinary collaboration with others kept him alive professionally, rescuing him from being in a **professional rut** "churning my wheels through the same old mud" (p. 29). He believed that the borrowing of perspectives, insights, and methods from other disciplines, as well as learning to apply them creatively, was a valuable personal learning process. He realized that all these experiences helped to suggest new ways of looking at a phenomenon, freeing him from the somewhat constricted mainstream sociological perspectives. In short, sociological practice helps to inject new ideas and approaches by rejuvenating the sociologist's tired spirit after dealing endlessly with the same old well-worn theories and ideas. Without a new exposure to interdisciplinary practical work sociologists may be merely tinkering and rehashing old ideas, relabeling and perhaps changing parts of their outward appearance, but old ideas nevertheless.

Associations and Professionalization

The establishment of specialized sociological associations plays a crucial role as the platform for generating further the passion and synergizing all the available and potential energies and resources towards achieving the vision and mission of a sociological specialty. In the United States, Keith (2000) urged the American Sociological Association (ASA) to do more to promote the development of clinical sociology in American universities, to venture beyond merely presenting a listing of sociology departments that offered programs in applied and clinical sociology. He suggested that ASA needed to be a proactive leader in this endeavor, such as helping to establish guidelines for applied sociology programs, accrediting programs that met these guidelines, working with specific employment sectors to create economic opportunities for graduates, and tracking the performance of professionally applied sociologists. According to him at the turn of the new Millennium, the discipline was analogous to **architecture without architects or medicine without doctors**. A particularly historic event occurred in 1978 when a **Clinical Sociology Association (CSA)** was formed in the United States. It was the first time that an Association in the country adopted the name **Clinical Sociology** in its name, a source of hope and inspiration for clinical sociologists worldwide. As we have seen, this victory of sorts was, however, short lived. The Association decided to change its name to the **Sociological Practice Association (SPA)** in 1986 on the pretext of attracting and incorporating a broader membership base for the Association, to include other practitioners.

For those who have advocated for the development of clinical sociology as a distinct specialty, this development incited concern and anxiety for the future. The specialty of clinical sociology seemed doomed to be overshadowed and pushed into the background within the wider but more amorphous scope of the **sociological practice**. For clinical sociologists, particularly for the authors of this book, the concept of the specialty has always been clear. For Wan Abdul Halim, clinical sociology was personally, and single-handedly created out of pure professional necessity and public support. While working alongside practitioners, in particular clinical psychologists, over 40 years, and being understudied by Wan Puspa Melati. for almost half of that period, clinical sociology has always been conceptualized as the sociological version of clinical psychology. The general public showed great excitement when they see clinical psychologists and clinical sociologists presenting approaches that complemented each other so perfectly enabling them to see the total reality of the situation like never before. On one occasion members of the audience stood up to ask, "Did you two have a written script because you complement and yet at time contradicting each other so perfectly."

The trajectory path of clinical sociology has always been clear to the author of this book because of the guidance inspired by the history of the development of clinical psychology. An additional inspiration was the development of social work practice, in particular clinical social practice, as well as the evolution of all other forms of social practice. The exact nature of other forms of sociological practice, at least in the minds of the authors of this book, has always been more variable, less theoretically developed, and often without clear **modus operandi** shared by different practitioners. So understandably psychologically deflating when the reversal of CSA into ASP occurred. It did not affect our work in Malaysia as we prodded on responding to requests and demands while fine-tuning out approaches. We were not particularly perturbed by the name change. In our local culture, when a child is frequently sick, the parent would change the child's name sometimes frequently, since the illness is attributed to the inappropriateness of the names given. So perhaps, CSA was analogous to a sick child whose name had to be changed. Sorry for the distraction.

However, the development that inspired new hopes to struggling clinical sociologists all over the world when two separate associations in the United States—**The Society for Applied Sociology** (ASA) and **The Sociological Practice Association** (SPA)—unite to form **The Association for Applied and Clinical Sociology** (AACS), with an international representation board members. Similarly, the setting up of the **International Sociological Association** in 1949 with 57 research divisions that include "Sociotechnics-Sociological Practice" and "Clinical Sociology" provide hope for clinically inclined sociologists around the world (International Sociological Association, 2019).

Among the main tasks of AACS are to review and certify individual clinical sociologists; outline code of ethics for practitioners as well as to monitor the development of public sociology, sociological practice, applied, and clinical work. In addition, the setting up of The Commission on Applied and Clinical Sociology (CACS) in 1995, which was renamed to The Commission on the Accreditation of Programs in Applied and Clinical Sociology (CAPACS) in 2010, is another milestone to further the development of Clinical Sociology through its accreditation of programs. Recently, CAPACS has evaluated and accredited the first international program. These positive developments helped to, at least temporarily and within certain localities, save the sinking Clinical Sociology ship, and resuscitated its drowning passengers, figuratively speaking, while ensuring that Clinical Sociology will not be another Titanic.

Still, in order to ensure the full development potential of clinical sociology more needed to be done. Its future development will require a more true application of sociological tools beyond research. These associations will then spearhead publicity campaigns, the recruitment of aspiring clinical sociologists, the offering of professional courses and practical training as well as eventually taking efforts to obtain practice licenses from the authorities in the respective societies they serve.

The eventual acquisition of a **professional status** for the specialty is of paramount importance. Sociologists have traditionally been highly critical of the idea of the **professionalization** of careers because they believed that this would lead to its misuse. They had been accusing many other established professionals of committing the abuse of their professional status. For some traditional sociologists, the idea of adopting a professional status is therefore an undeclared **taboo** which meant that it was seldom raised for any serious and objective reconsideration. A **profession** is defined in a dictionary as "a group or body, of some social standing, claiming expertise in an area of work" (Thomas & Pierson, 1995). A profession usually involves a set of skills and techniques evolved from a science or theory, which are applied to solve particular problems. A professional society or association is officially registered in order to regulate its activities and membership so as not to contravene the law. Its membership is limited to those who can demonstrate the possession of some specific competencies and qualifications as well as their readiness to adhere to its code of ethics.

In order to achieve full professional status, a particular specialty needs to undergo a step-by-step process of professionalization which, according to Wilensky (1964), involved a sequence of consecutive actions. It began with the presence of some individuals who were already involved full time in the performance of the occupation; the offering of training programs with an academic component in some universities; the setting-up of professional associations at a local level following by other branches at the national level; and finally the formalization of a **code of ethics** for its members.

Mayer (1972) analyzed the natural history of professionalization as involving 3 phases: A **pre-professional phase** where the focus was on the existence of specific problems being neglected by the society, or which were not being adequately dealt with by existing professionals. The second phase was the **emerging phase** where efforts were put to gather funds, conducting research on the problems concerned, obtaining public support, and offering specialized training programs. The final phase is the **established phase** where efforts were made for a clear job and salary classification and structuring as well as defining the boundaries and scopes of the profession. According to Haskell (1977), the **professionalization** process in social science involved a three-part process beginning with the establishment of a **community of inquirers** that distinguished itself from other groups and from the society at large as it established internal communication among its members; followed by efforts at organizing and **disciplining** its members; and finally by the efforts of its members to enhance their **credibility** in the eyes of the public.

Clinical sociology has much to learn from the past experiences of clinical psychology, how the latter struggled to become an acceptable specialty in the face of an initial lack of enthusiasm among mainstream psychologists. **Clinical psychology** has been initially described as a **schizophrenic** endeavor because of its dual emphasis on both the seeking of knowledge and the provision of human service to society which its critics considered as incompatible activities (Bellack & Hersen, 1980). The successful balancing of research and clinical skills, a hallmark of clinical psychology, has helped the profession to enlarge and develop over time until this originally small field which commanded little prestige and acceptance grew into "the largest area of specialization within American psychology" (Kirsch & Winter, 1983, p. 3). The success of clinical psychology to establish itself so successfully as the flagship of the psychology discipline serves as a source of inspiration to the clinical sociologists who are embarking on a similar journey and facing the same initial obstacles.

One of the reasons for the opposition by sociologists against **professionalization** is the accusation that those who support it are motivated purely by personal materialistic interests rather than by a genuine desire to serve better the community. Merton (1976) pointed out a basic contradiction that was built into role of the professional. On the one hand, the professionals were supposed to give the best possible service to their clients, to resolve the latter's problems, and empower them to become independent of the professionals. At the same time, it appeared to be in their interests to encourage a continuing dependency on the part of the clients on the professionals, guaranteeing the latter with a continuous means of livelihood.

In other words, the professionals have an institutionalized stake in maintaining the dependency relationship, as their critics would say, to "live off" the troubles of their clients. It is possible that professionals felt motivated to prolong a client's problem or suffering if it brought some form of rewards to them. Saks (1983) regarded **professionalization** as a form of "exclusionary closure based on **credentialism**" (p. 11), in other words, a strategy devised to limit and control the entry and exit of its members, motivated principally by the desire to safeguard the interests of the members and to enhance the market value of its services. The professions were seen as gradually deviating from what they claimed as their original purpose, which supposedly was to upgrade the professional standard of their service, developing what the critics label as **rigor professionis** characterized by "a loss of contact with the community outside the profession" (Heraud, 1979).

Adding to this barrage of criticisms, Townsend (1958) believed that a professional association would sooner or later develop several tendencies such as becoming inward-looking, diverting their attention away from providing services to their clients. He listed the negative tendencies that these associations tended to develop, such as to become engrossed with fierce internal power struggles as senior members try to entrench their positions to the resentment of younger members; exerting pressure for conformity and loyalty to tradition while innovative and creative ideas were considered as threats to the **status quo**; as well as a tendency to ignore the actual professional development of its members. The critics' apprehension toward the process of **professionalization** of many specialties were not totally without merit since many professional organizations do exhibit many or at least some of the negative trends and tendencies pointed out by the critics. Of course, the above list of criticism cited by Townsend (1958) can be equally directed toward any human beings, not only the professionals, such as politicians, bureaucrats, academicians, businessmen, and any form of informal and formal associations. The justification for this accusation certainly needs to be addressed and be discussed further, but it is necessary to avoid, using an analogy, the argument that knives need to be banned because it can be used as a murder weapon. The critics' talk of "living off the suffering of the clients" appears to describe the private medical profession to a large degree. Hopefully, it does not imply that the medical profession should be de-registered.

The emergence of the clinical sociologists on the scene makes the issue of professionalization, long considered as non-applicable to sociology, relevant once again. Clinical sociologists as practitioners need to weigh objectively the **pros** and the **cons** of the professionalization issue instead of dismissing it outright as irrelevant and unnecessary. The negative and positive aspects of professionalization needs to be re-weighed and reconsidered in view of the emerging clinical sociology specialty. Some sociologists feel that the **thinly veiled** attacks on the professions and the professionals by sociologists are often based on anecdotal illustrations that are seldom supported by objective evidence (Saks, 1983). Bryant (1976) believed that there was a new breed of new sociologists in the 1970s who were ready to reconsider the need for some form of professionalism. They firmly believed that such a move would help to establish some regulations and standards on how sociologists should perform. They believed that professionalization, that is, the establishment of a controlling body that oversees its members, would help to protect the clients better. Without a controlling body, the unethical sociologist would be free to exploit vulnerable and weak clients. Through professionalization, it is also hoped that the future development and growth of clinical sociology as a profession can be planned and charted rather than letting the future development of sociology depend on 'where outsiders happen to put their money in'.

Clinical sociologists need to anticipate the consequences if they make the decision **not** to professionalize. For example, it might place clinical sociologists in a disadvantageous position in their bid to become accepted as members of an interdisciplinary team since other specialists have opted for professionalization. A lack of professional structure, standards, and control over its practitioners may be used by others to exclude clinical sociologists from professional involvement which usually requires approval from licensing authorities. Some problems will also arise when some people claiming to be clinical sociologists do not subscribe to certain commonly accepted principles of ethical professional behavior. This may include the practice of certain dubious and controversial approaches and methods not based on sociological principles, such as the use of witchcraft or religious cult membership recruitment. Should clients end up being exploited by unscrupulous practitioners the victims may face some difficulties in trying to resort to a legal recourse. As professionals, clinical sociologists are required by law to drawing-up safeguards, rules, and regulations that prevent or punish professional abuse and neglect.

The debate concerning the professionalization of clinical sociology will probably continue among sociologists well into the future. For the clinical sociologists, however, this issue cannot be left hanging without some clear conclusion. It is something that needs to be resolved as the number of practicing clinical sociologists increase and the public wishes to see greater control on the growth of the specialty. It is possible that a group of clinical sociologists will choose to establish their professional body to regulate the profession, while others may prefer to practice without being affiliated with such a body. Should this occur, it is hoped that the two approaches are given equal recognition since they both have their valid justifications for choosing their respective courses of action, rather than having one actively opposing and denying the right for the other to exist. By law, however, the non-members will be required to use other designations to describe their career which they can choose from the many names used by other applied sociologists. What is clear is that sociologists need to be constantly vigilant against the traps of professionalization in order to avoid the weaknesses which are often associated, validly or otherwise, with the term **professionalism**. Payne and Cross (1993) discussed the idea of the **new professional**, as someone who successfully maintains a healthy balance between the **pure** and **applied** wings of discipline, rather than adopting the older "elitist, restrictive" (p. 8) model of professionalism.

Clinical sociology is here to stay, even if it does not follow the professional path. It has existed, at least in spirit if not in name, the day sociology itself was born as reflected in the wishes of its founders that sociology should directly address society issues and needs. What is left needing to be done is to embrace it with utmost commitment and passion for the ultimate benefit, or even the survival, of sociology as an invaluable and indispensable social science worthy of societal support and recognition. Every believer in the tremendous potential that clinical sociology can bring to sociology, and consequently to society, need to empower themselves to take whatever step, no matter how small or inconsequential they may seem to be, to activate its growth and development worldwide. The various stakeholders of clinical sociology, namely the students, academicians, educational administrators, financial sponsors, potential employers, professional associations, and so on will together need to identify the respective roles that they themselves can play individually or in collaboration with one another. It is only obvious that the sociologists themselves need to take the lead.

The support from sociologists who choose to restrict their role to that of teacher–researcher–commenter is also equally important for the continued survival of the discipline for according to Zetterberg (1962) there would always be the need for theoretical sociology that needed not necessarily be directly related to resolving the pressing social situation. As non-practitioners, they stood to gain from the work of the practitioners because, according to him, the practical application of social theory set "good standards for theorizing" (p. 189). Similarly, Etzioni (1965) agreed with this assessment. Tropp (1961) pointed out that grand theories inspire ideas in any discipline. According to him within the history of any science, there was "a graveyard of giant theories each slain in the search for truth but each in turn fertilizing the ground in which they are buried" (p. 30). In order for any clinical practice to prosper a strong theoretical foundation was always essential because it enabled basic philosophical issues to be thoroughly examined and debated. As Abrams (1981) saw it, through a process of **diffuse osmosis**, there was a slow release of findings and analyses which permeated the public consciousness until these ideas became public **common sense knowledge** without it being necessarily aware of the source of this information. It was difficult, he explained, to point-pin and to isolate the exact social impact of sociological knowledge on society since it typically had **no point or moment of impact**.

A Final Word or Two

Let us recap some of the salient points made, sometimes repeatedly and often **ad nauseum**, throughout this book. Basing on primarily earlier works within the English language sources, this book reiterates that clinical sociology introduces its own unique approach which sets it apart from other models in applied sociology, and even more significantly, from the approaches of other professions. The use of the term **clinical** is particularly significant because the basic approach of this specialty involves the application of systemic and systematic observation, analysis, diagnosis, synthesis and intervention techniques, and tools applicable to specific problem-solving situations. The term **clinical** has been universally applied to any activity performed by an expert in a practical, analytical, and objective manner usually involving some forms of diagnosis, solution identification, and intervention for the purpose of achieving particular change-goals.

Clinical sociologists deal with problematic situations that require social intervention at the **personal, family, group, organizational, community, societal,** and **global** levels of social reality. As practitioners, they have a wide choice of careers to choose. They do not have to restrict their options to the mainstream sociologist's roles as teachers and researchers. They may choose to practice in nonacademic settings, in public agencies, in voluntary organizations, or in the private sector. They may also serve in an academic setting while simultaneously being involved in consultancies outside the world of academia. They may choose any of the following specialized roles: as **social mediators, crisis interveners, school-career-family-or-marriage counselors, human rights advocators, addiction specialists, social impact experts, community organizers and developers, public health advocators, urban social planners, industrial relations practitioners, criminologists, probation officers, police community relations officers, parole officers, institutional managers and wardens, organizational development specialists, social empowerment specialists, social skill trainers, life course managers, community outreach workers, intercultural and interethnic relations officers, social inclusion advocators, gender sensitivity specialists, globalization specialists** and specializations in any other emergent social issues of the day. The list is inexhaustible and ever-expanding. Clinical sociology associations will have to work hard to promote the public confidence and acceptance of clinical sociologists as the appropriate and qualified candidates for the careers listed above. There is a long and laborious learning trajectory to undergo before clinical sociology can hope to earn this respect and gain a reputation of high esteem by society.

The main objective of this book is to promote awareness among sociologists and students currently studying sociology of the very existence of this exciting and challenging, and yet little-known, a specialty within sociology. It has the tremendous potential of bringing a new burst of excitement, life, and action into the rather drab world of armchair sociological contemplation. Now seems like a particularly appropriate time to review the role that sociology should and is capable of contributing to society. It is an appropriate follow-up to the achievements of the preceding century which had successfully created a niche for the sociology discipline as a legitimate social science within the academic world.

The plea made in this book is not for sociology to reinvent itself. Sociology does not have to do this. It has successfully established itself as an unquestionably important and legitimate social science, at least in the academic and research spheres. Sociology needs to expand itself true potential to the optimal level instead of being trapped by self-imposed limitations regarding to its rightful role and capabilities. Payne and Cross (1993) called for the making of a **new sociologist**, one possessing

> a range of skills at her or his disposal, with a knowledge of where and when to apply them and with a keen conceptual mind that is practiced in linking theory with data in a multitude of different ways (p. 8).

This **new sociologist** he envisaged should join the ranks of other new emergent sociologists of all persuasions and specialties which the discipline needed to produce from time-to-time as a response to the new challenges that society presents.

This book demonstrates the fact that clinical work is neither a totally new nor an alien idea within the sociological tradition. For the numerous reasons and circumstances elaborated throughout the book, the specialty remained relatively peripheral to mainstream sociology throughout most of the last century. Individual exponents struggled quietly to experiment with various clinical approaches, attaining success as well as failures, while at the same time defending themselves from skeptics and critics. These practitioners began to become more confident and aggressive in forming organizations or incorporating themselves and their activities as part of some larger organizations prominently in the United States but in a few other countries as well.

What has also been argued in this book is that by supplementing sociology with a clinical specialty the discipline has everything to gain with very little to lose. Clinical sociology lures the sociologists out of their cocoons, pushing aside the artificial traditional limitations and taboos which had kept them and their precursors off the clinical practice tuff. These self-imposed limitations were based on certain unfounded myths concerning the status of sociology—such as the claims that sociology was not ready and not matured enough to apply; that it should not apply because of the potential risks and controversies it would attract; that it would contaminate the discipline with subjective value-judgments; and that it already had proxies, i.e., other professionals, who, some claim, are perfectly capable of applying the sociological approach.

These myths are briefly examined and are largely found not to untenable and unjustified as a basis for sociologists to avoid performing clinical work. On the contrary, it is exactly for the purpose of making the discipline more matured and **street-wise**, of equipping sociologists with the skills of calculating risks and handling controversies; of dealing with personal and client's values and manipulation; and finally of providing clear and solid sociological tools and methodologies that full-fledged professional training in clinical sociology is urgently needed. In order to avoid the potential ethical and legal complications and **faux pas** professional training need to be made mandatory before a certified clinical sociologist is allowed to enter the field of practice. The pros and cons of the professionalization of the specialty is a complex question that **bona fide** clinicians need to address for themselves and by themselves rather than allowing non-practitioners to decide for them. By the same token, they, need to ensure that the so-called **evils** of professionalization, are at least minimized if they cannot be totally avoided.

Clinical practice promises the adventurous a different kind of challenge and experience as they enter the personal worlds of real people and real situations, this time not just out of curiosity, or wanting to "hang-out" with them, but for the purpose of helping them. These sociologists will become more acutely aware that their own **weltanschauung** (worldview) is only one of many, and that they need to respect the worldviews of others instead of dismissing them as mere **false-consciousness** or forms of social deviance, social disorganization or social pathology. Clinical sociologists can no longer see themselves from their egocentric views of the world, as once accused by Berelson (1966) when he wrote, "Sociologists are skilled at analyzing how other groups are sometimes caught up in their own social structures, but what about their own?" (p. 20). Clinical sociologists have to wrestle with reality rather than keeping it at arm's length as they begin to see themselves, like their clients, being caught in the web of social structure, of allowing their position, status and role as members of the academia to blind them from seeing the world beyond. Clinical sociology should help them to liberate themselves in the same way they try to liberate their clients from the confines of their restrictive worldviews.

A crucial point needing to be made, purposefully left to the last part of this book because of its extreme importance is the impact of practice on the practitioner as a person. He or she should be a socially-apt positive human being capable of gaining self-insight and respectful for others. Being directly involved in social situations, the personality traits and communication abilities of the clinical sociologist play a critical role in influencing the outcome of their work. Fletcher (1975) noted that sociologists would inevitably gain insights into their personal selves as they gained insight of others around them As a simple example, Hauser (1971) realized how his personal experience in social **actionism** taught him to be a better person, even with seemingly mundane habits as **managing time** more effectively and learning to become more **assertive** in dealing with other people's demands. After all, these are two of the many basic personal skills that practitioners often demand of their clients. It is important that they learn to practice them in their own lives as well.

Should clinical sociologists practice double standards in dealing with their social responsibilities, they would soon be confronted by their clients who naturally expect the practitioners to practice what they preach (Capelle, 1979). Who would dare to remind the old university professor of his forgetful and sometimes wayward ways? The practitioners will also invariably become more aware of the parallel between some of the problems faced by their clients and those that they themselves personally face at some points in their lives. Lee (1954) wants practitioners to look forward to exciting **intellectual adventures**, undergoing an unpredictable and exciting journey of discovery as he entered the client's world of experience. A decade later Lee (1966) described this involvement in clinical work as being in the middle of a constant flux of human relationships which constituted "the kind of assault by social realities which alone can modify one's ingrained social preconceptions" (p. 332) capable of making sociologists more conscious of both their own competencies as well as their inadequacies. Similarly, Rossi (1980) believed that applied work, besides stimulating the sociologists' intellectual growth and disciplinary strength, was able to bring a sense of excitement into their personal lives as well as generating a fresh personal sense of meaning and relevance of their work.

Straus (1987) agreed that clinical work was especially satisfying and meaningful because clinicians would get to feed their **sociology habit** as well as feeling that their life **count for something** as they helped clients to achieve goals. He realized that sociological practice could be an addictive venture since one could get **hooked** on the stimulating and exciting world of practice which promised to fill the sociologist's mind with **startling new ideas**. As early as 1939 Lynd (1939) pointed out that the experience of dealing with highly complex and unpredictable situations would be a **humbling** experience for sociologists although he realized that the suggestion that sociologists were not humble enough would be considered by some as **a bit of effrontery**. Lindesmith (1960) similarly felt that the experiences derived from dealing directly with social problems would reduce the tendency for one to be **over-subtle, over-theoretical, over-pretentious,** and **over-confident** with one's own views and assumptions concerning social reality (Shostak, 1966).

Sociologists have to learn a new language when performing clinical work, the everyday everyman language. This is a particularly daunting task for many sociologists who have habitually use **sociological jargon** to express their ideas' It is a language that can sometimes be notoriously obscure and abstruse, especially to the non-sociologists. Even sociologists themselves have unleashed barrages of attacks on their colleagues who fail to present their ideas more simply and clearly. In 1964 Horowitz (1964) criticized sociologists of an excessive use of jargon, of "burying themselves in the higher trivialities" (p. 36). The writer also warned that unless this habit was immediately rectified sociology would eventually become obsolete, finding itself "in an academic museum along with phrenology and alchemy" (Horowitz, 1964, p. 36).

In the same vein, Lindesmith (1960) refused to accept that sociology could not formulate its ideas in a simpler language which could be more easily understood by the layman. He considered much of sociological language as "common sense dressed up in fancy verbiage and sometimes it is just verbiage" (p. 272). Similarly, Collins (1982) reminded sociologists that they had acquired a bad reputation due to their fondness for abstract jargon. He cynically commented that after a reader has finally understood the abstractions and the technicalities of the language the latter would realize that very little had been said. Best (2003) went even further to consider the use of **sociologese** or **socspeak** itself as a **social problem**. As he put it, a sociology that failed to communicate its ideas more simply to the public should not escape from being labeled a social problem. He wanted sociologists to realize that in trying to **dazzle** their audience they only succeeded in losing the latter's attention. As practitioners, clinical sociologists will learn very fast how their failure to communicate effectively aborts their intervention efforts.

Practitioners also need to develop and project positive personal images of being mentally, emotionally, and physically stable and alert, capable of influencing and enhancing the level of confidence and positive energy in the client. A practitioner needed what Rosengren (1970) considered as a **positive personality**. Sociologists have to be aware of all aspects of their personality, including such things as personal grooming, mannerisms, and verbal and nonverbal communication styles. For example, clinical sociologists will have to take into consideration the need to make certain personal adjustments depending on whether they are dealing with children, adolescents, adults, the elderly, different ethnic groups, different social classes, and so on. All this will be considered as mundane, trivial, or simply unnecessary by the mainstream academic sociologists who do not have to establish and maintain a close rapport with their clients.

In 1985, Fritz (1985) documented the development of the clinical sociology specialty with painstaking detail, piecing together whatever limited information available, to provide novice clinical sociologists with a new sense of identity and history of being part of a global social movement pioneered by the likes of Wirth and many others. Many other sociologists in different corners of the world have ventured on their own into clinical work, often unaware of the emergence and the development of the specialty in other parts of the world. Much of their work has yet to be documented but they would certainly be undertaken when the specialty has become an established entity within the bosom of sociology. Fritz (1985) predicted that if national and international events encourage the development of the field and if a strong organizational structure for the field can be put in place, clinical sociology will blossom, and that it will become recognized as **mainstream sociology** rather than "just making tracks at the water's edge" (p. 19). To participate in this movement to promote clinical sociology is to acknowledge that the passionate pleas of earlier sociologists for a more practical and clinical sociology have not been in vain. Let's set into motion Etzioni's (1965) vision in the mid-sixties when he declared that applied sociology, in general, was poised to take off because "our wings have spouted; we are now ready to fly!" (p. 85).

Finally, it is abundantly clear is that the sociologists in developing countries need to go ahead to develop their clinical approaches and to offer training programs to interested students of their respective societies without waiting for the more developed societies to take the initiative. Clinical sociology in developing countries will need to incorporate the unique characteristics of the local culture into its practice. This specialty cannot be simply import clinical sociology as a finished product developed in some foreign countries. It has to be developed by local sociologists, by collaborating with social anthropologists, cultural psychologists, and indigenous social workers and social historians who are sensitive to the **nuances of cultural diversity** of the local communities in which they serve. The sociologists in the developing countries need to take this initiative into their own hands by taking immediate small steps and by networking among themselves as well as with practitioners from the developed countries. It is no longer acceptable for sociologists to simply respond to a public demand for intervention by offering the excuse **that this is not what sociologists do**. For those still having lingering self-doubts after arriving at this final point of this book, just a simple and obvious adage: **Practice makes perfect**.

References

Abrams, P. (1981). The collapse of British sociology? In P. Abrams, R. Deem, J. Finch, & P. Rock (Eds.), *Practice and progress: British sociology 1950–1980* (pp. 53–72). London: George Allen and Unwin. Adler, Adler and Fontana (1987).

Bellack, A. S., & Hersen, M. (1980). *Introduction to clinical psychology*. New York: Oxford University Press.

Berelson, B. (1966). Sociology in action: In population and in general. In A. B. Shostak (Ed.), *Sociology in action: Case studies in social problems and directed social change* (pp. 15–21). Homewood, IL: The Dorsey Press.

Best, J. (2003). Killing the messenger: The social problems of sociology. *Social Problems, 50*(1), 1–13.

Bradshaw, T. K., & McPherron, S. M. (1980). Issues and resources in undergraduate sociology curriculum. *The American Sociologist, 15*(1), 6–21.

Bruhn, J. G., & Rebach, H. M. (1996). *Clinical sociology: An agenda for action*. New York: Plenum Press.

Bryant, C. G. A. (1976). *Sociology in action: A critique of selected conceptions of the social role of the sociologist*. London: George Allen and Unwin.

Capelle, R. G. (1979). *Changing human system*. Toronto: International Human System Institute.

Collins, R. (1982). *Sociological insight: An introduction to nonobvious sociology*. New York: Oxford University Press.

Dowdall, G. W., & Pinchoff, D. M. (1994). Evaluation research and the psychiatric hospital: Blending management and inquiry in clinical sociology. *Clinical Sociology Review, 12*, 175–188.

Etzioni, A. (1965). Social analysis as a sociological vocation. *The American Journal of Sociology, 70*, 317–323.

Fletcher, C. (1975). *The person in the sight of sociology*. London: Routledge and Kegan Paul.

Fritz, J. M. (1985). *The clinical sociology handbook*. New York: Garland Publishing.

Hall, C. M. (1996). Clinical sociology in service-learning. *Clinical Sociology Review, 14*(1), 147–153.

Haskell, T. L. (1977). *The emergence of professional social science*. Urbana: University of Illinois Press.

Hauser, P. (1971). On actionism in the craft of sociology. In J. D. Colfax & J. F. Roach (Eds.), *Radical sociology* (pp. 425–439). New York: Basic Books.

Heraud, B. (1979). *Sociology in the professions*. London: Open Books.

Horowitz, I. L. (1964). An introduction to the new sociology. In I. L. Horowitz (Ed.), *The new sociology: Essays in social science and social theory in honor of C. Wright mills* (pp. 3–48). New York: Oxford University Press.

Howery, C. B. (1983). Undergraduate education. In H. E. Freeman, R. R. Dynes, P. H. Rossi, & W. F. Whyte (Eds.), *Applied sociology* (pp. 322–348). San Francisco: Jossey-Bass Publishers.

International Sociological Association. (2019). *Research networks*. Retrieved from https://www.isa-sociology.org/en/research-networks/research-committees

Kasarda, J. D. (1975). Policy change and grassroots inertia: The case of metropolitan services. In N. J. Demerath, O. Larsen, & K. F. Schuessler (Eds.), *Social policy and sociology* (pp. 45–55). New York: Academic Press.

Keith, B. (2000). Taking stock of the discipline: Some reflections on the state of American sociology. *The American Sociologist, 31*(1), 5–14.

Kirsch, I., & Winter, C. (1983). A history of clinical psychology. In C. E. Walker (Ed.), *The handbook of clinical psychology* (pp. 3–30). Homewood, IL: Dow Jones-Irwin.

Laue, J. H. (1978). Advocacy and sociology. In G. H. Weber & G. J. Mccall (Eds.), *Social scientists as advocates: Views from the applied disciplines* (pp. 167–200). Beverly Hills, CA: Sage Publications.

Lee, A. M. (1954). Sociologists in an integrating society: Significance and satisfaction in sociological work. *Social Problems, 2*(1), 57–66.

Lee, A. M. (1966). *Multivalent man*. New York: George Braziller.

Lindesmith, A. R. (1960). Social problems and sociological theory. Reproduced in A. B. Shostak (Ed.) (1966), *Sociology in action: Case studies in social problems and directed social change* (pp. 270–275). Homewood, IL: The Dorsey Press.

Lynd, R. S. (1939). *Knowledge for what? The place of social sciences in American culture*. Princeton: Princeton University Press.

Marshall, T. H. (1963). *Sociology at the crossroads. And other essays*. London: Heinemann.

Mayer, R. R. (1972). *Social planning and social change*. Englewood cliffs, NJ: Prentice-Hall.

Merton, R. K. (1976). *Sociological ambivalence and other essays*. New York: The Free Press.

Payne, G., & Cross, M. C. (Eds.). (1993). *Sociology in action: Applications and opportunities for the 1990s*. London: Macmillan Press.

Rosengren, W. R. (Ed.). (1970). *Organizations and clients. Essays in the sociology of service*. Columbus, OH: Merrill Publishing Company.

Rossi, P. H. (1980). The presidential address: The challenge and opportunities of applied social research. *American Sociological Review, 45*, 889–904.

Rossi, P. H., & Whyte, W. F. (1983). The applied side of sociology. In H. E. Freeman, R. D. Russell, P. H. Rossi, & W. F. Whyte (Eds.), *Applied sociology* (pp. 5–31). San Francisco: Jossey-Bass Publishers.

Saks, M. (1983). Removing the blinkers? A critique of recent contributions to the sociology of professions. *The Sociological Review, 31*(1), 1–21.

Schein, E. H. (2001). Clinical inquiry/research. In P. Reason & H. Bradbury (Eds.), *Handbook of action research: Participative inquiry and practice* (pp. 228–237). London: Sage Publications.

Shostak, A. B. (Ed.). (1966). *Sociology in action: Case studies in social problems and directed social change*. Homewood, IL: The Dorsey Press.

Smelser, N. J. (2000). Sociological and interdisciplinary adventures: A personal odyssey. *The American Sociologist, 31*(4), 5–33.

Straus, R. A. (1987). The theoretical base of clinical sociology: Root metaphors and key principles. *Clinical Sociology Review, 5*, 65–82.

Sussman, M. B. (1966). The sociologist as a tool of social action. In A. B. Shostak (Ed.), *Sociology in action: Case studies in social problems and directed social change* (pp. 3–13). Homewood, IL: The Dorsey Press.

Swan, L. A. (1984). *The practice of clinical sociology and sociotherapy*. Cambridge, MA: Schenkman Publishing Company.

Thomas, M., & Pierson, J. (Eds.). (1995). *Dictionary of social work*. London: Collins Educational.

Townsend, P. (1958). A society for people. In N. Mackenzie (Ed.), *Conviction* (p. 120). London: MacGibbon Kee.

Tropp, A. (1961). The relevance of sociology to the training of teachers and social workers. In *The Sociological Review*, monograph No.4. pp. 27–32. Keele, Staffordshire: University College of North Staffordshire.

Wilensky, H. (1964). The professionalization of everyone. *American Journal of Sociology, 70*(2), 137–158.

Woolf, W. J., Jr., & Bishop, J. M. (1980). Implications of competency-based education for undergraduate sociology. *The American Sociologist, 15*(1), 50–58.

Young, D. (1955). Sociology and the practicing professions. *American Sociological Review, 20*(6), 641–648.

Zetterberg, F. (1962). *Social theory and social practice*. New York: Bedminster Press.

Further Reading

American Sociological Association. (2003). *Careers in clinical sociology* (1st ed.). Retrieved July 23, 2013, from https://www.asanet.org/sites/default/files/savvy/images/employment/docs/pdf/clinsoc_45575v2.pdf

Ansoff, H. I. (1986). The pathology of applied research in social science. In F. Heller (Ed.), *The use and abuse of social science* (pp. 19–23). London: Sage.

Babbie, E. R. (1994). *What is society? Reflections on freedom, order, and change*. Thousand Oaks, CA: Pine Forge Press.

Bailey, R., & Brake, M. (1980a). Contributions to a radical practice in social work. In R. Bailey & M. Brake (Eds.), *Radical social work and practice* (pp. 7–25). London: Edward Arnold.

Bailey, R., & Brake, M. (Eds.). (1980b). *Radical social work and practice*. London: Edward Arnold.

Banton, M. (1965). *Roles: An introduction to the study of social relations*. London: Tavistock.

Bauman, L. J., Stein, R. E. K., & Ireys, H. (1991). A framework for conceptualizing interventions. *Sociological Practice Review, 2*, 241–251.

Bertrand, A. L. (1967). *Basic sociology: An introduction to theory and method*. New York: Meredith Publishing Company.

Bourdieu, P. (1993) *Sociology in question* (R. Nice, Trans.). London: Sage.

Bourdieu, P., & Wacquant, L. J. D. (1992). *An invitation to reflexive sociology*. Cambridge: Polity Press.

Bulmer, M. (1982). *The uses of social research: Social investigation in public policy-making*. London: Allen & Unwin.

Burkitt, I. (1997). Social relationships and emotion. *Sociology, 31*(1), 37–55.

Case, C. (1924). What is a social problem? *Journal of Applied Sociology, 8*, 268–273.

Churchman, C. W. (1979). *The systems approach and its enemies*. New York: Basic Books.

Colfax, J. D., & Roach, J. F. (Eds.). (1971). *Radical sociology*. New York: Basic Books.

Doyle, J. B., Wilcox, B. L., & Reppucci, N. D. (1983). Training for social and community change. In E. Seidman (Ed.), *Handbook of social intervention* (pp. 615–638). Beverly Hills, CA: Sage.

Gomm, R., Hammersley, M., & Foster, P. (2000). Case study and generalization. In R. Gomm, M. Hammersley, & P. Foster (Eds.), *Case study method: Key issues, key texts* (pp. 98–115). London: Sage.

Gouldner, A. W. (1971). *The coming crisis of western sociology*. London: Heinemann.

Green, C. S., Klug, H. G., Neider, L. A., & Salem, R. G. (1980). Careers and the undergraduate curriculum: An integrated program. *The American Sociologist, 15*(1), 30–39.

© Springer Nature Switzerland AG 2020

P. M. Wan, A. H. Wan, *Clinical Sociology*, Clinical Sociology: Research and Practice, https://doi.org/10.1007/978-3-030-49083-6

Harper, D. (1992). Small n's and community case studies. In C. C. Ragin & H. S. Becker (Eds.), *What is a case? Exploring the foundations of social inquiry* (pp. 139–158). Cambridge: Cambridge University Press.

Hochschild, A. R. (1998). The sociology of emotion as a way of seeing. In G. Bendelow & S. J. Williams (Eds.), *Emotions in social life* (pp. 3–15). London: Routledge.

Horowitz, I. L. (Ed.). (1971). *The use and abuse of social science*. New Brunswick, NJ: Transaction Books.

Index

© Springer Nature Switzerland AG 2020

P. M. Wan, A. H. Wan, *Clinical Sociology*, Clinical Sociology: Research and Practice, https://doi.org/10.1007/978-3-030-49083-6

MIX
Papier aus verantwortungsvollen Quellen
Paper from responsible sources
FSC® C105338

If you have any concerns about our products,
you can contact us on
ProductSafety@springernature.com

In case Publisher is established outside the EU,
the EU authorized representative is:
Springer Nature Customer Service Center GmbH
Europaplatz 3, 69115 Heidelberg, Germany

Printed by Libri Plureos GmbH
in Hamburg, Germany